The Scientific Principles of TEACHING

Bridging the Divide Between Educational Practice and Research

Nathaniel Hansford

Solution Tree | Press
a division of Solution Tree

555 North Morton Street
Bloomington, IN 47404
800.733.6786 (toll free) / 812.336.7700
FAX: 812.336.7790

email: info@SolutionTree.com
SolutionTree.com

Printed in the United States of America

Library of Congress Cataloging-in-Publication Data

Names: Hansford, Nathaniel (Nathaniel Joseph), author.
Title: The scientific principles of teaching : bridging the divide between educational practice and research / Nathaniel Hansford.
Description: Bloomington, IN : Solution Tree Press, 2024. | Includes bibliographical references and index.
Identifiers: LCCN 2024003787 (print) | LCCN 2024003788 (ebook) | ISBN 9781958590959 (paperback) | ISBN 9781958590966 (ebook)
Subjects: LCSH: Teaching--Methodology. | Education--Research. | Effective teaching. | Learning strategies.
Classification: LCC LB1025.3 .H3655 2024 (print) | LCC LB1025.3 (ebook) | DDC 371.3--dc23/eng/20240222
LC record available at https://lccn.loc.gov/2024003787
LC ebook record available at https://lccn.loc.gov/2024003788

Solution Tree
Jeffrey C. Jones, CEO
Edmund M. Ackerman, President

Solution Tree Press
President and Publisher: Douglas M. Rife
Associate Publishers: Todd Brakke and Kendra Slayton
Editorial Director: Laurel Hecker
Art Director: Rian Anderson
Copy Chief: Jessi Finn
Senior Production Editor: Christine Hood
Proofreader: Charlotte Jones
Text and Cover Designer: Fabiana Cochran
Acquisitions Editors: Carol Collins and Hilary Goff
Content Development Specialist: Amy Rubenstein
Associate Editors: Sarah Ludwig and Elijah Oates
Editorial Assistant: Anne Marie Watkins

ACKNOWLEDGMENTS

This book is dedicated to my amazing wife, Lindsey, who inspired me, reflected with me, and edited countless articles, chapters, and publishing submissions. I could never have done this without her.

Solution Tree Press would like to thank the following reviewers:

Lauren Aragon
Instructional Specialist, Innovation and Development
Pasadena ISD
Houston, Texas

Becca Bouchard
Educator
Calgary Academy
Calgary, Alberta

Doug Crowley
Assistant Principal
DeForest Area High School
DeForest, Wisconsin

John D. Ewald
Educator, Consultant, Presenter, Coach
Retired Superintendent, Principal, Teacher
Frederick, Maryland

Amber Gareri
Instructional Specialist, Innovation and Development
Pasadena ISD
Pasadena, Texas

Peter Marshall
Educational Consultant
Burlington, Ontario, Canada

Paula Mathews
STEM Instructional Coach
Dripping Springs ISD
Dripping Springs, Texas

Janet Nuzzie
District Intervention Specialist, K–12
Mathematics
Pasadena ISD
Pasadena, Texas

Rea Smith
Math Facilitator
Fairview Elementary
Rogers, Arkansas

TABLE OF CONTENTS

ABOUT THE AUTHOR

Nathaniel Hansford has worked as a teacher, teaching every grade from preK–12, in places like South Korea, the United Kingdom, the subarctic of Quebec, and Ontario, Canada. In 2022, he won the Literacy Leader of the Year award from the Ontario International Dyslexia Association. Nathaniel has written hundreds of articles on the science of teaching. He is most interested in using meta-analysis research to help teachers implement methodologies that have been proven to work.

Nathaniel graduated from Lakehead University in Thunder Bay, Ontario, Canada, with a Bachelor of Arts in education and history. He also holds eleven additional teaching qualifications, including a specialist in reading and in special education.

To learn more about Nathaniel's work in education, visit www.teachingbyscience.com, or follow him @Natejoseph19 on X (formerly Twitter).

To book Nathaniel Hansford for professional development, contact pd@SolutionTree.com.

INTRODUCTION

Near the start of my teaching career, in 2014, I worked on a small reserve for Eeyou First Nations people in northern Canada. My students were far behind academically, for a myriad of reasons. I taught grades 9–11 English and history, and I wanted to find more ways to help my students. At the time, I followed a rather traditional approach to teaching. I would lecture on a topic, give my students a little bit of time to practice a skill, and then move on, regardless of whether they showed mastery. This was how I had been taught in high school. However, I could tell my students were struggling.

I took several courses on reading and special education to learn how to better help my students, ultimately obtaining a specialist qualification in each. However, I was deeply dissatisfied with the courses I took. My instructors often made strong statements about what teaching methodologies were best practice and did not have citations to support their claims. I remember being particularly concerned when I read in my textbook that reading instruction that occurs too early can damage children's brain development (Copple & Bredekamp, 2008). The claim appeared outlandish, and the authors cited "research" without citing any actual study. I began to dive deeper into education research on my own, starting with meta-analyses.

The Divide Between Educational Practice and Research

Once I started this process, I noticed that there was a real divide between what was popular in education and what was supported by scientific research. I had been taught that inquiry-based learning, balanced literacy, learning styles, and cooperative learning were the keys to good education, and yet I could find little evidence to support any of these ideas. Indeed, there was a great deal of evidence that some of these pedagogies might be counterproductive.

I grew more and more frustrated by this divide. I called my colleague, Joshua King (the cofounder of PNG Education), who was also a teacher and equally frustrated by the lack of research to support popular claims in education. In 2018, we decided to create a podcast together that focused on reviewing education research and interviewing accomplished researchers. We called the podcast *Pedagogy Non-Grata*, which means *the science of teaching, not welcome.* We explored popular topics in education instructional methods and did our best to answer the question: Is it evidence based?

At the time of writing this book (2023), I have recorded a few hundred podcast episodes (many with my original cofounder), written more than two hundred articles, conducted multiple large-scale meta-analyses, and written a few dozen research studies. That said, I am first and foremost a teacher. And I wrote this book with the intent of providing other teachers with an easy-to-read guide on current best practices in education across subjects and grades. Moreover, I wanted to provide a user-friendly research framework that empowers teachers to determine for themselves what teaching factors are evidence based. Teachers are constantly inundated with new pedagogical recommendations from their school boards, administrations, and education influencers.

My goal in writing this book is to help teachers by giving them the tools to sort out the facts from the fads. My goal is not to teach teachers how to teach but rather to help them learn to evaluate for themselves what are effective and ineffective teaching methods and discover a greater sense of self-efficacy and agency. If teachers were to take one thing away from this book, it would not be a recommendation to use any single teaching strategy but rather how to determine for themselves if a teaching strategy is evidence based.

About This Book

This book begins by providing some general guidance for reading education research. It summarizes the scientific research on foundational concepts for learning sciences and explores the research on popular teaching methodologies and their scientifically demonstrated *efficacy*. Finally, it examines the impact of different types of education policies on student academic achievement. Chapters 1–3 provide fundamental background knowledge for interpreting and understanding education research. Chapters 4–14 cover theories of learning, intelligence, and instruction for general education practices. Chapter 15 uses secondary meta-analysis to examine the efficacy of specific pedagogies, and finally, chapters 16 and 17 examine education policies.

More specifically, chapters 1 and 2 focus on how to read and understand different kinds of education research—they work as an interpretation tool to better comprehend the contents of the book. Chapter 3 explores the principles of evidence-based teaching that connect different pedagogies. Chapter 4 examines the meaning of intelligence and whether one can measure it. Chapter 5 discusses the evidence for and against a growth mindset. Chapter 6 explores how best to utilize feedback. Chapter 7 discusses the benefits of active versus passive learning. Chapter 8 presents some common myths about special education and learning disabilities and some of the research around this. Chapter 9 reviews the research on cooperative learning and how best to use it.

Chapter 10 explores the developmentally appropriate practice movement. Chapter 11 reviews the research on action research frameworks, such as response to intervention (RTI), multitiered systems of support (MTSS), collaborative inquiry, and the literacy assessment planning and instruction cycle (LAPIC). Chapter 12 discusses thoughts and issues regarding the current multiple intelligences theory framework and how it compares to learning styles. Chapter 13 explores the scientific research on constructivist teaching, while chapter 14 examines research on different forms of differentiation. Chapter 15 contains a secondary meta-analysis on the most popular teaching methods, and chapter 16 explores the education systems of the countries with the highest PISA achievement scores. Finally, chapter 17 examines the most unique and constructivist education systems in the world. The book concludes with an epilogue in which I offer my concluding thoughts on the most pressing debates within academic research on teaching. A glossary follows to help those who might need more specific information about the various research terms used throughout the book.

I wrote this book based on the available scientific evidence. I attempted to conduct my research from as neutral and objective a position as possible and then base my recommendations on that research. I did not want to provide a prescriptive guide to instruction; rather, I wanted the reader to fully understand why I came to various conclusions.

My goal is not to provide teachers with a framework or guide for learning about the science of teaching; instead, I want to give them the tools they need to be critical consumers of educational materials themselves. Of course, science is constantly evolving, as new studies are being published every day. Use this guide to help inform your understanding of the many complex topics that influence high-quality teaching, and then continue to learn from everything that comes next!

CHAPTER 1

How to Understand the Types of Education Research

The majority of this book is based on available scientific research. However, in my experience, most teacher education programs do not train teacher candidates in interpreting scientific research; this can be a difficult task. I often receive messages on social media from teachers, telling me how difficult it is to understand education research.

To make this book easier to understand and empower teachers as critical consumers, the first two chapters act as a guide to reading and interpreting research. They are not based on a standard set of interpretation guidelines, as there is intense debate on how to interpret research. Instead, they are based on my experience reading and writing about hundreds of meta-analyses and studies. In these chapters, you will explore the following.

- The difference between evidence based and research based
- The three types of education research
- How to evaluate the quality of a study
- How to interpret research results

Evidence Based Versus Research Based

Evidence based is commonly used as a label for teaching practices; however, it rarely means what people think it means. For example, both inquiry-based learning advocates and direct instruction advocates refer to their practices as evidence based. However, the types of evidence they are using are vastly different. When a teaching method is evidence based, it means there is research evidence showing that the method increases academic results (also referred to as *efficacy*). The terms *researched based* and *evidence based* are often used interchangeably when referring to pedagogical products, such as instructional programs. However, the terms have slightly different meanings.

When a product is described as *evidence based*, it means that the product has research specific to that product, showing its demonstrated effectiveness. However, when the product is *research based*, it means that the product was developed based on existing research. But not all types of research evidence are equal. In this chapter, I attempt to provide a basic understanding of how to assess the efficacy of a teaching method and the strength of the evidence behind it.

Three Types of Education Research

There are three main types of education research: (1) qualitative, (2) quantitative, and (3) synthesis. When a product or program lists *qualitative research* or *theoretical research*, like a *white paper*, this means it is research based. When a product or program lists a *quantitative study*, this means it is evidence based. *Synthesis research*, such as literature reviews, meta-analyses, or secondary meta-analyses, synthesize the results of many studies into one paper. Very few products or programs have synthesis research supporting their efficacy. However, meta-analyses have been conducted on many popular pedagogies.

Qualitative Research

Qualitative research tends to be observational and rationalist. Researchers usually observe teachers using a specific teaching strategy and then record their observations and hypotheses regarding those observations (McGill Qualitative Health Research Group, n.d.). Qualitative research can be a great place to start the research process because it gives hints as to what strategies might be interesting to explore further. It can also be useful to explain why one strategy works better than another or how a strategy might best be used. For example, qualitative studies should not be used as a definitive source of efficacy or the lack thereof. The scientific method is based on two fundamental ideas: (1) the generation of hypotheses and (2) the testing of hypotheses. Qualitative studies help with the first part of this equation by providing a systematic framework to make observations and build better hypotheses. However, they do not measure the impact of a pedagogy or product. This means they cannot be used to demonstrate efficacy. Ultimately, a qualitative study is just a very well-thought-out anecdote.

Quantitative Research

The second main type of research is *quantitative research*, which usually seeks to create an experiment and measures the results of the experiment using statistical analyses. The analyses typically yield *effect sizes*. This type of research gives you an idea of how much of an effect you might reasonably expect if you replicate the procedures and conditions reported in the study (McGill Qualitative Health Research Group, n.d.).

There are many effect size calculations used in the literature, but the most common one is referred to as *Cohen's d*. In best practice, Cohen's *d* is calculated by dividing the *mean difference* between the *treatment group* and *control (or comparison) group* by the *standard deviation (SD)* of the *outcome measure* you care about. In an experimental study, a treatment group receives the teaching method being tested (the *treatment*), and the control group does not. The researcher then calculates an effect size to measure the *magnitude* of the effect between the two groups.

But what does all this actually mean? What are the effect size and magnitude? And what are some of the ways quantitative research can be weakened by flawed design? The following sections look more closely at these topics.

EFFECT SIZE AND MAGNITUDE

Unlike *statistical significance* (the likelihood that a result was random), effect sizes are meant to be interpreted by their magnitude (Brydges, 2019), which means that they measure the size of a study result.

Effect sizes are *standardized mean differences*. This means they are supposed to replace a mean difference. Effect sizes standardize results by controlling the level of deviation in data. Ideally, an effect size is calculated by taking the mean difference between a treatment group and a control group and dividing it by the standard deviation. One way you could conceptualize an effect size would be to see it as the percentage to which a treatment group does better than a control group, after correcting for variability within the data. So, at the risk of oversimplification, an effect size of 0.20 would essentially indicate a 20 percent improvement caused by the treatment or tested variable. Conventionally, an effect size below 0.20 usually signifies that the results were negligible. Within education research, the average education study presents an effect size of 0.40 (Hattie, 2009).

This is actually a higher effect size when compared to other fields of study; however, some common practices in education research can inflate effect sizes. Anything in the range of 0.30–0.59 should likely be described as *moderate to strong*. Effect sizes greater than 0.80 are considered *high*, meaning that there is strong evidence that the teaching method works to improve learning outcomes. And effect sizes above 1.20 should be considered *very strong*, meaning there is very strong evidence that the teaching method works (Sullivan & Feinn, 2012).

It is important to remember that scientists speak in degrees of probabilities, not absolutes. Effect sizes cannot be interpreted in isolation; they are always closely connected to and determined by the research procedures that produced them. Given adequate *controls*, or high-quality research procedures with rigorous outcome measures, the higher the effect size, the greater the efficacy of that strategy.

Figure 1.1 provides a guide to interpreting effect sizes.

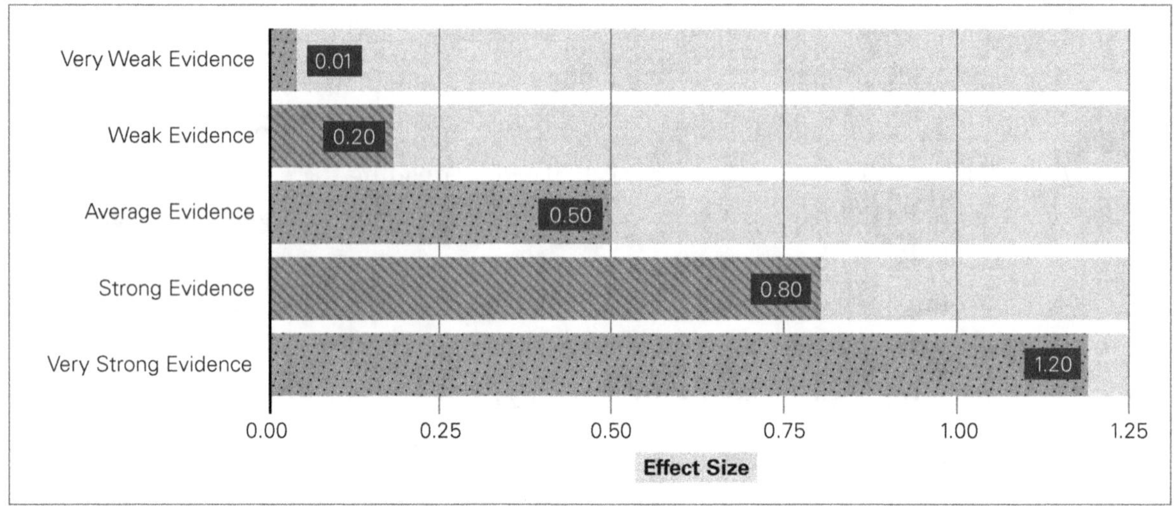

Source: Hansford & King, 2022. Used with permission.

FIGURE 1.1: Guide to interpreting effect sizes.

The purpose of using effect sizes with experimental research is to estimate the magnitude of the effect or measure the impact of a teaching method. This is what makes them quantitative. Effect sizes are meant to standardize results so studies can be universally compared. While universality is the theoretical goal, in practice, it is difficult, as studies range significantly in degrees of quality.

POOR STUDY DESIGN

Not all experimental studies are created equal. Some can be poorly designed. As an anecdotal example, I once came across a study that included an experiment group and a control group. In the experiment group, a teacher read a book to students and then had students read the book to themselves. In the control group, the teacher just had students read the book to themselves. The results of the study showed that the *experimental group* outperformed the control group for comprehension. In their conclusion, the researchers claimed that this proved the efficacy of *ear reading* (or being read to).

This study was poorly designed for two reasons: (1) students got to read the story twice in the experimental group and only once in the control group; and (2) struggling readers understood the text better if a teacher read it to them first. However, this does not prove the efficacy of ear reading as an instructional strategy for reading comprehension, as the study design did not properly test the impact of ear reading on reading comprehension.

When looking at quantitative papers, researchers usually want to see a rigorously designed experiment in which a treatment group was compared to a control group. Within education research, the treatment group receives the teaching method being tested, and the control group does not. There also needs to be a sufficiently sized and representative *sample*, random assignment of participants to treatment or *control conditions*, well-justified measures ranging from more sensitive to more global, and procedural controls to verify that *experimental conditions* were delivered as planned. That said, many education studies do not use a control group at all. They simply have a pretest and a posttest for the intervention and measure the effect size of the results. However, the problem with this study design is that you have no idea whether the intervention caused the improvement. Such nonexperimental designs leave open the possibility that the passage of time (or some other unmeasured event) caused the improvement in performance.

A pre–post design cannot test the efficacy of an experimental method of instruction compared to any other form of instruction. When conducting an experiment, researchers should test whether this teaching method works better than another form of instruction, with the most common form of instruction being ideal for the control group. When researchers do an experiment, the time frame also matters, as the longer the experiment is, the lower the effect size typically becomes, possibly due to the novelty of the tested method wearing off or because the instructors are fatigued with implementing the treatment with *fidelity* (consistency).

Three other things that should make you leery when reading research include: (1) small sample sizes, (2) researcher bias, or (3) lack of randomization.

Small Sample Sizes

When a study uses a smaller sample, this can affect the range of results and end up creating distorted effect sizes on both ends of the spectrum. Novice research interpreters often memorize this rule about research—larger sample sizes are, in general, better. You also must account for what it takes to have an adequate sample, and in fact, simply larger samples are not always better. The sample must be selected with regard to the research question, the existing literature, the intended methods, the baseline performance, demographic characteristics, anticipated effects, and managed for *attrition*, which can be a sign of manipulated data.

Attrition might take place if students who started in the study were removed. Some attrition is normal, as students often drop out of studies due to absenteeism or illness. However, a large amount of attrition can be a sign that data have been manipulated. For example, authors might be tempted to remove the lowest-performing students from a study. Attrition can be a sign of data manipulation, especially when it is disproportionate between the treatment and control group (What Works Clearinghouse, n.d.).

Remember that samples are often nested in specific contexts. The success of an intervention in a study does not prove an intervention works universally, but rather only in that context. For example, a phonics intervention would have different effects in a kindergarten class than in a grade 12 class.

Researcher Bias

Researcher bias can be another concern. Often, I observe that researchers invested in an idea publish studies with more positive results than researchers who are testing other people's hypotheses

(Open Science Collaboration, 2015). While some of this difference might be the impact of bias, some of it might also be the result of expertise. For example, Sarah Powell is one of the world's leading experts in word-problem mathematics instruction. She is the founder of the Science of Math movement, which includes a collection of researchers dedicated to advancing the teaching of mathematics through evidence-based strategies. She was part of the largest-ever meta-analysis of word-problem instruction (Powell & Fuchs, 2018).

Who is going to get better results in a word-problem study, Powell or a first-year graduate student? Similarly, teachers with greater experience with a teaching method might produce better outcomes than teachers using the method for the first time. While this is not necessarily wrong, the goal of education research is to find results that are reproducible by the average teacher.

Lack of Randomization

Simple *randomization* can create a lack of equivalence between control and experimental groups at the beginning of an experiment, and such differences weaken the research study (What Works Clearing House, n.d.). While a study with a control group is almost always going to be better than a study without one, an experimental group and a control group should be randomly assigned (What Works Clearing House, n.d.). This is less important than some of the other points mentioned; however, it can still matter. For example, it would not be ideal for the control group to have the weakest students and for the experiment group to have the strongest students, as that obviously would bias the results.

Even if there is one well-done study, researchers should not typically place a high value on individual studies, because there is usually a range of results in education research. This is often the part of science that the public gets wrong. This doesn't just happen in education but in science in general. For example, I recently did a secondary meta-analysis on morphology instruction (teaching students about the meaning of word parts; for example *-ed* means past tense), and I found one study with an effect size of 0.29 and another with an effect size of 1.24. Obviously, both effect sizes cannot best represent the effect of morphological instruction, so there needs to be a method to best determine what is referred to as the *scientific consensus*. This is where meta-analysis and secondary meta-analysis come into play.

Synthesis Research

As noted previously, synthesis research, such as literature reviews, meta-analyses, or secondary meta-analyses, synthesize the results of many studies into one paper. The following sections describe meta-analysis and secondary meta-analysis in more detail.

META-ANALYSIS

Meta-analysis looks at all the studies in an area of research and tries to use statistical analysis to find the most normalized results (Sánchez-Meca & Martín-Martínez, 1998). Ideally, a meta-analysis accounts for the sample sizes in different studies when calculating a mean effect size. However, this is only possible when researchers publish enough data, which isn't always the case. Research must begin somewhere, after all. When this happens, meta-analysis researchers will sometimes take an average of the effect sizes reported while ideally removing any *outlier* effect sizes. Based on my research, meta-analysis is by far the best way to determine the efficacy of a teaching intervention (Hansford & Schechter, 2023).

However, not all meta-analyses are created equal. For example, I came across a meta-analysis on individualized instruction with an effect size of 2.35 (Steenbergen-Hu, Makel, & Olszewski-Kubilius, 2016). This is an extremely high effect size; however, it was based on four studies, which leaves me skeptical about the validity of this outcome. Phonics, on the other hand, usually has a result of 0.40–0.60 (Hattie, 2023g), depending on the meta-analysis. Some of these meta-analyses have hundreds of studies behind them, so this makes me more confident in the research behind phonics than the research behind individualized instruction, although both are evidence-based strategies. There is a balance here in that very promising teaching methods that are newer or less well-researched can still be valid; you just can't know with certainty that they're valid. They could be. You could also over- or underestimate reality. But when a method has accumulated hundreds of studies, you might be more confident in estimating a "typical" effect of the teaching method.

SECONDARY META-ANALYSIS

Secondary meta-analysis is a strategy popularized in education by John Hattie (2009) and is something I often do myself through my books and on my website. Secondary meta-analyses are meta-analyses of multiple other meta-analyses. (How meta is that?) Some scholars, such as Robert E. Slavin (2018) and Dylan Wiliam (as cited in Pedagogy Non-Grata, 2019b), have criticized secondary meta-analysis for taking too broad of an approach, as it can be used to collate research that is hard to compare (for example, different student populations, sample sizes, effect calculations, and types of research).

However, I am a big fan of this type of research, as it allows people to easily digest large amounts of education research quickly to identify which teaching strategies have strong evidence to support them and which do not. For example, figure 1.2 (page 12) shows an infographic from my 2021 secondary meta-analysis on commonly used teaching strategies (Hansford, 2022h). This figure shows the *mean effect size* found for a large number of teaching methodologies, according to dozens of different meta-analyses at the same time.

By using this graph, teachers can quickly determine the relative effectiveness of a teaching method and compare it to the effectiveness of other popular teaching methods. This is useful when looking at competing methods. While some forms of instruction can be used synergistically, like phonemic awareness and morphology, others—systematic phonics, balanced literacy, and whole language, for example—are diametrically opposite pedagogies and cannot be used simultaneously. As teachers can typically only use one strategy at a time, it makes sense to compare their overall effectiveness.

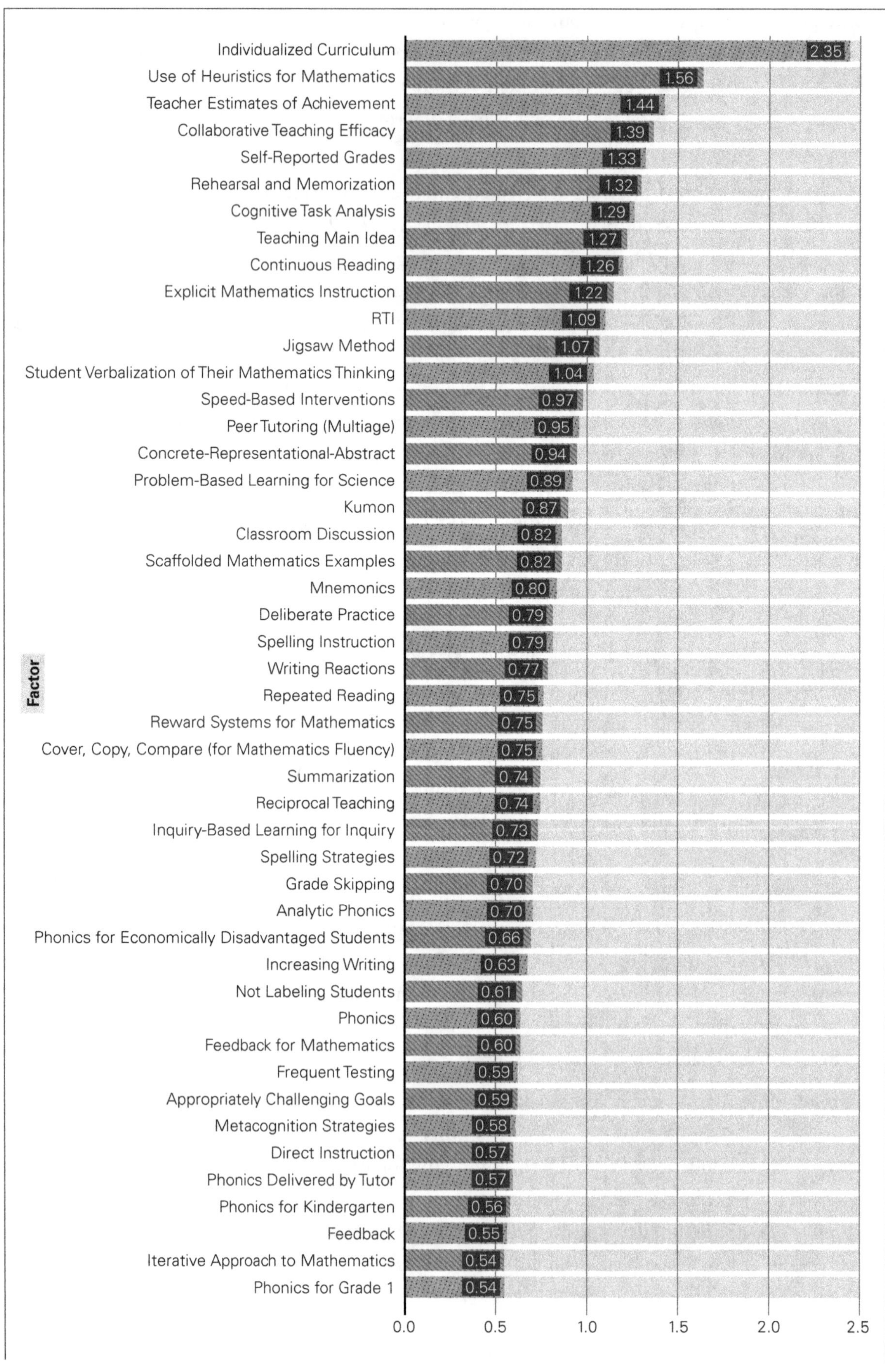
Individualized Curriculum
2.35
Use of Heuristics for Mathematics
1.56
Teacher Estimates of Achievement
1.44
Collaborative Teaching Efficacy
1.39
Self-Reported Grades
1.33
Rehearsal and Memorization
1.32
Cognitive Task Analysis
1.29
Teaching Main Idea
1.27
Continuous Reading
1.26
Explicit Mathematics Instruction
1.22
RTI
1.09
Jigsaw Method
1.07
Student Verbalization of Their Mathematics Thinking
1.04
Speed-Based Interventions
0.97
Peer Tutoring (Multiage)
0.95
Concrete-Representational-Abstract
0.94
Problem-Based Learning for Science
0.89
Kumon
0.87
Classroom Discussion
0.82
Scaffolded Mathematics Examples
0.82
Mnemonics
0.80
Deliberate Practice
0.79
Spelling Instruction
0.79
Writing Reactions
0.77
Repeated Reading
0.75
Reward Systems for Mathematics
0.75
Cover, Copy, Compare (for Mathematics Fluency)
0.75
Summarization
0.74
Reciprocal Teaching
0.74
Inquiry-Based Learning for Inquiry
0.73
Spelling Strategies
0.72
Grade Skipping
0.70
Analytic Phonics
0.70
Phonics for Economically Disadvantaged Students
0.66
Increasing Writing
0.63
Not Labeling Students
0.61
Phonics
0.60
Feedback for Mathematics
0.60
Frequent Testing
0.59
Appropriately Challenging Goals
0.59
Metacognition Strategies
0.58
Direct Instruction
0.57
Phonics Delivered by Tutor
0.57
Phonics for Kindergarten
0.56
Feedback
0.55
Iterative Approach to Mathematics
0.54
Phonics for Grade 1
0.54
Factor
0.0
0.5
1.0
1.5
2.0
2.5

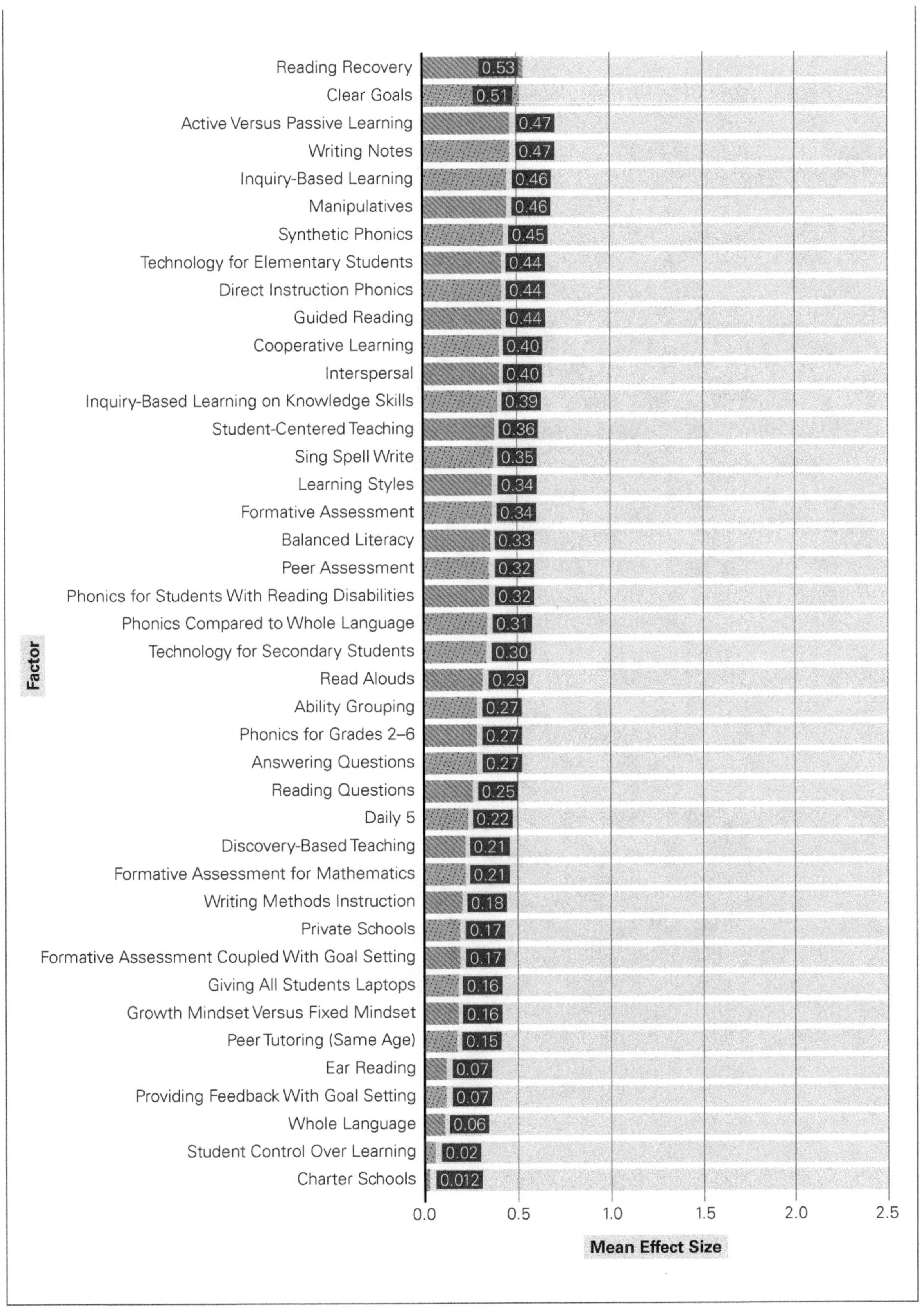

Source: Hansford, 2022b. Used with permission.

FIGURE 1.2: Teaching strategies ranked by effect size.

Summary Points to Remember

Following is a list of highlights and significant points outlined in this chapter.

- ☑ For a teaching method to be truly evidence based, it needs support from multiple studies with control groups that compare the effect of adding interventions.
- ☑ It is important to look for multiple studies because education research tends to show a lot of variability.
- ☑ Meta-analyses are the most practical way to look at large amounts of research because meta-analysis systematically reviews studies, which limits the risk of cherry-picking.
- ☑ While teachers could try to identify the most rigorous study as opposed to reading a meta-analysis, this would require reading all studies and having an advanced understanding of study design. It is far simpler for teachers to rely on meta-analyses. It lowers the potential for bias, in comparison to trying to pick the best studies.
- ☑ Generally, effect sizes within meta-analysis provide an easy-to-use metric that allows readers to quickly gauge the overall effectiveness of a teaching method.

Reflection Questions

Individually or with your team, use these questions to reflect on the information in this chapter.

1. What surprised you most in this chapter?
2. What type of questions are best answered by qualitative research?
3. What type of questions are best answered by quantitative research?
4. Why is it important for studies to use a control group?
5. Why is randomization beneficial?
6. What are the advantages and disadvantages of meta-analysis?

How to Read and Interpret Education Research

Chapter 1 (page 5) was a beginners' guide to reading education research. In this chapter, I attempt to extend that knowledge to a more intermediate level. This chapter addresses some of the difficulties and required nuances for interpreting education research. These first two chapters are an attempt to add some clarity for the novice to reading scientific research.

This chapter goes deeper into understanding elements of education research, discussing the reasons why education study results tend to be inflated, how study quality affects research results, how sponsorship can add bias to results, how different control group designs can affect study results, and the importance of considering the context behind study samples. All of these elements can have a profound impact on the validity and reliability of a study.

Inflation

In education research, effect sizes tend to be exaggerated by a combination of factors. On average, education studies produce an effect size of 0.40 (Hattie, 2009). However, the average effect sizes change across different scientific fields of study and therefore are not comparable between disciplines (Brydges, 2019). This is likely due to the differences in what researchers are trying to influence and the tools used for influencing it. For example, teaching kindergarten students their ABCs might show a powerful impact on reading outcomes. However, anyone who has spent a considerable amount of time in the gym knows it takes a lot of effort and time to develop muscles. Therefore, it makes sense that education studies would show larger impacts than studies on bodybuilding.

There are likely many factors inflating the average effect size in education research, but in this section, I focus on the following.

- File drawer problem
- Quality of education studies
- Structure factor

File Drawer Problem

In a 2019 interview, esteemed education writer and researcher Dylan Wiliam pointed out the file drawer problem (as cited in Pedagogy Non-Grata, 2019b). The *file drawer problem* is the noted phenomenon of researchers not publishing studies with insignificant results (those results remain in the "file drawer"). In fact, most journals will not accept studies that produce nonsignificant results, often defined by effect sizes below 0.20 or *p values* above 0.05.

Well-conducted meta-analyses and research syntheses should attend to the potential for the absence of weaker and null effects for specific teaching methods arising from the file drawer problem. For example, some meta-analysis scholars will use a *funnel plot analysis*, which compares the sample size of a study to the effect size found. Figure 2.1 shows an example funnel plot comparing systematic phonics instruction with balanced literacy instruction.

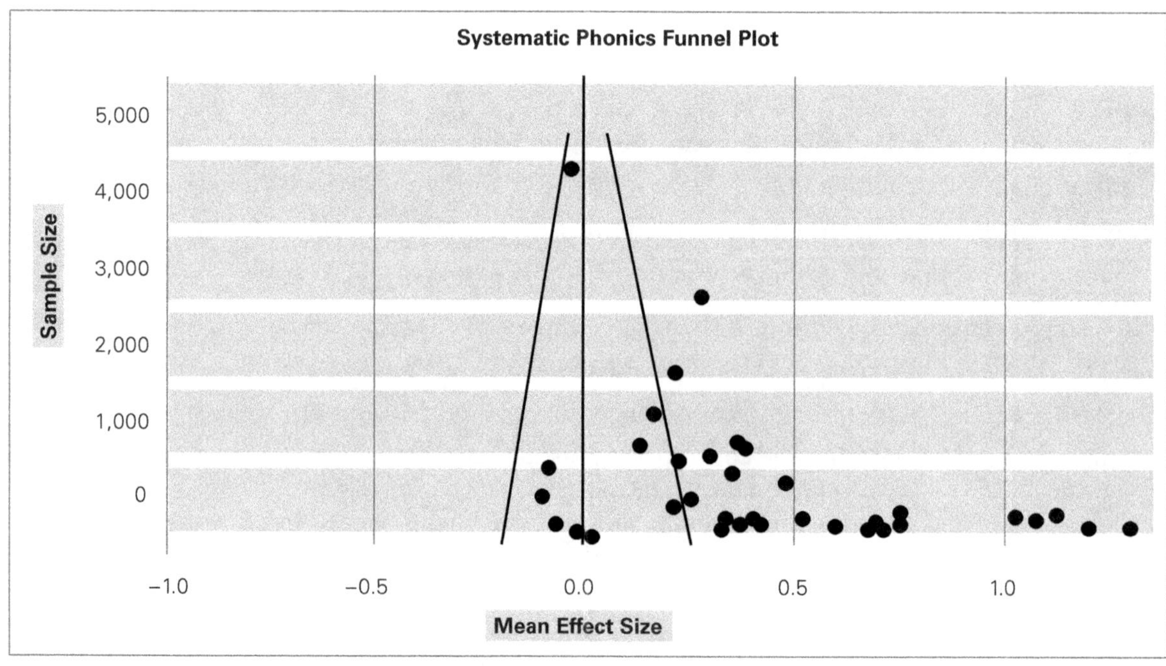

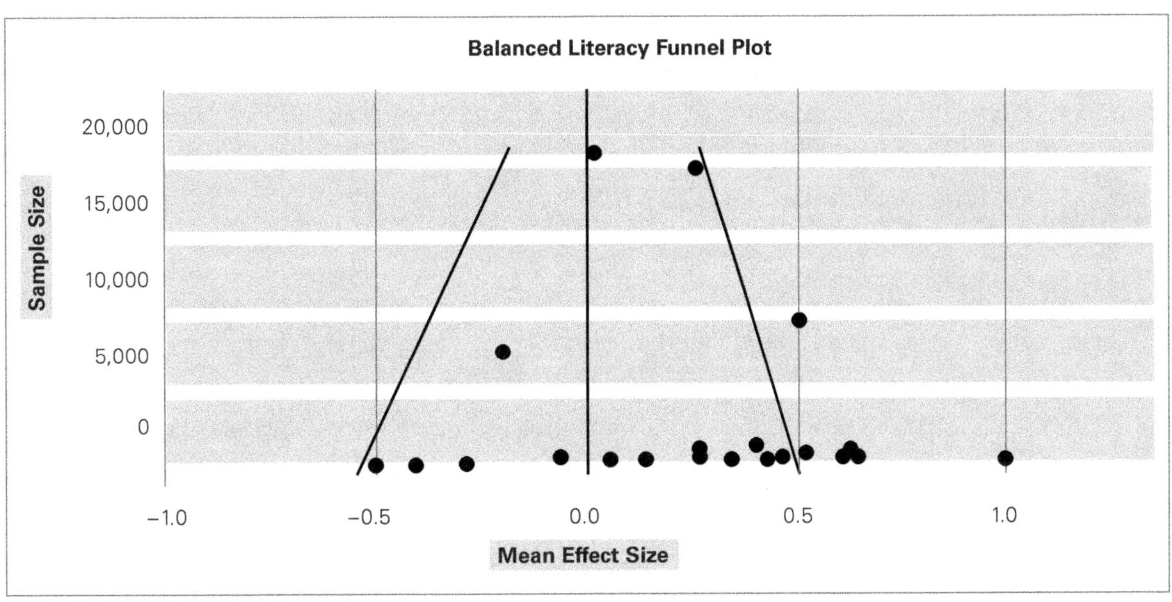

FIGURE 2.1: Systematic phonics versus balanced literacy funnel plot examples.

In a funnel plot, the vertical axis shows the study's sample size. The horizontal axis shows the mean effect size found. If smaller studies were published, regardless of the results, one would see a symmetrical pyramid. In theory, this should happen because small studies are more prone to larger effect sizes, both positive and negative. This occurs because outliers have a greater potential impact on the overall statistical mean.

Conversely, the larger the sample size, the closer the effect size should be to the center of the horizontal axis. This should occur because the larger studies are less impacted by outlier data. However, as figure 2.1 shows, both systematic phonics meta-analysis and balanced literacy meta-analysis showed a larger number of studies clustered in the bottom-right quadrant, suggesting that small-sample studies are more likely to be published when they have a large effect. This makes sense, as most of these studies are sponsored by companies trying to sell their products.

Some university researchers are starting to help increase the ethical standards in education research by *preregistering studies*. This means that studies are on the record before they begin. Preregistration is becoming more common and should help reduce the likelihood that studies are left unpublished due to null or negative findings. By preregistering studies, authors agree to publish their studies, regardless of the results. However, most researchers do not preregister.

Quality of Education Studies

Another problem is likely tied to the quality of education studies in general. Only in the early 2000s has education research shifted to prioritize more rigorous experimental evaluation of teaching tactics (Torgerson & Torgerson 2001). The Institute for Education Sciences, which is the main funding body for education research, has organized and allocated funds for research according to research type, ranging from development to effectiveness and replication trials ("examinations of associations between variables; iterative design and testing of strategies or interventions; and assessments of the impact of a fully developed intervention on an education outcome"; as cited in What Works Clearing House, n.d.). Each type of research has specific methodological requirements that are rigorous and lead to causal conclusions over time (Odom et al., 2005). Papers before 2000 often used weaker, nonexperimental designs that weakened confidence in the research findings (Torgerson & Torgerson, 2001).

Structure Factor

Additionally, there is what I would call the *structure factor*. In general, teaching methods that are more structured have greater effect sizes than those that are not. For example, according to Hattie (2023c), direct instruction outperforms inquiry-based learning; inquiry-based learning outperforms problem-based learning; and problem-based learning outperforms discovery-based learning. That said, most studies that have a control group assign no specific teaching methods or strategies to the control group, which is called *business as usual*. On one hand, it makes sense to evaluate a treatment by comparing it to what currently exists in terms of instruction. However, this is not always defined in a study, as a control group could be using an alternative program that is equally structured, or the control group conditions could reflect a less structured approach.

Research that creates more competitive or rigorous counterfactual conditions is rarer but offers a more rigorous test of the intervention, although business as usual is conventional and reflects what the benefit would be if the experimental teaching method were used in a setting similar to that in which the research study was conducted. For example, many intervention studies on special education instruction provide students in the treatment group with intensive one-on-one instruction but then provide no additional instruction to students in the control group. This type of design biases the result in favor of the treatment group.

In more rigorously designed studies, the treatment group and the control group receive equal levels of instruction. Even studies that provide equivalent treatment often do not fully explain what that treatment looks like. Moreover, the treatment group often receives multiple treatments at the same time. This can result in a *random effect* because it is impossible to know which variable is generating the results. In the most rigorous study designs, all instruction between the control group and the treatment group are identical, except for the variable being tested. These types of studies can measure for the *fixed effect* of the treatment, as opposed to the random effects of an experiment.

Following are definitions specifying the difference between a fixed effect and a random effect in study design.

- **Fixed effect:** All instruction and variables are the same in both the treatment and control group, except for the teaching method or factor being studied.
- **Random effect:** The instruction or variables are different for more than just the teaching method or factor being studied.

To help put this all in context, I reference my own meta-analysis on reading comprehension (Hansford, McGlynn, & King, 2023). My colleagues and I examined 501 studies with our initial screening criteria. Only seventy-three of these studies were experimental, only thirty-six of those used standardized measures, and only seven of those studies measured a fixed effect (Hansford, McGlynn, & King, 2023).

For all these reasons, education researchers should adopt the mindset that teaching methods with higher effect sizes are more likely to be useful. That said, there might be a time and place for implementing methods with smaller effect sizes. Ultimately, the reason I got into this research was the realization that there is an *opportunity cost* to different teaching methods, as we can only use so many at a time; and yielding the benefits from one teaching method means missing the benefits of other teaching methods. Everything you do in your classroom takes time, both in its learning curve and its implementation; that is why it is important to use teaching strategies proven to be highly effective.

However, the time costs of different methods are not equal. Some teaching methods require significant investment in teacher professional development before they can be implemented; others require a lot of work to implement. For individual teachers, I suggest using a low-time-cost teaching strategy with a small to moderate impact rather than one with an extremely high time cost and a moderate to high impact because low-time-cost teaching strategies can be easily combined, and high-time-cost ones cannot.

Ultimately, the best strategies are both easy to implement and *high yield*. One might refer to this paradigm as the *impact-to-time ratio*. Formally, this concept is referred to as *incremental cost-effectiveness ratio (ICER)* and is a systematic type of cost-benefit analysis (Barrett, Gadke, & VanDerHeyden, 2020).

Quality

As you undoubtedly realize at this point, not all studies are created equal. However, in meta-analysis, researchers often place an equal weight on studies of different quality levels. Unfortunately, the higher quality or more structured a research paper is, the lower the effect size tends to be (Plonsky & Oswald, 2014). This trend of lower effects for higher-quality research might be because researchers remove some of the inherited research bias from the study. As discussed earlier, most studies show a positive benefit, as negative studies tend not to get published, and study designs often bias the treatment group.

This is why it is important not to take any positive benefit as meaningful but rather look for a minimum effect size. Because higher-quality studies are more tightly controlled, it is less likely that random benefits are part of the effect size. As pointed out earlier, control group studies tend to have lower effect sizes than studies without control groups. That said, there are many different control group designs, all aimed at reducing some of the randomness of study results. Moreover, some more recent meta-analyses have been using *covariance calculations* and *multilevel modeling* to control different levels of quality (Stuebing, Barth, Cirino, Francis, & Fletcher, 2008).

The gold standard of group experimental designs is the *randomized controlled trial (RCT)*. This means people are randomly assigned to the control group and experimental group. This is meant to stop researchers from doing unscrupulous things like putting all the strongest students in the experimental group. However, more importantly, randomized controlled trial studies usually ensure the groups start at equivalent levels so as not to bias the results. This is especially important, as some quasi-experimental studies will include groups that are so nonequivalent that the treatment group will improve substantially less but still show a positive effect size (What Works Clearing House, n.d.).

For context, look at a hypothetical example in figure 2.2.

Group	Pretest Mean (SD)	Posttest Mean (SD)	Effect Size (*d*)
Control (*N* = 17)	10 (1.2)	18 (1.8)	
Treatment (*N* = 19)	15 (1.3)	20 (2.3)	0.96

FIGURE 2.2: Hypothetical study results.

This example is typical of a results section for a quasi-experimental study. The mean represents the average result; the standard deviation is the number in parentheses and represents the range of results; *N* represents the number of students; and *d* represents the Cohen's *d* effect size. In figure 2.2, the treatment group had a positive effect size of 0.96, suggesting that the teaching method was very successful. However, the control group started 50 percent lower than the treatment group at the pretest and improved significantly across the duration of the study. The study design here was not equivalent and created results that did not reflect the success or failure of the teaching method.

As noted previously, more structure almost always beats less structure. This is why some researchers, rather than just having the control group, have no structure, assign teachers in the control group to a specific alternative intervention, and give both groups equal training. For example, rather than having a phonics group and a business-as-usual control group, they have a phonics group and a balanced literacy group. This type of approach is likely fairer, especially if neither group knows if they are the control group or the experimental group. However, studies with this design tend to have, on average, lower effect sizes. This means that studies with more rigorous designs, such as case studies, require larger effect sizes to be considered significant (Plonsky & Oswald, 2014).

Indeed, Luke Plonsky & Frederick L. Oswald (2014) suggest that for case studies, an effect size should be above 0.40 to be considered statistically significant. Ultimately, the more fairly conducted and structured the study design, the lower the effect sizes tend to be.

For these reasons, some scholars might argue against meta-analysis that includes less rigorous study designs. And in some cases, they might be right. Would you rather look at one well-conducted study or four poorly conducted studies? Unfortunately, there are several reasons that make this reductionist approach less useful.

- Lack of high-quality research studies
- Discounted majority of older research
- Understanding of low-quality research effect sizes
- Sponsorship

Lack of High-Quality Research Studies

Many education topics do not have high-quality research studies behind them, so if researchers only base hypotheses on areas where there are high-quality studies, they exclude most of the research and are, therefore, limited in the research-based hypotheses they can make. However, this is not reflective of the scientific process. A more useful position would be to recognize that evidence is always fluid and never perfect and to be cognizant that we can only speak in degrees of probabilities, not absolutes.

So, when you see strong results found in multiple high-quality studies and within a meta-analysis, you can be reasonably certain that the strategy is effective. When you have multiple poorly done studies with high effect sizes, however, a more useful observation might be that the strategy appears evidence based, according to the evidence you have now, but there needs to be more high-quality research. As important, the lack of high-quality research to back up a result doesn't mean you, as a teacher, shouldn't put a strategy to use. Consider again the cost to implement. Even if an effect size is inflated, if the cost to implement the strategy is low, it might still be worth your time and effort to utilize.

Discounted Majority of Older Research

Another issue with ignoring lower-quality research is that it forces educators to discount the majority of older research. In my experience in conducting multiple meta-analyses, very few studies from the 1980s and 1990s used randomized controlled trials or statistically corrected test groups. So, if we ignore this research, we end up having to throw out large amounts of the body of research. This might be advisable at some point, but within the field of education, there is not a big enough base of high-quality research to make this practical.

Understanding of Low-Quality Research Effect Sizes

The understanding of effect sizes in education research mostly comes from low-quality studies (Plonsky & Oswald, 2014). Because most of the research is low in quality, the natural comparisons being made are with the contextual understanding of what is the normal range for effect sizes in education research. For example, embedded mnemonics (Shanahan, 2021), RTI (Tran, Sanchez, Arellano, & Swanson, 2011), and speech-to-print (Vernon-Feagans et al., 2012) are all popular teaching strategies that have shown high effect sizes in the research. However, the vast majority of studies on these three topics are based on case studies and quasi-experimental studies, not randomized controlled trials (Hansford, 2022d). If you conduct a meta-analysis that excludes all but the highest-quality research, it makes sense to lower your benchmarks of what's considered strong, moderate, and weak effects.

Sponsorship

Within education, some researchers might conduct studies to get specific results. Researchers critical of a specific strategy tend to get fewer positive results than researchers who are promoting the same strategy. This can be especially problematic when researchers are sponsored by a company seeking to prove a specific outcome. For example, most language program studies are conducted by the same companies selling the products. Researchers trying to get a specific result can accomplish this through a variety of means. They can provide more instruction to the treatment group, exclude negative results, engage in *p-hacking* (using many measurements but only publishing the significant ones), or conduct a large number of studies and only publish the ones with the highest results. Of course, this potential source of bias is why meta-analysis researchers try to use rigorous study designs—to correct for this bias. However, this solution does not always work.

For example, I recently conducted a non-peer-reviewed meta-analysis of a popular language program. Within the body of research were seven studies. Five of these seven studies were conducted by a research firm and showed effect sizes that were, on average, forty-five times higher than the two studies conducted by independent authors. These five studies also excluded outcomes that were negligible or negative and repeated moderator variables under different names, which inflates the mean effect (Joseph, King, & McGlynn, 2022). While this is an extreme example, it helps to remember that not all studies are equally trustworthy.

Samples

It is impossible for a well-controlled study to look at an entire population. Instead, researchers study a sample of a population. However, a sample can only ever be representative of the participants involved. Therefore, it's important that researchers use samples that are large enough to both provide meaningful results and reflect the demographics of the population under study.

Sample Size

Sample size refers to the number of participants in a study. Large sample sizes, on average, tend to produce more normalized results than smaller sample sizes. As smaller sample sizes can distort a standard deviation calculation, it can make the data look both more or less random than it actually is. For example, let's say you have a sample of only six students, and all of them get a result within 5 percent of each other. This creates an extremely low standard deviation and an extremely high effect size. Now, let's say within a sample of fifty students, most, on average, have a range of results within 10 percent of each other, with outliers ranging up to 40 percent in either direction. Now, if you have another study with a sample size of six students with two large outliers, then your standard deviation will suddenly become extremely high, and the effect size will be extremely low.

Of course, in general, you probably should not place a high weight on studies that have sample sizes below twenty. This is not to say studies with low sample sizes should be ignored, but rather, you should take these studies with a grain of salt.

Demographics

Size is not the only consideration when examining samples, as different demographics tend to show different results. For example, generally speaking, younger students progress more rapidly in learning than older students (for example, elementary school compared to high school). So, it follows that in a study, the younger the study sample, the larger the expected effect sizes. This phenomenon is caused, in part, because the scope of expected learning and the potential to be farther behind is less with younger students.

Wiliam was the first to point out this phenomenon to me (as cited in Pedagogy Non-Grata, 2019b); however, I have found the same trend within my own meta-analyses (Hansford & King, 2022; Hansford, McGlynn, & King, 2023; Joseph, King, & McGlynn, 2022). Indeed, different teaching methods and interventions can have drastically different results with students in different grades. For example, phonics interventions tend to have by far the highest results between preK and grade 2, whereas problem-based learning tends to have the highest results on students in grade 12 or those in postsecondary education (Camilli, Vargas, & Yurecko, 2003; National Reading Panel, 2000; Stuebing et al., 2008).

For these reasons, it is likely inappropriate to include studies in a meta-analysis that are not from what should be the targeted demographic. Similarly, students in a socioeconomically disadvantaged district might see very different outcomes than students in a prosperous district. For example, would study results from a rich private school be easily comparable to study results from a disadvantaged school? In private schools, students are more likely to be advantaged and, thus, more likely to be ahead in the curriculum. This has the potential to lower the study results because students have less total progress to make. Again, demographics are an important consideration when putting together a sample for a research study.

Types of Effect Size Calculations

While Cohen's *d* is likely the most commonly used effect size within education research, it is not the only one. Education researchers also commonly use *Hedge's g*, which is used to normalize the results for smaller sample sizes. Hedge's *g* is calculated by dividing the results by the pooled standard deviation (National Institute of Standards and Technology, 2018). When the control group has substantially different standard deviations from the experimental group, *Glass's Delta* is recommended instead, which only uses the standard deviation of the control group (University of Connecticut, 2000). A *Pearson effect size* is used when examining the effect of two variables to determine correlation (University of Connecticut, 2000). For example, you would use a Pearson effect size if you wanted to examine the correlation between parent income and student achievement. While all these calculations are different, they are meant for researchers to use under specific circumstances to normalize results within a standard interpretation.

Some authors criticize meta-analyses that include studies with different types of effect size calculations; however, as most of these calculations are meant to be interpreted the same, I cannot say I agree with the criticism (Pedagogy Non-Grata, 2019b). Sometimes, instead of using an effect-size calculation, authors will use a *p* value, which is used to determine the likelihood of significance when accounting for the degree of variability. It is represented as a decimal. A *p* value of below 0.05 indicates a less than 5 percent chance that the results are random statistical noise. In other words, the lower the *p* value, the more likely results are not just statistical noise. Researchers are essentially trying to measure the degree to which the study results might be random versus meaningful (Dahiru, 2008).

Comparisons

So, how do educators compare low-quality and high-quality research if they generate different effect sizes? The reality is to consider the value of findings from the understanding that evidence is fluid, varies in quality, and any effort to summarize (while aiding practical conclusions) simultaneously loses some of the nuance that is relevant to those conclusions. While the state of the literature is far from perfect, researchers have to work with the available body of scientific evidence. This is why you need to consider the quality, quantity, and impact of research to truly understand if something is evidence based (Hansford & Schechter, 2021).

Yes, high-quality studies included with meta-analysis will, on average, drag down an effect size, and yes, low-quality studies will, on average, increase an effect size. But that does not mean study results are solely impacted by study quality. For example, in the meta-analysis on phonics Joshua King and I conducted, we used Pearson effect sizes and *p* values to determine what factor had the highest impact on effect sizes. We found that the pace of instruction had almost double the impact that study quality did (Hansford & King, 2018).

How to Be a Critical Reader of Research

Being a critical reader of research requires examining the research in degrees of probabilities, not absolutes. Moreover, it is not as if all well-controlled studies have effect sizes below 0.40 and all poorly controlled studies have effect sizes above 0.70. Indeed, I have come across multiple well-done studies with effect sizes above 1.0 and multiple poorly done studies with effect sizes below 0.20. Ultimately, we must all understand that research quality influences the possible result of meta-analysis and therefore should inform our conclusions or interpretations of average or median effects (Hansford & Schechter, 2021).

Ideally, a large enough sample size and number of studies should correct for most errors. Take phonics, for example. According to Hattie's (2023g) database, phonics is one of the most well-studied topics in the literature, with over one thousand studies conducted. Within individual studies, I have seen negative and above 2.0 effect sizes; however, within meta-analyses, I have seen a much narrower range of results. The majority of meta-analyses on phonics had an effect size within the relatively small range of 0.40–0.70 (Hattie, 2023g). Hattie (2023g) conducted the largest meta-analysis (a secondary meta-analysis) on phonics and found an effect size of 0.57. When the vast majority of meta-analyses on phonics consistently find the methods to have a moderately high effect size, I feel confident in saying that phonics has a moderately positive result and therefore is, therefore, evidence based (Hattie, 2023g).

Some might argue that the degree of variability within the research suggests that you need to disregard meta-analysis and focus on parsing out the best-constructed studies on each topic; however, I disagree with this approach for several reasons. First, even within well-constructed studies, you still see a large variability. The human condition is complex, and determining the effect of a human intervention is challenging. Second, this approach discounts most of the research. But last and most important, it de-democratizes research, as it is easier for teachers and less trained individuals to read one meta-analysis than it is to read every study on a topic and choose the best one.

Without meta-analyses, we must largely rely on the ability of benign and brilliant scholars to interpret the literature for everyone else, as the "sage on the stage" so to speak. However, the problem with this approach is it requires individual teachers to find trustworthy scholars to interpret the evidence for them. This methodology has been the most popular method for understanding scientific literature. However, there is great risk in relying on the most popular scholars to give opinions because they may not be the most informed but rather the best at marketing. It is this practice and belief system that has allowed pseudoscientific practices, such as learning styles, to become popular within the field of education.

Using meta-analysis empowers teachers to be able to quickly and easily interpret the efficacy of different teaching interventions within the literature. I believe this might be the real reason meta-analysis is sometimes criticized by researchers within the field of education. Meta-analysis has the ability to prove pedagogies people have spent their entire academic life promoting and researching are futile. Furthermore, it diminishes the importance of those scholars who have aspired to be the sage on the stage, as it gives people the ability to interpret the literature for themselves, without spending a lifetime reading every published study.

Summary Points to Remember

Following is a list of highlights and significant points outlined in this chapter.

- ☑ Interpreting the results of individual studies requires far greater expertise than interpreting the results of meta-analyses. Therefore, it makes more sense for educators to look at meta-analyses rather than individual studies.
- ☑ Effect sizes are imprecise measurements and should be interpreted in degrees of probabilities, not as absolutes. However, they provide the easiest and simplest metric for teachers to interpret research results.
- ☑ Higher-quality studies tend to produce lower effect sizes, which means interpreting scientific studies should account for quality, quantity, and impact.

Reflection Questions

Individually or with your team, use these questions to reflect on the information in this chapter.

1. What factors might lower an effect size, and how might that impact your understanding of research?
2. What factors might increase an effect size?
3. What factors might make an effect size less accurate?
4. How do you know if something reported as science is true?
5. What do you think are the most important variables to consider when evaluating the rigor of a study and why?

CHAPTER 3

The Five Scientific Principles of Teaching

Evidence-based teaching methodologies do not exist in isolation. There are fundamental principles that connect the best teaching methodologies and pedagogies. In this chapter, you will learn about the principles of effective instruction behind popular evidence-based teaching methods and strategies.

Each year, Hattie (2023c) conducts a secondary meta-study to identify the 256 most effective teaching factors (or methods) and their order of importance based on current findings and the newest research. While in my own research, I have typically looked at teaching methods or pedagogies, such as phonics, morphology, repeated reading, and so on, Hattie (2023c) looks at a much broader scope of factors. Factors can include things like pedagogies such as phonics, but they can also include things like class size, demographics, and income levels.

Asking teachers to read about 256 different teaching factors and their applications in the classroom every year would be impractical, overwhelming, and largely unproductive, given the fact that so many strategies could never all be meaningfully implemented in a single classroom. That said, many of the most successful factors Hattie (2023c) identifies overlap with each other in their application. For example, learning goals, feedback, assessment as learning, and metacognition strategies are all evidence-based pedagogical strategies that improve learning. All these strategies function on the same basic principle: they increase the clarity of learning expectations so students are better able to understand what teachers want them to learn (Hattie, 2023c).

In 2018, Joshua King and I wrote an article in which we highlighted the connecting principles between pedagogies that Hattie (2023c) had identified as high yield within his work. Since then, I have endeavored to update this research based on Hattie's (2023c) current database of meta-analyses. I also attempted to improve on this analysis by more critically examining the studies within Hattie's (2023c) database. Many of the studies he includes are either correlational, unpublished, or only relate to older students, such as those of college age (Hattie, 2023c).

As I updated the research for this book, I strived to increase the quality of the research included. The next section reviews the meta-analyses related to what I call the scientific principles of teaching. In previously released versions of this research, I relied on the meta-analyses in Hattie's (2023c) database. However, as noted, not all these meta-analyses are comparable. To improve the quality of this analysis, I have removed all meta-analyses that were correlational, unpublished, on older students, or based on single-case research.

The Five Scientific Principles of Teaching

At the writing of this book, I could identify five core principles behind most evidence-based teaching methods: (1) quality time under instruction, (2) clarity of expectations, (3) specificity of teaching, (4) appropriately challenging curriculum, and (5) reflective teaching practices. These principles can help create a framework for evidence-based teachers to better understand the efficacy of the strategies they are already using and more easily identify new avenues for supporting student success. Let's explore each of these.

Quality Time Under Instruction

All students are capable of higher learning, but it is important to remember that different students learn at different rates. The amount of educational stimulus each student needs to learn a concept may be different, but all students need a minimum amount of educational stimulus to understand a given topic or skill. It is through exposure and practice that we learn, not osmosis, and therefore, I hypothesize that the most fundamental scientific principle in teaching is quality time under instruction. For example, very few of us could learn trigonometry in just one hour. The more we are exposed to information, the more likely we are to learn it. But each of us learns at different rates, so while one person may only need three hours of instruction to learn how to do this type of mathematics, another person may need eight hours or more before they achieve the same level of understanding. Students who take longer to learn new information may feel that they are not as smart as other students, but it is important to understand that the rate at which we learn is not a limiting factor on how much we can learn, rather just the efficiency with which we learn it (Stuebing et al., 2008).

Figure 3.1 shows effective teaching strategies that are either time intensive or increase the amount of time students must spend learning.

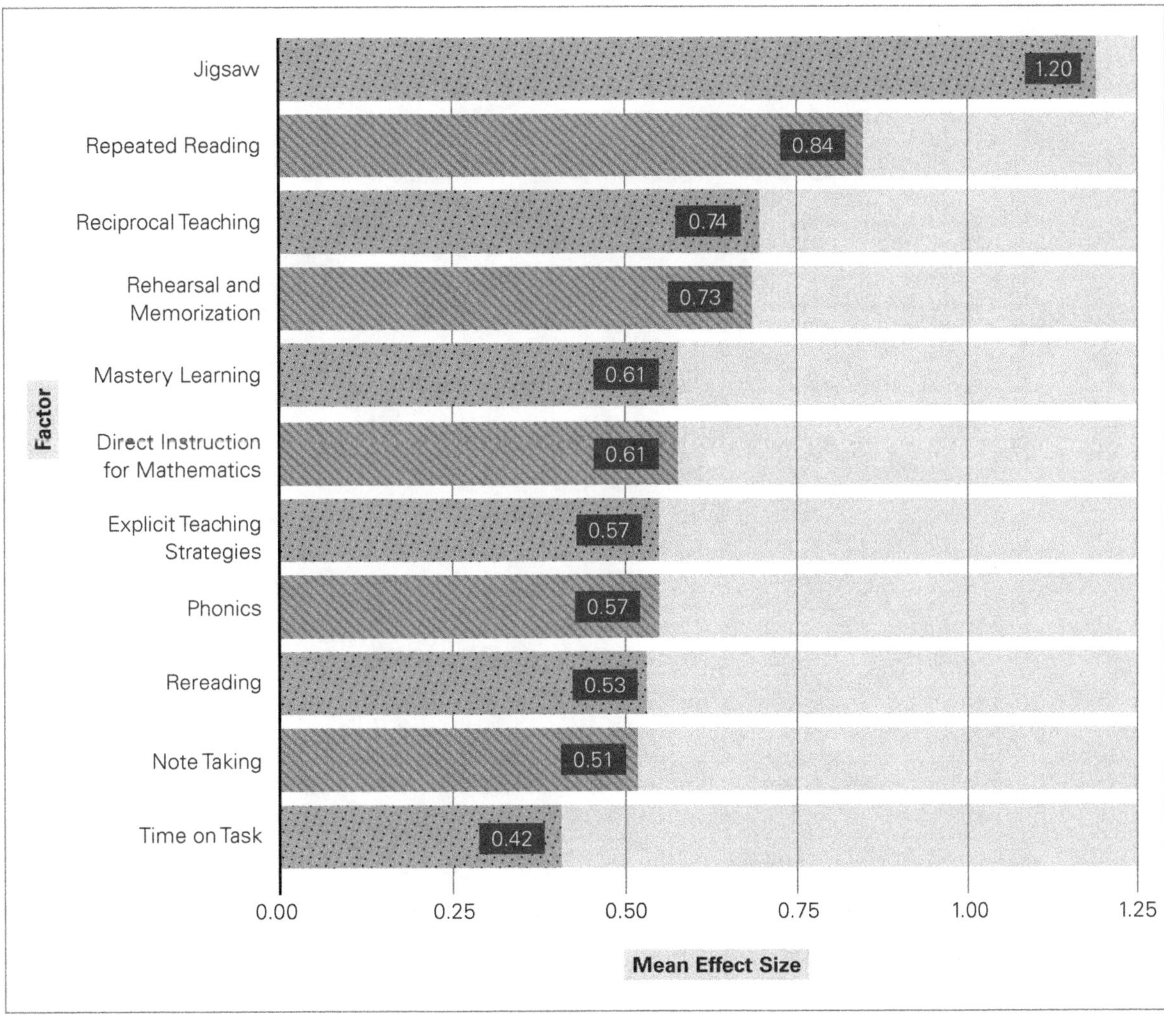

Source: Hattie, 2023c.

FIGURE 3.1: Teaching strategies that increase quality time under instruction.

For example, according to Hattie (2023c), *jigsaw* (which incorporates peer-tutoring) is the only high-yield cooperative learning strategy (meaning it shows an effect size above 0.40). With jigsaw, students must read, study, and then teach the learned content to their classmates. The entirety of a jigsaw class is spent studying or peer-tutoring. All time is spent on the actual learning process. This is different from other cooperative learning strategies, like round robin and think-pair-share, in which the greatest emphasis is placed on students sharing their opinions on subject matter—a process that promotes empathy and open-mindedness but often limits the time for studying core materials or practicing their application.

The principle of quality time under instruction is based on scholarly research, which I believe shows that tasks requiring more study or practice tend to result in greater increases in student learning. Unsurprisingly, then, the empirical evidence also shows that teaching factors that lower student instructional time typically produce only moderate or weak results (Hattie 2023c).

Figure 3.2 shows those teaching methods and factors that are likely to minimize student instructional time.

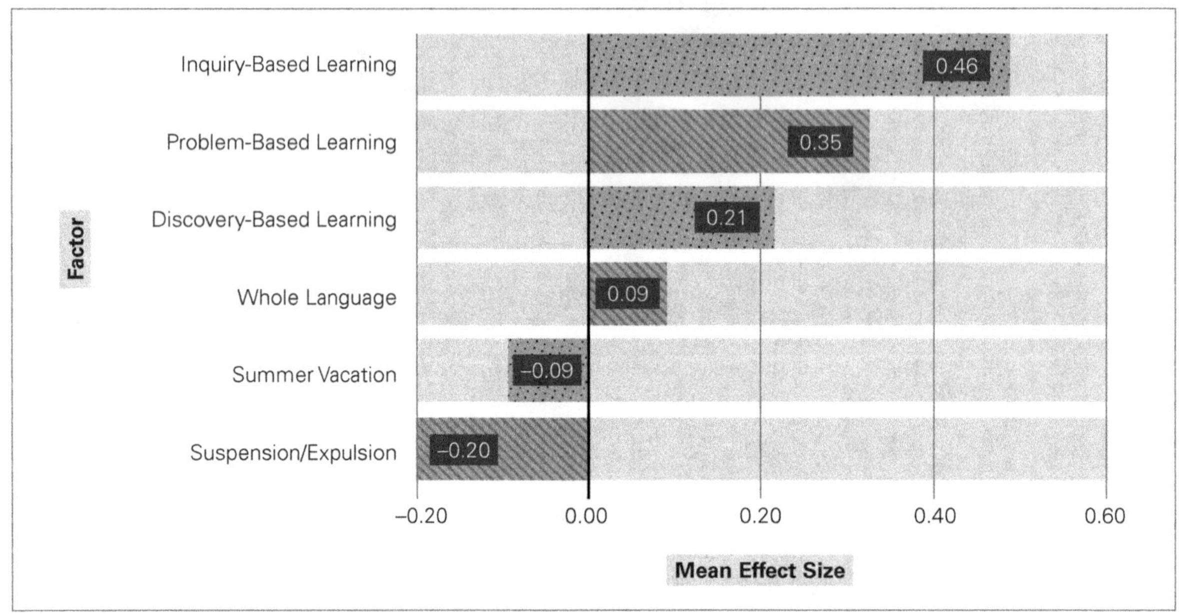

Source: Hattie, 2023c.

FIGURE 3.2: Teaching methods and factors that decrease instructional time.

Several of the factors and pedagogies in figure 3.2 work contrarily to those in figure 3.1 (page 29). For example, direct instruction is a teaching strategy in which the teacher directly and actively explains a concept to students, which is an opposing concept to discovery-based learning and inquiry-based learning, both of which are strategies that focus on decreasing a teacher's instructional time. Whereas direct instruction methods focus on having teachers explicitly explain curricular content, discovery-based and inquiry-based teaching methods focus on having teachers foster situations in which students learn the material on their own.

According to Hattie's (2023c) secondary meta-analysis, direct instruction has an effect size of 0.57; inquiry-based learning has an effect size of 0.47; and discovery-based teaching has an effect size of 0.21. Within this trend, we can clearly see that the more explicit instruction students receive, the better they do.

Similarly, phonics instruction and whole-language instruction are also contradictory strategies. Many whole-language advocates believe students should learn to read simply by practicing reading and often advocate that reading practice should largely be an independent student learning process (National Reading Panel, 2000). Phonics advocates suggest, instead, that students need explicit instruction from their teacher on how to decode words (National Reading Panel, 2000). In both instances, the teaching strategy that requires more explicit instruction outperforms the teaching strategy that requires less explicit instruction.

Essentially, I would hypothesize that the more time students spend directly engaging with curriculum materials, the more likely they are to absorb those materials and be able to meaningfully apply and scaffold that knowledge during assessments and later studies. Explicit instruction, as such, helps set up students for success by ensuring that time spent in class focuses on building a strong foundation of understanding, so students never feel surprised by what they are asked to do during an evaluation.

Clarity of Expectations

Many of the most proven teaching strategies within evidence-based education rely on increasing the clarity of learning expectations for students (Hattie, 2023c), such as success criteria, formative assessment, and clear learning goals. As a teacher, I believe we should be seeking to demystify the learning process. The better students understand the teacher's expectations, the more possible it is for them to reach those expectations. Interventions that embrace this principle help teachers better communicate to students what assessment standards and assessment success look like.

As a student, I remember getting back essays and not really understanding why I got the marks I did. When we use interventions that increase the clarity of expectations, this is precisely the type of scenario we are looking to avoid. Figure 3.3 features teaching strategies that increase the clarity of expectations for students, in one way or another.

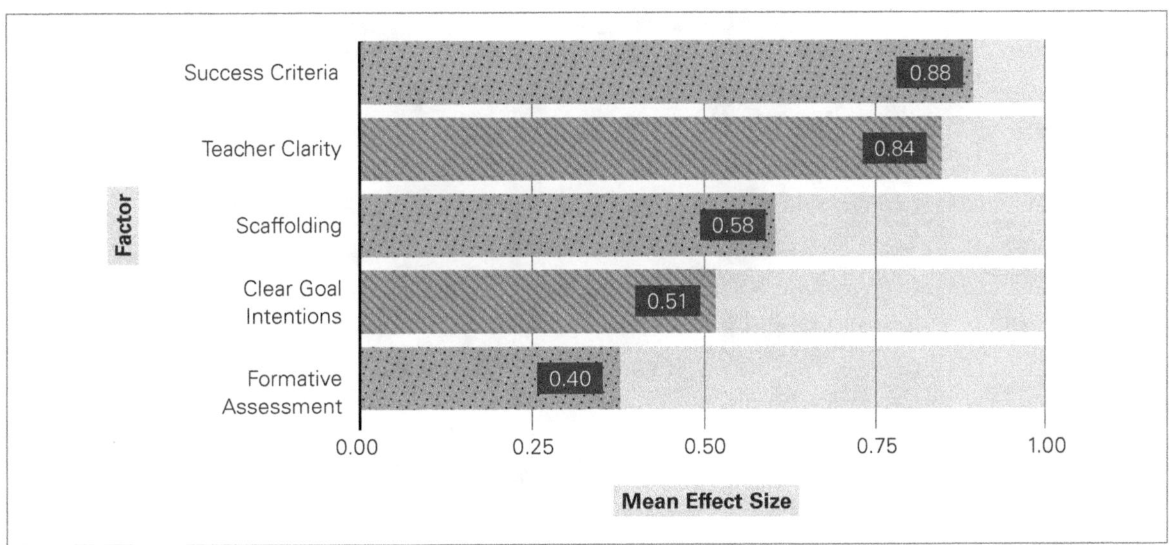

Source: Hattie 2023c.

FIGURE 3.3: Teaching strategies that increase clarity of expectations.

Success criteria, for example, is one of my favorite teaching tools, as it is both an incredibly effective strategy and requires very little additional work or expertise on the part of teachers. This strategy involves communicating your marking expectations to students using tools such as rubrics and exemplars. By making success criteria more transparent, teachers make it easier for students to accomplish what they want them to accomplish.

Specificity of Teaching

To evaluate students on their mastery of a learning target, both teaching and assessments need to specifically focus on this target. If you recognize that students do not learn through osmosis, you should also recognize that most of the teaching should specifically prepare students for assessments, unless our primary learning goal is to prepare them for *application questions* (questions students must use to apply previously learned concepts to completely new abstract situations). However, even if you want to specifically prepare students for challenging situations that can arise in life and in higher education, you must actually teach the application process as a learning goal itself and not just assess for it. In other words, it is fundamentally important to teach specifically to the tests.

I selected the teaching strategies in figure 3.4 because they either target a specific skill, like phonics (targets decoding), phonemic awareness (targets identification and manipulation of phonemes), and repeated reading (targets fluency), or because they are strategies to help teachers be more specific in their teaching, like deliberate practice.

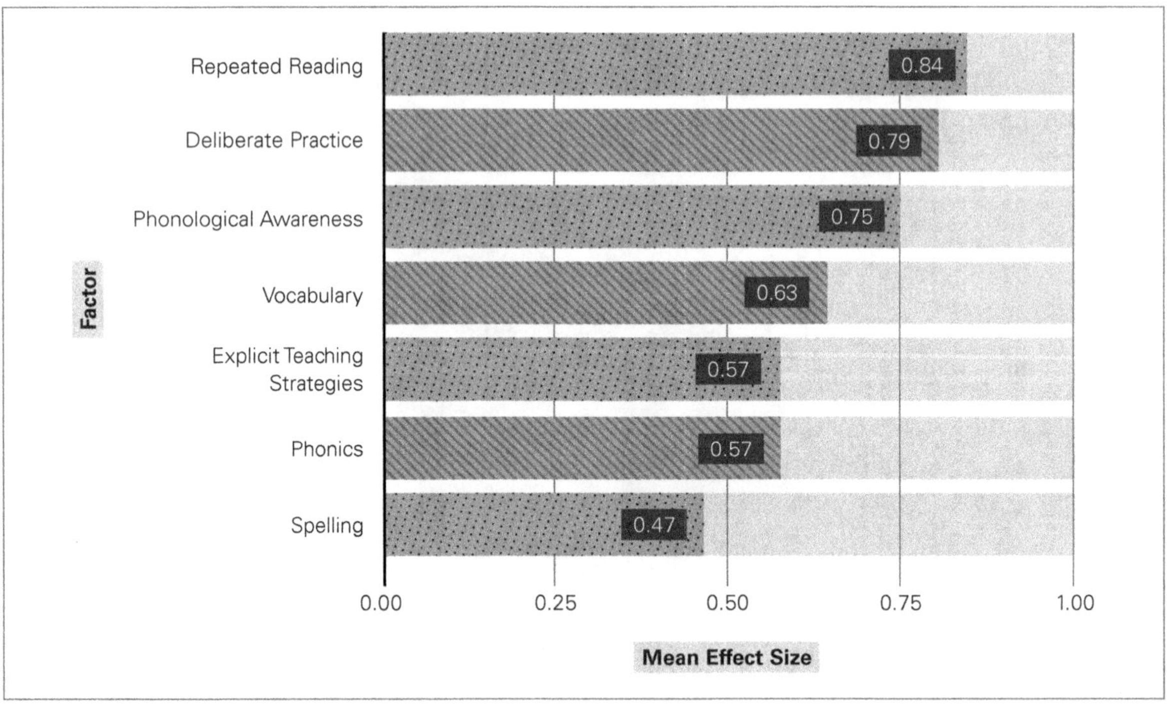

Source: Hattie, 2023c.

FIGURE 3.4: Teaching strategies that increase specificity of instruction.

It is important to remember that deeper levels of learning do not happen by accident. All students will learn some things independently and without teacher direction. However, teaching that is targeted at improving a student's understanding of a specific idea or concept is more likely to be successful. For example, interventions like spelling instruction, vocabulary programs, phonetic instruction, and repeated reading are all effective interventions that aim to increase a student's understanding of a specific component of literacy. Conversely, whole-language instruction takes a more general, less specific approach and has an effect size of only 0.06, according to Hattie (2023c).

Ultimately, specificity helps give teaching more direction. I remember being a new teacher and thinking, "How can I fill a six-hour day with educational content for my students?" I was not so much trying to teach my students specific concepts as I was just trying to fill my students' days. Teachers should, as often as possible, ask themselves, "How can I connect what I am teaching to specific curriculum expectations?"

Appropriately Challenging Curriculum

Extrapolating from the implications of the Pygmalion effect (Perera, 2023) and labeling theory (Nickerson, 2023), one should recognize that keeping high expectations for students is one of the most important teaching strategies. However, high expectations can be a double-edged sword if we do not recognize when students have learning gaps keeping them from meeting those expectations.

One of the easiest mistakes teachers can make is to lower the learning expectations for students too much when students are struggling to reach learning goals. Learning expectations should always be higher than a student's current ability, leaving them room to improve and grow. These expectations, however, should never be so high that students do not have the appropriate scaffolding to achieve them. To use this principle effectively, teachers should recognize that different students have different levels of abilities and therefore need different levels of difficulty in their curriculum. That said, the goal should always be to push each student to achieve his or her own highest levels of potential.

In the 1960s, coauthors Robert Rosenthal and Lenore Jacobson found that giving teachers falsified IQ tests changed student levels of success in a classroom (as cited in Good, Sterzinger, & Lavigne, 2018). If a teacher saw high IQ test results for a student, that student's class achievement increased. The inverse was true as well; if a teacher saw low IQ tests for a student, that student's class achievement decreased (Good et al., 2018). When we believe students are capable of success, we are more likely to challenge them, expect more of them, and believe in them. It is essential to give students a curriculum that challenges them, as it suggests that their teachers believe they are capable of higher levels of success.

Of course, it is possible to set expectations for students too high and present them with a curriculum that is too challenging, but in my experience, educators are far more likely to under-challenge students than they are to over-challenge them. In the 1980s, Thomas L. Good, Natasha Sterzinger, and Alyson Lavigne (2018) conducted an observational study that asked teachers to rank the capability of students in a class from highest to lowest. He then measured the teacher-student interactions for the top four and the bottom four. The bottom four students received systematically weaker teacher instruction, fewer opportunities to respond, were more likely to have incorrect responses, or were simply ignored.

Figure 3.5 (page 34) shows the factors that influence appropriately challenging expectations for students.

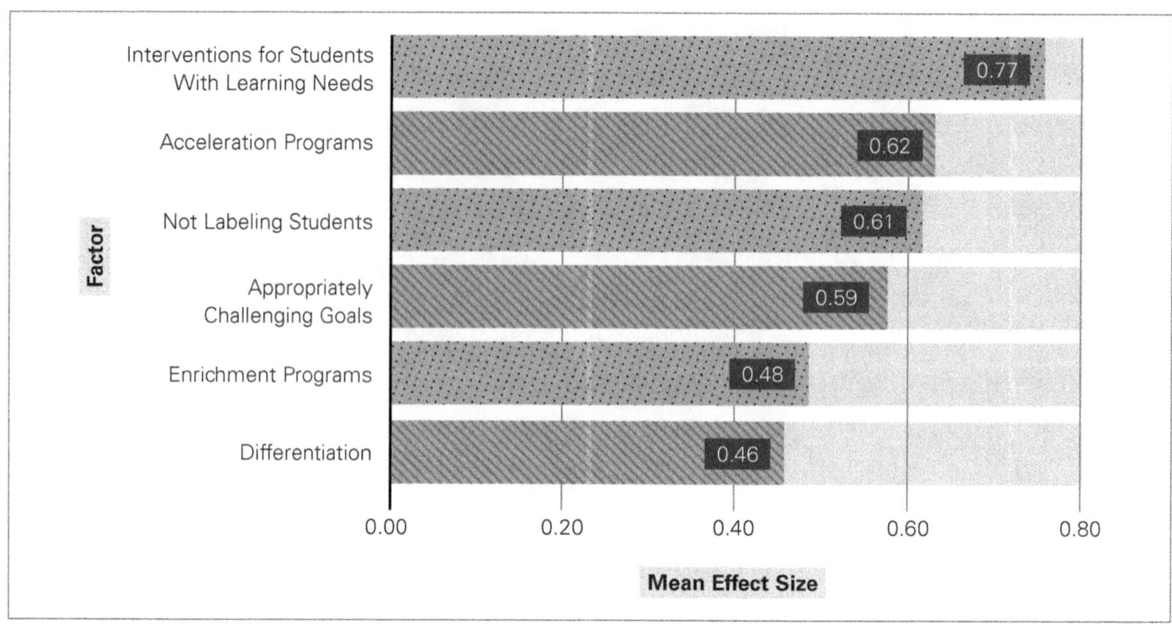

Source: Hattie 2023c.

FIGURE 3.5: Factors that influence appropriately challenging expectations for students.

All the factors in figure 3.5 highly correlate with student achievement and involve maintaining appropriately challenging expectations. Indeed, within Hattie's (2023c) secondary meta-analysis, he studied appropriately challenging learning goals, which showed a mean effect size of 0.59.

Reflective Teaching Practices

Collective self-efficacy was one of the number-one student achievement factors on Hattie's (2023c) list, with an effect size of 1.36, in large part because it promotes reflective teaching. No one is perfect, no human being is always right, and no single teacher is better able to serve all students all the time. No matter the endeavor, it is important, as a teacher, to reflect on your performance and be willing to adapt or evolve your practices according to what is working and what is not. This idea is fundamental to the principle of evidence-based teaching, which is to say, being evidence based requires a certain degree of self-scrutiny above and beyond merely keeping up to date on new teaching strategies or current best practices.

The principle of reflective teaching practices can be found in a variety of popular teaching strategies such as RTI or collaborative inquiry. Reflective teaching is a necessary precursor to understanding how we, as educators, can grow our own practices. Other frameworks and methods for improving reflective practices include:

- Team teaching
- Multitiered systems of support (MTSS)
- The literacy assessment, planning, and instruction cycle (LAPIC)

Teaching Methods Aligned With the Five Scientific Principles of Teaching

Figure 3.6 shows many teaching methods that align with the five scientific principles of teaching. For example, direct instruction can both increase the quality time under instruction in a classroom and the specificity of instruction. Teaching methods that overlap can be some of the most effective.

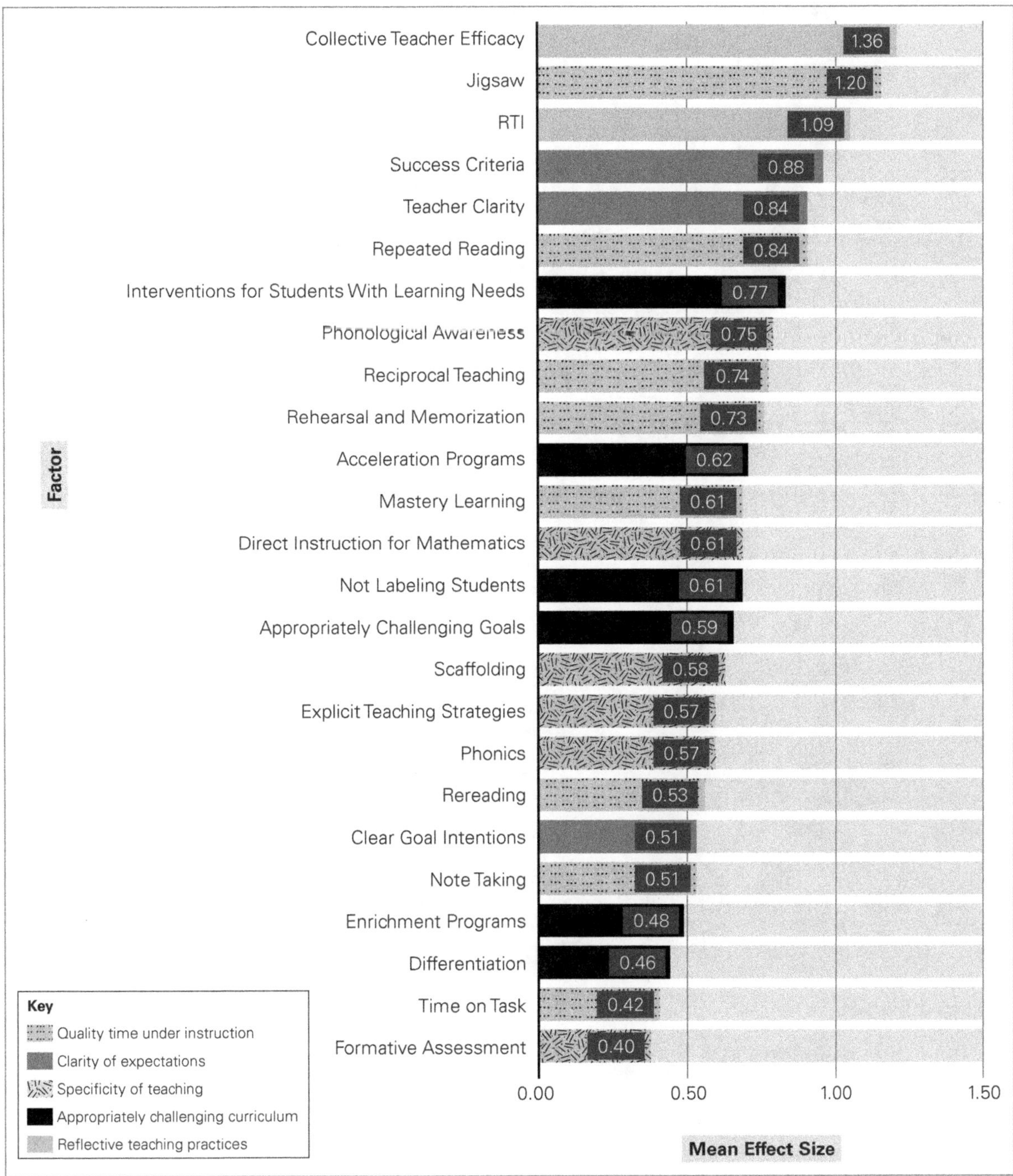

Source: Hattie 2023c.

FIGURE 3.6: Teaching methods aligned with the five scientific principles of teaching.

Keeping these connected principles in mind can be an effective way of creating a kind of framework for thinking about useful strategies. For example, I implement self-reported grades in my classroom with the goal of using it to increase the clarity of my expectations. Having this type of framework to reference when designing lessons can allow teachers to be more mindful and deliberate in implementing learning strategies.

Summary Points to Remember

Following is a list of highlights and significant points outlined in this chapter.

- ☑ All students can learn given enough time and high-quality instruction.
- ☑ Providing students with clear and high expectations, explicit instruction, and sufficient time is the simplest way to improve educational outcomes.
- ☑ As educators, we are always learning; being reflective in our practice helps us improve instruction over time.

Reflection Questions

Individually or with your team, use these questions to reflect on the information in this chapter.

1. Which of the five principles do you feel best embodies your own teaching practices? Why?
2. Which of the five principles could you better utilize in your practice? Why would that work well in your class?
3. Which principle do you think is most important, according to your experience, and why?
4. Which principle do you think is least important, according to your experience, and why?
5. Which of the five principles surprised you the most, and why?

CHAPTER 4

Intelligence and IQ Tests

This chapter provides an overview of intelligence, why it is difficult to measure, and the potential downsides to making instructional decisions based on IQ tests. Psychological assessments can be valuable tools when used correctly. However, they have possible downsides when used inappropriately. As teachers, it's important to understand the potential benefits and practical limitations of psychological assessments so you can make better instructional decisions.

Intelligence as a Concept

At first glance, the answer to the question, What is intelligence? might appear to be so simple that exploring the concept is irrelevant. However, our understanding of what intelligence is, as educators, affects how we envision student learning, approximations of what our expectations for students should be (such as for those receiving intervention), and how we work with students in special education. Ultimately, this question is far more central to how we behave as teachers than we might intuitively believe. Intelligence is not the skills one has mastered or the knowledge one has accumulated, but rather, it is the potential to acquire and retain new skills or knowledge (Goddard, 1946).

Designing intelligence tests is challenging, therefore, because it is almost impossible to build a test that isn't based on preexisting skills. Imagine, for instance, that you have a student who struggles to learn mathematics. To help this student, you spend extra time practicing mathematics with them until they can outperform many of their peers. Now imagine that this student is given an intelligence test with many mathematics questions, and they score high. Did the student improve mathematical intelligence, or simply memorize a large number of mathematics concepts and procedures?

Even more confounding is the fact the brain constantly rewires itself to become better at the skills practiced through a process referred to as *neuroplasticity* (Puderbaugh & Emmady, 2022). This means someone can become "smarter" by studying. In reality, intelligence is probably a fluid concept rather than a fixed one (Puderbaugh & Emmady, 2022).

Early 20th-century psychologists developed intellectual assessments to try and quantify a person's raw intellectual potential. The most famous of these assessments is, of course, the IQ test, and to this date, school boards all around the world still use these to diagnostically assess students' individual needs (Stough, 2015). However, these tests do not measure true intelligence but rather a proxy of intelligence; as such, their results are only valid when identifying large deviations.

To quote IQ researcher James Flynn (1987), "The hypothesis that best fits the results is that IQ tests do not measure intelligence but rather correlate with a weak causal link to intelligence" (p. 171). If an IQ test was testing intellectual ability rather than intellectual preparedness, you would not be able to study for it and improve your result, but companies who sell these tests admit that it is possible to study for them to increase your score (Genius Tests, n.d.).

Risks of Intelligence and IQ Tests

This section explores the potential downsides that exist with using IQ tests to inform teaching practices. There are three potential downsides of IQ tests: (1) they tend to be culturally and institutionally biased toward the dominant group in society; (2) they come with an inherent risk of creating self-fulfilling prophecies (for example, students with higher IQ scores get more positive attention and continue to improve); and (3) they have been used to justify oppression and systemic racism.

Cultural and Institutional Bias

It may feel tempting to be dismissive of the idea of bias in an intelligence text, but the data tell a different story. For example, White middle- or upper-class students tend to do better than non-White, working-class students (Rushton & Jensen, 2005). However, race is not a scientifically validated concept, but rather a social construct. While minor differences can be seen between groups of people, these differences do not show a significant impact on the human genome. Therefore, if we realize that differences in IQ exist, the explanation for these differences must be social and not biological (Cunningham et al., 2004). In other words, the test measures academic preparedness rather than the actual raw intellectual potential. Remember, the human brain, regardless of race or socioeconomic status, literally rewires itself to become better at the tasks people practice (Puderbaugh & Emmady, 2022).

As such, if a student comes from an economically disadvantaged home, with few books, lower-quality nutrition, and less educated parents who do not have the luxury of time to help with homework, that student is likely not going to perform well on an intelligence test. However, this low IQ score is not an authentic indicator of the student's actual intellectual potential.

One early study that really demonstrates this fact was conducted by Sandra Scarr and Richard A. Weinberg in 1976. This study looked at 130 Black children who had been adopted by wealthy White families. The results showed that these children outperformed the average White student on IQ tests. Comparatively, Black students at that time, on average, performed worse than White students (Scarr & Weinberg, 1976). This study shows that the prime factor in determining intelligence test outcomes is social and not biological.

The Self-Fulfilling Prophecy

Using IQ tests is not a risk-free endeavor. Labeling theory and the Pygmalion experiment teach us that making prejudgments about a student has an extremely large impact on student achievement (Bernburg, 2009; Good et al., 2018). If a teacher prematurely or incorrectly assesses a student as having an intellectual disability, they risk creating a self-fulfilling prophecy (Good et al., 2018). When a student in this situation does poorly, the teacher might blame the student's intellectual disability and discount his or her own accountability. The teacher might modify their own expectations for the student, and even their marking can be potentially biased by these labels. While it is extremely tempting to think that we are above being biased, the reality is that bias has a subtle and pernicious effect that is difficult for any human being to avoid.

Justification for Oppression

Even more troubling is how labels regarding intelligence can affect racialized and oppressed communities. The Canadian government, for example, used English IQ tests as justification to forcibly sterilize immigrants who could not speak English in the early 20th century (Marsh, 2015). Unfortunately, because of socioeconomic factors, students of color are far more likely to be identified as having a learning disability or intellectual disability (Shifrer, Muller, & Callahan, 2011). As educators, it is crucial that we avoid making unnecessary or unqualified judgments about a student's intelligence that could potentially create a labeling bias—which is not to say that it is always inappropriate to use an intelligence test but rather that we should be extremely careful with its application.

Possible Benefits of Intelligence and IQ Tests

While intelligence tests are both imprecise and risky, they still have some potential benefits. They can have some practical application benefits if used carefully by professionals on the extreme ends of the spectrums. For example, if a sixth-grade student scores well below a first-grade level on an intelligence test or in the very bottom percentile of a school's population, it would seem reasonable to believe that the student might have an intellectual disability, and the test could, therefore, be used as a justification to provide that student with modified learning goals. However, I would point out that many factors can skew a test—for example, giving a student an intelligence test in English when it is not his or her first language (Hiermeier & Verity, 2022) or giving a student an intelligence test after they have stayed up late and are too tired to give their best effort (Wang et al., 2013).

It is important to remember that we, as teachers, are not psychologists, and barring some other special training, we're not qualified to use these tests. Intelligence tests can be potentially dangerous tools. We do not want to see professionals using these tests on a frequent or casual basis. Most importantly, we want to make sure we are not callously identifying students of color or students living in poverty as having an intellectual disability and then creating self-fulfilling prophecies.

Summary Points to Remember

Following is a list of highlights and significant points outlined in this chapter.

- ☑ IQ tests are not precise and, therefore, only large deviations should be seen as meaningful.
- ☑ When reading IQ tests or psychological assessments, consider how other factors influenced the results, such as socioeconomic factors, attendance, prior instruction, sleep, and so on.
- ☑ Only trained psychologists should be conducting psychological and IQ/intelligence assessments with students.

Reflection Questions

Individually or with your team, use these questions to reflect on the information in this chapter.

1. How can your understanding of intelligence shape your teaching practice?
2. How should your understanding of intelligence shape your teaching practice?
3. What risks of institutional racism or bias come with IQ tests?
4. When might an intelligence test be useful?
5. What factors might influence the result of an intelligence test?

CHAPTER 5

Growth Mindset

Growth mindset is a popular metacognition strategy coined by Carol S. Dweck (2016), who defines it as a state of being in which individuals respond to challenges by asking how they can overcome them, as opposed to *if* they can overcome them. Within this framework, ability and intelligence are flexible rather than fixed. Adopting this mindset is supposed to help people to work through adversity and challenge instead of giving up. Given its popularity, it's also a concept that is often misunderstood and misapplied.

This chapter reviews what it means to have a growth mindset, whether there is value in teaching students about growth mindset, and if there are any specific benefits to having a growth mindset.

My Journey With Growth Mindset

My journey with growth mindset began in 2018, when I received training in response to intervention (RTI). This training was a large part of what sparked my interest in evidence-based teaching.

The trainers at the time talked about the value of adopting a growth mindset. They taught us not only to teach students to adopt this concept but also that we should adopt it for how we approach instruction. We were told not to ask if students were capable of higher levels of success, but instead to believe students are capable of higher levels of success as long as we provide them with the appropriate instruction. When students struggle, we are supposed to ask ourselves how we can ensure their success.

I found this mantra incredibly empowering for a multitude of reasons. First, it was an inspiring message, and it fit with my preconceived notions of how a good teacher should act. Most importantly, I felt it empowered me to better serve my students. At the time, I worked in a remote indigenous school that was struggling. Within my school, many students and families were affected by intergenerational trauma caused by the residential school system. Most teachers were fresh out of college, looking for professional experience. There was a high staff turnover rate, and we were often short on qualified teachers. Additionally, many of the wealthiest students' families paid to send their children to school in a nearby town. These factors, among other socioeconomic factors, contributed to an obvious achievement gap.

I felt like I was witnessing, firsthand, institutionalized racism and its effects. The dropout rate was high, truancy was rampant, graduation rates were low, and problem behaviors were frequent. There was a palpable feeling of "us versus them" between the school and the community. Some parents found that the school reminded them of their own negative experiences and often did not trust the teachers. Teachers felt overwhelmed and frequently blamed the community. Many staff, students, and community members did not view the school as a "real" school. During my last two years working there, I was the upper-secondary language and history teacher. I was bound and determined to teach the students how to write essays, as I had high hopes that some of them would go to college. I distinctly remember some students telling me, "This is an Indian school; we don't do real work here." I felt hopeless.

When you work at a school that is truly struggling, it can sometimes be easier to give up on students. The learning gaps are large, challenging behaviors are more frequent, and there tends to be a general air of defeatism within the building. Adapting a growth mindset gave me the hope I needed to be a better teacher and better serve my students.

Truthfully, I don't think I was doing a good job as a teacher before my RTI training. I primarily used an inquiry-based model, in which there was minimal explicit or systematic instruction. My focus was not on building knowledge but on engagement. I thought if I could just make school fun, everything else would click into place. My thought process was often more about filling my instructional hours than meeting instructional goals. However, once I started to track students' progress with the RTI model, I quickly saw that my students were not learning, at least not at the rate I wanted.

With this newly adopted growth mindset, I felt more responsible for my students' learning and began to make changes. My teaching became a fluid and evolving process of improving my own practices rather than a mindless replication of how I remembered being taught.

Fast forward to 2024: I have spent the last six years researching, writing, blogging, and podcasting about my own journey with evidence-based instruction. Indeed, I have now written almost two hundred articles on the subject, recorded hundreds of podcast episodes, and published multiple books on the science of teaching. If I had not been so hooked on the idea of a growth mindset, I am not so sure I would have even done all that research and writing. I know a growth mindset has helped me on my journey as an educator. Moreover, I didn't just apply this mindset to my teaching craft but to other areas of my life, such as professional development, personal finances, and personal fitness.

With these experiences in mind, a growth mindset can be powerful for teachers to apply to working and teaching in difficult settings. It is important to ask, "How can I help these students succeed?" rather than "Can these students succeed?"

The Research on Growth Mindset

In 2018, I wrote a blog post called "The Scientific Principles of Teaching" with the cofounder of *Pedagogy Non-Grata*, Joshua King. This blog post ranked six principles that we felt were common influencing factors behind pedagogies that Hattie (2023c) had found to have a high-yield impact. We made growth mindset one of those principles and ranked it at number five.

In 2021, I went on to write and self-publish a book inspired by that blog post, also titled *The Scientific Principles of Teaching* (Hansford, 2022h). The cover of the book shows a pyramid with growth mindset as the fifth ranking.

The original blog post became a crowning chapter of the book, and, at the time, I was not aware of any meta-analyses on the topic. However, Josh and I noticed that several of the high-yield pedagogies identified by Hattie in his secondary meta-analysis appeared connected to growth mindset, including teacher estimates of achievement, collective-self efficacy, RTI, metacognition strategies, student-self efficacy, and teachers not labeling students (Visible Learning, 2018). This led both of us to hypothesize that growth mindset was fundamentally important for excellent education.

Within the chapter on growth mindset, I advocated that teachers encourage students to develop a growth mindset and adopt one for themselves. Of course, growth mindset sharing connections with other evidence-based pedagogies is not direct evidence of efficacy in itself. This chapter was the most hypothetical of the book, as rather than laying out direct evidence for or against pedagogies, it made a theoretical case for my hypotheses regarding education. And it brings me no joy to say that a large part of my hypothesis has now been thoroughly disproven.

Several days before writing this book, Brooke N. Macnamara and Alexander P. Burgoyne (2023) published a meta-analysis of sixty-three studies on the impact of growth mindset interventions on students' academic growth. Much to my chagrin, their results put a large hole in my hypothesis that a growth mindset is a fundamental principle of good teaching. Across all studies, they found an average Cohen's *d* effect size of 0.05. Considering effect sizes below 0.20 are considered negligible, this is very low and suggests that there is no statistical benefit for growth mindset interventions. Moreover, the authors noted that most of the studies were of low quality and that sponsorship bias was a major issue. When the authors controlled for quality, they excluded all but six studies and found a mean effect size of 0.02. This meta-analysis clearly indicates that teaching students to develop a growth mindset has, on average, no meaningful benefit of any kind for academic achievement (Macnamara & Burgoyne, 2023).

Jeni L. Burnette and colleagues (2023) also conducted a meta-analysis on growth mindset. Within this meta-analysis, the authors used a very rigorous inclusion criteria and only accepted randomized controlled trial studies. In total, they located fifty-three independent testing samples. Again, the authors found a negligible effect size for the impact of teaching a growth mindset on academic achievement ($d = 0.14$). However, they also found in their analysis that growth mindset instruction was positive for student mental health ($d = 0.32$; Burnette et al., 2023). This suggests that while the benefit of growth mindset on academics appears to be low, the primary benefit of growth mindset is on students' well-being. This is important to note, as growth mindset is a very low-cost intervention (both from a time and money standpoint) and thus, if it benefits students, it does make sense to implement it.

Of course, meta-analysis generally tells the *what*, not the *why*. It would be interesting to know if the reason growth mindset instruction fails to show any significant benefit on academics is because there is no real practical application or if it is because students don't tend to respond to or buy into mindset interventions.

It reminds me of the studies on mindfulness training. Some adults would claim mindfulness training has revolutionized their lives. According to Louise Delegran and Alex Haley (2023), *mindfulness training* is meant to help people achieve a mental state in which "nonelaborative, nonjudgmental, present-centered awareness in which each thought, feeling, sensation that arises . . . is acknowledged and accepted as it is." However, studies on teaching mindfulness to students also tend to show very low results across various types of research measures (Bauer et al., 2019). In my own practice, I have found that students rarely seem to buy into mindset-related training.

While it is clear that I was wrong about growth mindset training being essential to good teaching, I still cannot quite concede that there is no benefit to the strategy or adopting a growth mindset. I would like to make the case for not entirely throwing away the concept of growth mindset. The academic merit of teaching growth mindset is clearly limited, but that does not mean there is no emotional or holistic value for students. Moreover, while growth mindset appears to be a low-value practice, it also is a low-cost one. Other low-value practices, such as discovery-based learning, not teaching algorithms, or three cueing, come with a potential risk of harm to students, as I discuss in chapter 13 (page 89).

However, I don't see a potential harm factor to growth mindset instruction, short of teaching it instead of other high-value practices. Additionally, I think it's worth considering if growth mindset instruction might help students develop a better sense of perseverance over the longer term, even if it does not improve academic outcomes, over the short or medium term. In my own teaching practice, I spend five minutes explaining the concept to my class at the beginning of the year. Then, when students make closed-minded statements, like "I can't learn mathematics," I identify the statement as being a product of a fixed mindset and encourage them to persevere. While the potential benefit of this practice is likely low, so is the potential harm, in my opinion.

That said, it is quite clear that there is little to no empirical evidence for an overall effect for teaching students to adopt a growth mindset for improving academic outcomes. However, I still think there is value in teachers adopting a growth mindset about students. I maintain that adopting a growth mindset has helped me as a teacher. I also think most of the indirect research I referenced at the beginning of this chapter (Visible Learning, 2018)—the secondary meta-analyses on RTI, teacher estimates of achievement, student-self efficacy, and teachers not labeling students—was focused on teacher practices, not student practices.

While there isn't a large body of research that specifically examines the benefits of teachers believing in students, we do have research showing that what teachers believe about their students' abilities matters. According to Hattie (2023i), Robert Ridge's 1989 meta-analysis on the correlation between teacher expectations and student achievement shows a mean Pearson effect size of 0.62. Inversely, research shows that low teacher expectations have harmed students of color, in particular, when their teachers did not believe in them.

Rosenthal and Jacobson have done a lot of research confirming this phenomenon (as cited in Good et al., 2018). In the 1960s, they conducted a series of studies that all showed a benefit to teachers holding high expectations and beliefs for their students. In the most famous of these experiments, they administered IQ tests to students and then gave randomized fake results back to their teachers (as cited in Good et al., 2018). The students who received the fake positive IQ tests went on to outperform the other students in their class.

In one experiment, Rosenthal and Jacobson even replicated their results on rats (as cited in Good et al., 2018). They pooled groups of researchers together to train rats. They told one set of researchers that the rats they were working with had below-average intelligence, and another group of researchers that the rats they were working with had above-average intelligence. The rats in the second group outperformed the rats in the first group (as cited in Good et al., 2018). Researchers since Rosenthal and Jacobson observed:

> High-achieving students received teacher actions and opportunities that supported their achievement (for example, teachers asked them more challenging questions and stayed with them by providing clues when they initially responded incorrectly). In contrast, low-achieving students received less stimulation. (as cited in Good et al., 2018)

I see some of this debate playing out on social media regarding the reading wars. There is a growing movement of teachers who are adopting what they refer to as the *science of reading* (SOR). Typically, these teachers support using a structured literacy approach as opposed to a balanced literacy approach (Hollingsworth, 2023). I often see SOR teachers discussing how, before they started to research the science of reading, they just believed some students could not learn how to read. These same teachers will often tell you how switching to an SOR approach changed how they viewed their most struggling readers and that instead of asking themselves if these students could read, they started to ask how they could help these students learn to read. Adopting a growth mindset was of great personal and emotional value to me as an educator and an evidence-based practitioner.

So truthfully, I might be holding onto some emotional bias here, as normally, I would not continue to endorse a practice after finding a meta-analysis that presents strong evidence that a practice is not effective. That said, I still believe there is value in teachers adopting a growth mindset for how they teach their students, as I think believing in students' potential is of the highest worthiness for our profession.

However, there is a big difference between casually including instruction on growth mindset as part of your daily routine and hiring consultants to come into a school to provide intensive growth-mindset training. Similarly, I have seen some schools in my career that have placed an intense focus on growth-mindset instruction to the point that you might call it the bedrock of their curriculum practice. I would think that as long as growth-mindset instruction is not used in the place of other high-value pedagogies, there is no potential for harm and some potential for benefit.

Summary Points to Remember

Following is a list of highlights and significant points outlined in this chapter.

- ☑ Growth mindset is a time- and cost-efficient pedagogy.
- ☑ The scientific evidence that it might help student achievement is weak. However, there is stronger evidence that it helps with student mental health.
- ☑ Growth-mindset instruction should not replace other high-value pedagogies.
- ☑ To avoid the pitfalls of labeling, it is important to adopt the idea that *all students can learn.*

Reflection Questions

Individually or with your team, use these questions to reflect on the information in this chapter.

1. What surprised you most in this chapter?
2. Do you believe all students are capable of success? Why or why not?
3. How can you better maintain a positive mindset about your students? Why do you think growth mindset instruction shows such small benefits for students, according to the research?
4. Do you believe growth-mindset instruction is worth the time cost?
5. Do you think some students might benefit from growth mindset training? Why or why not?

Feedback

Giving students effective feedback can be one of the most difficult parts of teaching. Providing feedback on learning tasks and assessments is obviously paramount to explicit instruction. However, it's time-consuming, and students often don't put the same effort into reading feedback that teachers put into writing it. I have seen some teachers stay late every night, diligently marking and writing comments on every piece of work their students complete.

I have little doubt that feedback can help students; however, I have often wondered if this practice of marking each assignment is truly a time-efficient strategy. I can't even count the number of times I have seen a student check their mark on a test and throw out the paper before reading the comments. So, it does beg the questions: How valuable does feedback tend to be? What kind of feedback is most effective, and how can you best use it?

In this chapter, I review three meta-analyses to try and answer these questions.

Three Meta-Analyses on Feedback

Of the three meta-analyses studies on feedback detailed in this chapter, the first (Study 1) was conducted in 2015 by Fabienne M. Van der Kleij, Remco C. Feskins, and Theo J. H. M. Eggen. It examines forty experimental and quasi-experimental studies and is focused on computer-based learning. The second meta-analysis (Study 2) was conducted in 2020 by Bennedikt Wisniewski, Klaus Zierer, and John Hattie and looks at 435 studies on the topic of feedback in general. This study was by far the largest ever conducted on this topic. However, it also used weak inclusion criteria, so the results could be inflated. The final meta-analysis (Study 3) was conducted in 2016 by Huiyong Fan, Jianzhong Xu, Zhihui Cai, Jinbo He, and Xitao Fan and examines sixty-one studies. However, the analysis was purely correlational. Of these three meta-analyses, Study 1 is the most rigorous; however, it only examines feedback in the context of computer-based learning.

Study 1

Study 1 (Van der Kleij et al., 2015) examined forty experimental or quasi-experimental studies on the topic of feedback for computer-based learning in K–12 and college. The authors looked at three types of feedback: providing an explanation, indicating if an answer was correct, or providing the correct answer (Van der Kleij et al., 2015). The authors measured the results using a Hedge's *g* calculation (Van der Kleij et al., 2015). (For more about this calculation, see Types of Effect Size Calculations in chapter 1, page 23.) Figure 6.1 shows the results of this study.

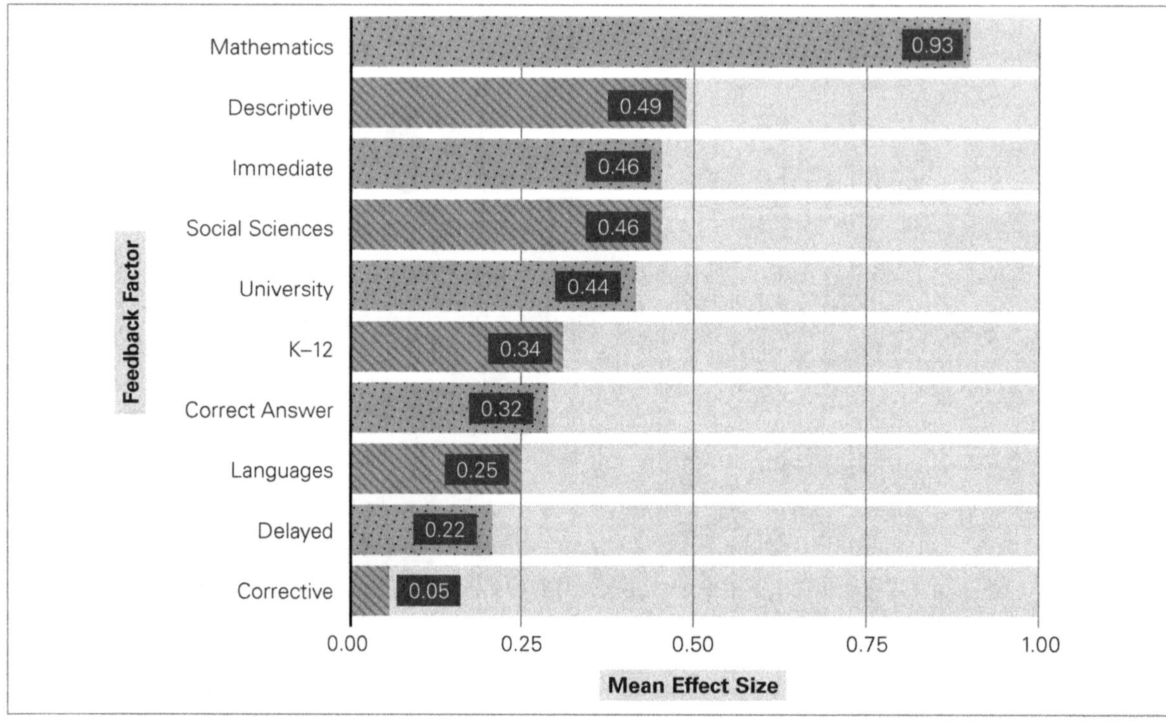

Source for data: Van der Kleij et al., 2015.
Source: Hansford, 2022c. Used with permission.

FIGURE 6.1: When and how feedback is best used.

These results suggest that feedback is most useful when it's immediate and descriptive. They also suggest that feedback that is delayed or only indicates if an answer is correct is far less helpful. These results also suggest that feedback is most important for students in grades 7 and higher and in mathematics. This seems logical, as these students might have a greater sense of responsibility, and mathematics can be highly procedural—meaning small errors can cause much lower outcomes. This study did have two limitations. First, it was only for computer-based learning; and second, only fourteen effect sizes were for students in grade 12 or lower, which means the results could be unreliable for lower elementary students.

Study 2

Study 2 (Wisniewski et al., 2020) is a meta-analysis of 435 studies on feedback. The authors found a mean Cohen's *d* effect size of 0.55. However, they also included case studies that were of low quality and did not use a control group (Wisniewski et al., 2020). If studies that did not include control groups were excluded, a mean effect size of 0.42 was found. The authors also calculated several interesting *moderator variables results* (moderator results look at subsets of data to see how findings change across variables, such as demographics, study design, or measurement; Wisniewski et al., 2020), as shown in figure 6.2.

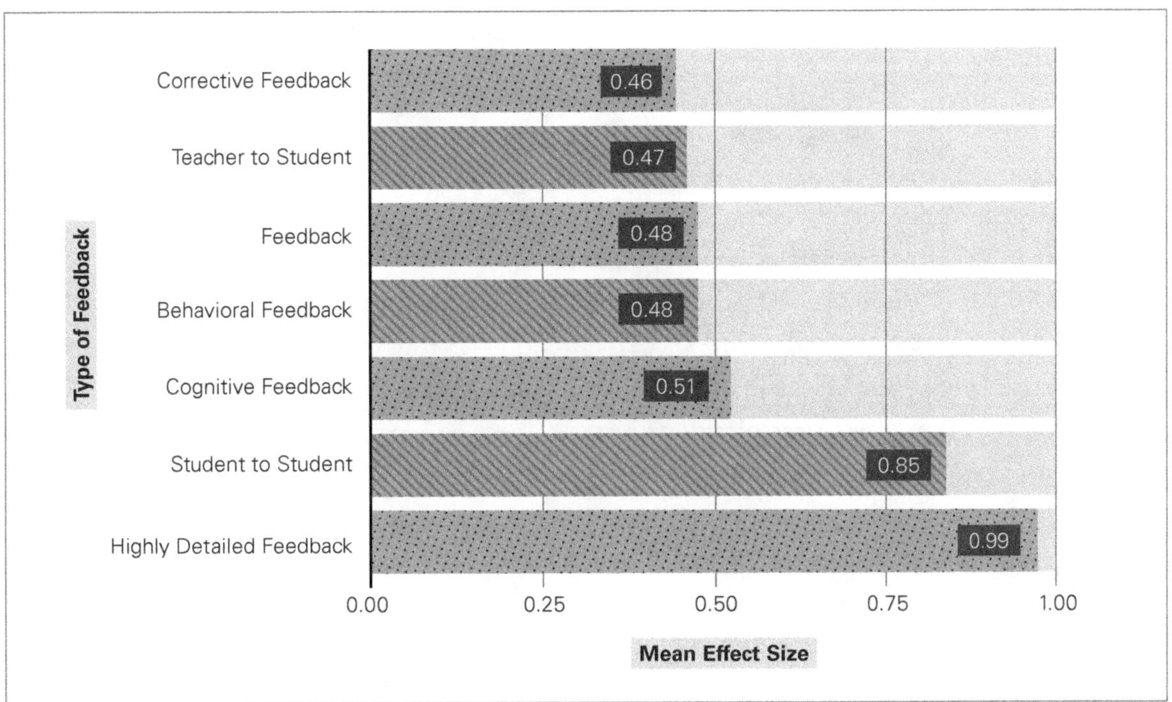

Source for data: Wisniewski et al., 2020.
Source: Hansford, 2022c. Used with permission.

FIGURE 6.2: Types of feedback organized by effect size.

These results reinforce the fact that more descriptive feedback is likely to have better results than less descriptive feedback. It also suggests that students might be more willing to listen to feedback if it comes from a peer (Wisniewski et al., 2020). However, this meta-analysis has several limitations.

First, the authors included low-quality studies that inflated the results, which makes the *moderator data* in figure 6.2 (page 49) less reliable (Wisniewski et al., 2020). (*Moderator analysis* breaks down the results of a meta-analysis according to specific sub-categories, such as age, subject, or assessment type.) Second, the authors did not code for grades or subjects, which means it is unknown if these results are reliable in earlier grades (Wisniewski et al., 2020). This is especially problematic when considering that Study 1 showed lower results for younger students (Van der Kleij et al., 2015).

Study 3

Study 3 (Fan et al., 2016) looked at twenty-eight studies on homework. The results showed that marked homework (r = 0.51) showed more than double the outcomes of unmarked homework (r = 0.22; Fan et al., 2016). This meta-analysis had two limitations: (1) it included *nonexperimental studies* and (2) it used a *correlational effect size* (Fan et al., 2016).

Aggregation of the Studies

These three studies are not definitive, but they do suggest that feedback is important, especially for mathematics and older students. They also suggest that the importance of feedback is not to evaluate students but rather to help them learn via explanations. However, detailed written feedback can be very time-consuming, so the following are some practical suggestions to maximize the time efficiency of providing feedback.

- **Offer detailed success criteria:** Clearly explain to students how you will be marking an assignment before they start working. This frontloads feedback so students understand your expectations and reduces the amount of feedback required after the assignment is complete.
- **Use self-assessment and peer assessment:** In a peer or self-assessment, students mark themselves based on the success criterion and rubrics they received. While you might not accept all the marks students provide, this can expedite your marking process. Plus, these strategies don't just cut down on marking time; they help draw students' attention to your expectations and clarify any misunderstandings.
  I particularly like to use self-assessment on complex formative assignments. For example, if you are teaching students how to write a five-paragraph essay, you might have them self-assess their first two attempts based on a rubric or success criteria and only mark their final attempt. Similarly, you write mathematics problems on a white board and have students check each other's work, but still mark the final test yourself. These types of strategies decrease time spent marking daily student work and increase student learning.
- **Use conferencing:** In my own practice as a teacher, I like meeting with students one on one to discuss areas for feedback, as I can talk a lot faster than

I can write. This allows me to check for understanding and give students more detailed feedback within a smaller amount of time.

- **Include group feedback:** If you notice a lot of students are making the same mistake, rather than writing the same comment down repeatedly, discuss it as a class or in small groups. This strategy saves you from having to write the same comment over and over again.
- **Randomly mark questions:** If you assign work that includes a lot of practice questions, rather than checking each question, consider checking a random sample of questions. This is especially practical for marking mathematics work, as it allows you to assess if students understand the material without taking up too much time.
- **Don't assign homework you're not marking:** The meta-analysis in Study 3 demonstrates that there is a minimal benefit to homework that is not marked (Fan et al., 2016). So, if you don't have the time to mark it, why invest the time in creating it? Instead of giving homework every night, consider giving more meaningful homework that you can take the time to mark.
- **Give higher-quality feedback less frequently rather than lower-quality feedback more frequently:** The featured research in this chapter demonstrates that there is little benefit for marking student work with just a checkmark or an *X*. So, consider giving less total feedback but focusing on providing higher-quality feedback. For example, rather than marking one hundred mathematics questions as simply right or wrong, choose five questions, identify mistakes students are making, and explain how to correct those mistakes.

Summary Points to Remember

Following is a list of highlights and significant points outlined in this chapter.

- ☑ Homework is only valuable if students put effort into completing it and you're going to put effort into marking it.
- ☑ Feedback is important, but focus on giving students more detailed feedback, not more frequent feedback.
- ☑ Providing feedback in a timely manner makes the feedback more meaningful for students.
- ☑ Strategies like group feedback, self-assessment, conferencing, and success criteria can help make your feedback more time efficient and less laborious.

Reflection Questions

Individually or with your team, use these questions to reflect on the information in this chapter.

1. How are you using feedback effectively? How can you improve what you are doing?
2. What do you think has been your biggest mistake with feedback?
3. Based on the results of these studies, how do you think you could use feedback more efficiently?
4. When might feedback be most important?
5. How do you get students to pay attention to feedback?

Active Learning Versus Passive Learning

In *active learning*, the student actively participates in the learning process. *Passive learning* is learning in which the student receives knowledge from a teacher or a text without interacting with the process. For example, you might describe reading and listening as passive learning processes, whereas you might describe discussing and writing as active learning processes. Both types of instruction have a place in the classroom. However, you should consider the proportion of active versus passive learning implemented in the classroom.

This chapter reviews the difference between active and passive learning, which type of learning leads to higher achievement results, and why you need to understand how active learning versus passive learning can affect research results when analyzing education research.

Active Learning and Passive Learning in Practice

All learning that takes place in the classroom is either passive or active. *Passive learning* occurs when the learner receives knowledge without having to interact with that knowledge in any way, whereas *active learning* occurs when the learner must interact with this knowledge. Most learning skills can be easily broken down into these categories, as shown in table 7.1.

TABLE 7.1: Passive Learning Activities Versus Active Learning Activities

Passive Learning	Active Learning
Reading	Writing
Listening	Speaking
Watching	Acting

Source: Hansford, 2022h. Used with permission.

It is important to understand the difference between active and passive learning for two reasons.

1. **Students will likely benefit from engaging in active learning:** For example, it is likely not enough for students to just read, listen, or watch something. If you want students to remember that curriculum, they need to have a chance to interact with that information, whether by speaking, writing, or acting (Freeman et al., 2014).
2. **The difference between passive and active learning can be a confounding factor for education studies:** For example, according to Hattie's (2023c) database, there have been fourteen meta-analyses on teaching to learning styles, with a mean effect size of 0.34. However, by trying to teach to different learning styles, it is likely that teachers are increasing the number of active learning strategies unintentionally as well. So, if a teacher wants to teach students characterized as having an interpersonal learning style, they need to add a speaking component. However, speaking is also a form of active learning. If they wanted to engage kinesthetic learners, again, they would have to add an active learning component via actions or motion.

The Research on Active and Passive Learning

According to a meta-analysis by Scott Freeman and colleagues (2014), instruction that emphasizes active learning outperforms passive learning, on average, by an effect size of 0.47. This suggests a moderate benefit for active learning over passive learning. Interestingly, this study also showed a large reduction in the number of students who failed—in fact, failing grades dropped by 150 percent.

While this meta-study may appear to be less useful because it was conducted on university students, it is currently (to the best of my knowledge, as of the writing of this book) the only meta-study on the topic. It is also important to remember that studies on postsecondary students tend to have lower effect sizes, so these results might have been higher in an elementary or secondary setting (Pedagogy Non-Grata, 2019b). Moreover, it is likely that highly motivated students in a university setting would have lower deviations in achievement than students in elementary school.

However, as educators, we cannot eliminate passive learning instruction, as the ability for students to take information via passive modalities is an important life skill. For example, reading is largely a more passive skill than writing, but students must be able to read to be successful. That said, reading and writing instruction are inherently linked, as shown in the Steve Graham and Michael Herbert (2011) meta-analysis, which showed that writing instruction has a large impact on students' reading ability. The effect sizes for writing instruction on reading outcomes was higher than the effect sizes found in the National Reading Panel (2000) meta-analysis for reading instruction on reading outcomes.

It's important to note that active and passive learning do not need to be taught in an entirely dichotomous way. For example, you can have students take notes when they read or listen to lectures. Similarly, you can teach many individual skills by bringing in more active learning components. For example, decoding instruction often involves teaching students the correlation between sounds and letters, and then having them practice reading and identifying those sounds. However, encoding instruction typically teaches spelling by having students write down the spelling patterns associated with sounds. By focusing more on encoding instruction, you essentially teach students the same skill while making the process more active. Spelling is an inherently more complex part of literacy, and by focusing on the spelling side of instruction, you can provide a greater overall learning benefit for students.

It's not only important to consider the impact of active versus passive learning in classroom instruction, but also when interpreting education research. If a treatment increases the amount of active learning, it is likely to increase the effect size. This leaves the question of how we separate the impact of active learning from other teaching methods, like teaching to learning styles. One cannot just subtract the effect size of active learning from the actually studied teaching pedagogy. Active learning, for example, has a higher effect size than teaching to learning styles. This is not to say that teaching to learning styles has no effect other than via active learning, but rather, active learning can be a confounding factor when examining education research.

Summary Points to Remember

Following is a list of highlights and significant points outlined in this chapter.

- ☑ Active learning is learning that requires active participation from the student, typically writing, speaking, or acting. Research shows that on average active learning benefits student achievement more than passive learning (Freeman et al., 2014).
- ☑ Both active learning and passive learning are important and, therefore, both should be included in daily lessons. While writing and speaking might better help students

remember important facts, reading and listening for information are crucial skills for students to develop.

☑ Teaching methods, like teaching to learning styles, likely show small benefits for students not because it uniquely targets learning styles, but because it increases the amount of active learning.

☑ When you read education research, be cognizant of the impact of active learning versus passive learning. For example, a study that has students read and then spell a word will likely show higher outcomes than a study that just has the student read the word.

Reflection Questions

Individually or with your team, use these questions to reflect on the information in this chapter.

1. How do you balance active and passive learning in your classroom?
2. Is there a specific subject that might benefit from adding active learning components, and why?
3. Do you personally learn better passively or actively? Why do you think so?
4. Why is passive learning an important component in the classroom?
5. What do you think is an ideal ratio of active versus passive learning? Explain your thinking.

CHAPTER 8

Special Education

Most developed nations require schools to provide students with special support for exceptionalities; this is a relatively new phenomenon that evolved out of the 1980s as part of the American civil rights movement, but the movement to provide special education was largely championed by parent activists. It generated increased attention and awareness for severe intellectual needs and learning disabilities (Bennett, Dworet, & Weber, 2013).

This movement has been socially positive for education. More students are allowed in mainstream schools, and educators are promoting greater empathy and, moreover, academic benefit. But there is always the risk of creating negative self-fulfilling prophecies when educators label students (Bernburg, 2009). In my experience, the literature on special education is often of low quality, and this has led to many myths that can distract from the science on the matter.

This chapter reviews the history of special education, the inherent risks and benefits of special education, and common mythologies that surround it.

Meta-Analyses on Inclusion and Mainstreaming

Hattie (2023d) identifies nine meta-analyses on inclusion and mainstreaming, with a mean effect size of 0.25. All nine meta-analyses showed a positive benefit, including one meta-analysis that looks at the impact of inclusion on students without learning difficulties. More importantly, within his database, Hattie (2023d) identifies a large 1990 meta-analysis by Sheryle Dixon on the impact of inclusion on special education students' well-being, showing a large effect size of 0.65 (Hattie, 2023c). These results suggest that inclusion is beneficial for all students, but especially for the well-being of those who would otherwise be excluded from mainstream education (Hattie, 2023c).

Hattie (2023f) also provides strong support for the use of special education *pullout instruction* (instruction that takes place outside the classroom). He identifies seven meta-analyses on mathematics intervention instruction, showing a mean effect size of 0.60, and seven meta-analyses on reading intervention instruction showing a mean effect size of 0.84 (Hattie, 2023f). Comparatively, there are four meta-analyses of class-based ability grouping, showing a mean effect size of 0.27 (Hansford, 2020). This suggests that pullout instruction is potentially three times more powerful than ability grouping for reading instruction and two times more powerful for mathematics instruction.

Figure 8.1 shows that, on average, ability grouping has a far lower impact on student achievement than pulling students out of class for intervention-based instruction.

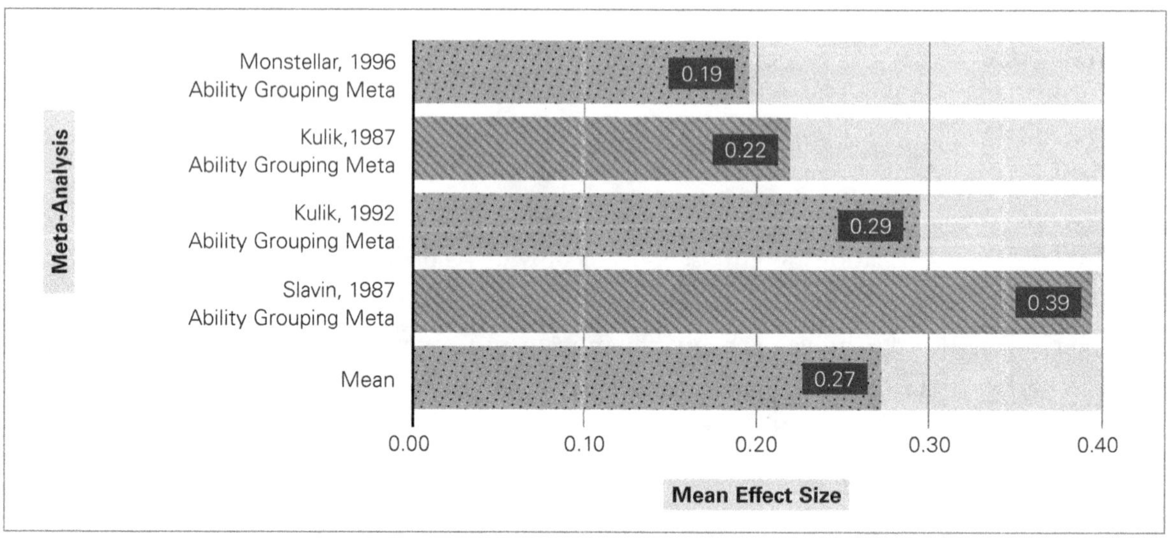

Source: Hansford, 2022h. Used with permission.

FIGURE 8.1: Ability grouping meta-studies.

While special education is a crucial component to effective schooling, there are common mythologies that exist regarding special education, and there are potential pitfalls within any special education program. In the following section, I unpack some of these myths and pitfalls.

The Myths Surrounding Learning Disabilities

The following are myths that I have heard while working at elementary schools since starting my professional teaching career in 2012. I do not believe these myths come from a place of malice; however, I think it is important to correct the record on these ideas. Most of these myths relate to what some believe about learning disabilities, as there is a great deal of confusion on this topic.

Myth: Learning Disabilities Include Diagnoses Such as ASD and ADHD

People sometimes assume that learning disabilities, behavioral disorders, and intellectual disabilities are all the same type of issue; however, each issue is radically different. According to the *Diagnostic and Statistical Manual of Mental Disorders (DSM-5)*, a *learning disability* is diagnosed by identifying that a student has a specific learning gap (American Psychiatric Association, 2013). If a student has multiple learning gaps (not caused by insufficient or ineffective education), it is considered an *intellectual disability*. While this is sometimes referred to as the diagnosis of *multiple learning disabilities*, the two diagnoses are distinctly separate and should not be confused. Someone with a learning disability, by definition, does not have an intellectual disability (American Psychiatric Association, 2013).

Behavioral disorders, including attention-deficit hyperactivity disorder (ADHD), autism spectrum disorder (ASD), and oppositional defiant disorder (ODD), while correlated with learning disabilities, do not have any direct relation with learning disabilities. Referring to a student with ADHD or ASD as having a learning disability is, therefore, by definition, incorrect (Elmaghraby & Garayalde, 2021). Of course, none of this is to say that students with ADD or ADHD do not deserve support. However, it is important to clarify that these disorders are not learning disorders.

Myth: Learning Disabilities Are Always Neurological Conditions

Although learning disabilities can be caused by neurological factors, they do not exclusively have to be. According to the American Psychiatric Association (2013), a *learning disability* is diagnosed by identifying that a student is far below grade level in a specific subject by a licensed psychologist, after having received what is deemed as sufficient instruction. They are not diagnosed with an MRI test or a genetic test. In fact, a learning disability can be caused by psychological, sociological, or neurological factors. For example, if a student dislikes foreign language classes, they might not apply themselves in a subject like French, creating the appearance of a nonneurological learning disability. However, the idea that a student could have a neurological disability that extends to a new language and not their first language is obviously incorrect.

While learning disorders can be caused by neurological factors, learning disabilities are diagnosed by their symptoms, not by their cause. Therefore, it's important not to make sweeping declarations about the causes of learning disabilities. Instead, the focus should be on the treatment for learning disorders, which is more explicit instruction.

Myth: Having a Learning Disability Means You Cannot Learn

All students are capable of learning. If a student falls behind in a subject, he or she may simply need more time, motivation, or support than other students to learn the specific material. Even if the student has a neurological learning disability, they can still learn the curriculum; however, the student's response to learning stimuli may be lower than that of other students (Barquero, Davis, & Cutting, 2014).

Myth: Having Dyslexia Means You Flip Letters and Words

While some students diagnosed with dyslexia have reported flipping their letters and words (American Psychiatric Association, 2013), students are diagnosed primarily by being far below grade-level ability in reading despite having received adequate instruction. Flipping letters is also common to all beginning language students. The specific problem of students flipping letters and words could be a potential red flag of some dyslexic cases; however, it is not dyslexia itself. Indeed, as Max Colheart points out in an interview on *Pedagogy Non-Grata* (2021), dyslexia can have a wide range of symptoms and causes. However, the treatment is almost always the same—explicit language instruction (Pedagogy Non-Grata, 2021).

Important Considerations for Teaching Students With Learning Disabilities

The following are some practical considerations for teachers working with students who have learning disabilities. It is my hope that these considerations will give teachers a framework for thinking about how best to help students identified as having learning disabilities.

More Intervention Time

If educators fail to realize that students with learning disabilities can still learn, they might unnecessarily lower academic expectations and excuse students from work. However, once teachers understand intelligence and how learning happens, it becomes abundantly clear that the first step for a learning-disabled student is to give them extra learning time and work to help them catch up (Torgesen, 2009).

As an analogy, if a basketball player could not perform a layup, a coach would not excuse that player from layups. Instead, the coach would make sure the player spent more time practicing layups. The same concept applies to teaching. If a student is falling behind in mathematics or literacy, that student needs to spend more time practicing the specific skills they are struggling to master.

A literature review by Laura A. Barquero, Nicole Davis, and Laurie E. Cutting (2014) on the impact of reading interventions on neurobiology showed that the brains of students identified with dyslexia had physical differences when scanned under MRI machines. More importantly, though, the same study showed that short reading intervention programs could begin to reverse some of these physical differences (Barquero et al., 2014). This suggests that, with enough high-quality reading interventions, it may even be possible to overcome many of the challenges of dyslexia. If such a strategy works for dyslexia, it seems likely that it might work for other learning disabilities.

The truly challenging part of teaching students with learning disabilities is not choosing the best strategy to help but rather triaging their needs. A 2009 literature review by Joseph K. Torgesen showed that 95 percent or more of students could read at grade level, provided they were given enough small-group intervention instruction. Indeed, in all the studies he analyzed in which schools achieved a 95 percent or higher success rate, struggling readers were offered a minimum of eighty hours of extra instruction within the year (Torgesen, 2009).

Patricia G. Mathes and Carolyn A. Denton conducted a similar literature review in 2002 and found the same result: 96 percent or more of students could learn how to read, provided schools offered a minimum of eighty hours of intervention instruction for struggling readers. Both studies also showed that results were even better if a structured literacy approach was used, as opposed to a balanced literacy approach (Mathes & Denton, 2002; Torgesen, 2009).

Taking an identified student out of literacy class to practice literacy with a special education teacher does nothing except lower the specificity of that student's learning in relation to the classroom teacher's assessments. Special education interventions must take place *in addition* to the student's regular learning, which can mean working with the student during recess, gym, art, or music. It also might mean keeping the student after school or having the student report early. This might seem harsh for the student; however, this might be the only way for the school and its educators to truly make a difference toward the student's long-term learning success.

The Impact of Labels

Labeling theory claims that giving students labels, like *dyslexic*, *ADHD*, or *intellectually disabled*, can potentially negatively impact how those students perceive themselves. If you tell a student that they have dyslexia, that student could potentially stop trying as hard to learn how to read, or they may become convinced that learning this subject is impossible for them (Gold & Richards, 2012).

Moreover, the same risk is present with a teacher. If a teacher knows that a student has a learning disability, it might make the teacher feel less accountable for that student's success. For example, a literature review of this topic showed that teachers gave the most attention to the students they believed to be the brightest and the least amount of attention to the students who were struggling (Good et al., 2018).

After all, working with a student with a learning disability does require more effort than working with one without this challenge. To be clear, this does not mean you should not diagnose students with learning disabilities when applicable; rather, you need to be mindful of the possible impact on your own unconscious bias.

Ultimately, students with learning disabilities and exceptionalities need to be diagnosed so they can receive the support they require; however, labeling students can lead to negative self-fulfilling prophecies. I believe the best tool for dealing with this problem is applying a growth-mindset metacognition strategy—both the teacher and the student must internalize the idea that the student can learn. Teachers need to be conscious of never making a student feel incapable, and they need to encourage students to work toward overcoming their difficulties rather than internalizing them and viewing such challenges as hurdles instead of boundaries.

Summary Points to Remember

Following is a list of highlights and significant points outlined in this chapter.

- ☑ Identifying students' exceptionalities is important, so you can provide them with the necessary support.
- ☑ Pullout intervention instruction is more effective than ability grouping.
- ☑ All students are capable of higher learning with enough support and time.
- ☑ Students with learning disabilities can still learn difficult concepts and procedures, provided they are given enough time and support.
- ☑ We, as educators, are all prone to unconscious bias and need to be aware of how our biases can have unintended consequences on student learning.
- ☑ Learning disabilities, behavioral disabilities, and intellectual disabilities are distinctively different types of disorders.

Reflection Questions

Individually or with your team, use these questions to reflect on the information in this chapter.

1. What myth surprised you the most, and why?
2. What times of the school day do you feel would work best for pullout instruction? What are some ways students with special needs can get extra time with instruction?
3. How does labeling potentially affect your understanding of students and their learning?
4. When does inclusion or mainstreaming become too difficult to accomplish?
5. How can you make inclusion or mainstreaming more effective?

CHAPTER 9

Cooperative Learning

Cooperative learning is a popular constructivist pedagogy. However, there are many different types and subtypes of cooperative learning, and they don't all improve learning outcomes. When reviewing the research on cooperative learning, it makes the most sense to look at individual types of cooperative learning and individual benefits as opposed to taking a holistic approach.

In this chapter, you will learn about the history of cooperative learning, different types of cooperative learning, the overall efficacy of cooperative learning as a pedagogy, and how best to maximize the benefits of cooperative learning.

Types of Cooperative Learning

According to David W. Johnson and Robert T. Johnson (n.d.), *cooperative learning* is a model of teaching popularized in the 1960s and largely based on the work of educational psychologist B. F. Skinner. This model of teaching includes a multitude of strategies; however, there are three main types of cooperative learning.

1. *Formal cooperative learning* consists of "students working together, for one class period to several weeks, to achieve shared learning goals and complete jointly specific tasks and assignments" (Johnson & Johnson, n.d.).
2. *Informal cooperative learning* consists of "having students work together to achieve a joint learning goal in temporary, ad-hoc groups that last from a few minutes to one class period" (Johnson & Johnson, n.d.).
3. *Cooperative base groups* consist of "long-term, heterogeneous cooperative learning groups with stable membership" (Johnson & Johnson, n.d.).

Some of the most popular cooperative learning strategies include round robin, think-pair-share, four corners, and jigsaw. These are just a few examples, but there are countless other cooperative learning strategies.

- In *round robin*, the teacher divides the class into small groups, and then each student gives their opinion on a topic.
- In *think-pair-share*, students first brainstorm about a topic or question, then discuss their ideas with a partner, and finally, share with the class.
- In *four corners*, the teacher assigns each corner of the room one of the following values: *strongly agree, agree, disagree,* and *strongly disagree*. The teacher then reads a statement, and the students move to the corner associated with the value they most identify with. Once in the corner, students discuss their opinions with their peers.
- In *jigsaw*, the teacher divides the room into stations, and each station has a booklet of information about a specific topic. The teacher then divides the class into small groups. One student from each group goes to a different station to learn about the topic and become an "expert." They then return to their original group to share what they have learned.

Cooperative learning was such a popular concept when I was getting my education degree that there was an entire class on it. There are many scholars and consultants who make a living off promoting and studying different types of cooperative learning models. However, if we look at meta-analyses, some of the cooperative learning study results have been quite underwhelming.

The Research on Cooperative Learning

Eva Kyndt and colleagues conducted a meta-study on cooperative learning in 2013, which looked at sixty-five different studies on the topic using a Hedge's g effect-size calculation. According to the study, there were eighty-five examples of positive effect sizes associated with cooperative learning, one negative example, and forty-eight examples where there was no discernible difference. According to their analysis, which had strict inclusion criteria, there was an average effect size of 0.31, with a p value of less than 0.01 (Kyndt et al., 2013).

These results suggest that there is a small but statistically significant benefit for cooperative learning strategies for student learning within the academic literature. However, almost all studies and meta-analyses show positive results; what really matters is what teaching strategies work best. This suggests that one can assume with a great deal of confidence that while cooperative learning is usually a positive intervention for students, the impact on student achievement is exceptionally low.

Hattie (2023a) identifies twenty-seven meta-analyses on cooperative learning, with a mean effect size of 0.45. However, some of these meta-analyses are unpublished, some are correlational, some are not specifically on cooperative learning pedagogies, one is on gifted students, and some study college-age students (Hattie, 2023a). If you only look at the published meta-analyses that specifically examine the impact of cooperative-learning pedagogies on academic achievement, you get a very different result (see figure 9.1).

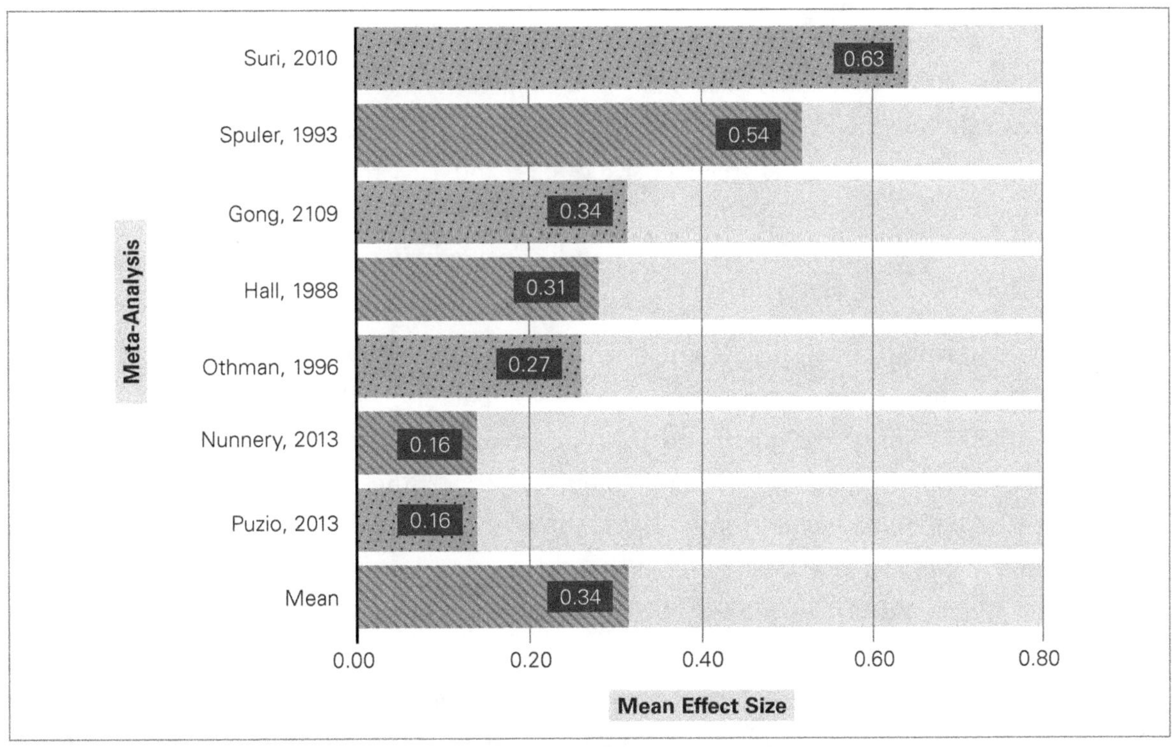

FIGURE 9.1: Secondary meta-analysis on the impact of cooperative learning on academic achievement.

These results suggest an overall low effectiveness, especially if you recognize that the Suri (2010) and Spuler (1993) studies appear to be outliers. Moreover, it should be noted that the studies by Shanan Chappell and John Nunnery (2013) and Kelly Puzio and Glenn T. Colby (2013) specifically looked at the impact of cooperative learning on reading and mathematics achievement and show negligible results (as cited in Hattie, 2023a).

At first glance, it appears that cooperative learning lacks the evidence that would suggest it is worth the effort for the average teacher to implement. However, like with most education topics, there is some nuance to cooperative learning. One confounding issue is that not all cooperative learning strategies are equally effective. For example, while the research shows that cooperative learning, in general, is largely ineffective, the jigsaw strategy is noted as high yield. A 2014 meta-analysis by Veli Batdi showed a mean effect size of 1.20. While this may appear confounding when you consider how jigsaw differs from other cooperative learning strategies, it makes perfect sense. In jigsaw, each student spends an entire period learning, memorizing, reading, researching, and teaching.

Comparatively, many other cooperative learning strategies are far less intensive and focus on students sharing their feelings. For example, within the think-pair-share strategy, there is very little time devoted to learning material, compared to the jigsaw strategy, in which students are expected to spend most of the class time learning. Ultimately, this demonstrates perfectly how time under quality instruction is the first principle of evidence-based teaching.

While cooperative learning strategies may not increase student achievement by significant amounts, there is considerable research showing that it has other benefits. As Johnson and Johnson (n.d.) point out, quantitative research suggests that cooperative learning dramatically increases the time students willingly spend on a task. When compared to individual learning and competitive learning, cooperative learning has an effect size of 0.76 and 1.17, respectively, for time spent on a task (Johnson & Johnson, n.d.). Moreover, in cooperative learning situations, students are more likely to view their work positively, compared to individual learning and competitive learning, with effect sizes of 0.57 and 0.42 respectively (Johnson & Johnson, n.d.).

Cooperative learning strategies have also been shown to increase the quality of student bonds, reduce bullying, and decrease drop-out rates when compared to individualistic and competitive teaching models. In 2005, Johnson and Johnson conducted a meta-analysis that examined 106 individual studies, which showed that cooperative learning had an effect size of 0.67 for improving positive peer relationships when compared to individual learning, which had an effect size of 0.60 when compared to competitive learning (Johnson & Johnson, 2005). In 2018, Mark J. Van Ryzin and Cary J. Roseth did a quantitative analysis on the effect of cooperative learning on reducing bullying. The study looked at fifteen rural middle schools. Each teacher was given a book on cooperative learning and three training sessions. Their study found an effect size of 0.37 for reducing bullying incidents and a 0.69 effect size for reducing student perception of victimization (Van Ryzin & Roseth, 2018).

Ultimately, cooperative learning was not developed as a learning strategy to primarily increase student learning. Like many pedagogies of the 1960s, it was as much of an academic movement as it was a social response. Cooperative is and was an attempt to democratize the classroom, an attempt to depart from the authoritarian teaching styles of the previous decades.

As much as the social priorities of pedagogical movements are not the priority of my research, I cannot say that the social value of pedagogy is irrelevant. There is always an implicit and explicit curriculum. Students learn from *how* we teach almost as much as *what* we teach. When all teaching is done through direct instruction and all work is done competitively or individually, students learn that knowledge comes from authority and the individual matters more than the collective, whereas inquiry-based learning and cooperative learning teach the opposite (Inlay, 2016).

As previously discussed, while cooperative learning does not appear to significantly impact academic achievement, it does appear to increase the holistic well-being of students by a significant margin. Furthermore, while cooperative learning does not appear to significantly increase learning, it does not *decrease* learning, and with the right execution, it potentially can be a high-yield strategy. Nonetheless, cooperative learning does come with some opportunity costs. It requires significant research and planning time, and if a teacher struggles with classroom management, complex cooperative learning lessons might be a barrier to classroom learning.

Ultimately, teachers should strive to become familiar with cooperative learning strategies and implement more of them as they become more confident. However, I don't think it should be a priority for new or struggling teachers. Alternatively, cooperative learning should be a priority for more experienced teachers and for classes with bullying issues.

Summary Points to Remember

Following is a list of highlights and significant points outlined in this chapter.

- ☑ Research shows that cooperative learning has a negligible to small benefit on academics.
- ☑ Research shows that cooperative learning can reduce bullying and increase student well-being.
- ☑ Most cooperative learning strategies focus on students sharing their feelings; instead, teachers should focus students on learning curriculum material.
- ☑ Research shows that cooperative learning is better for motivation than individualistic-focused learning.

Reflection Questions

Individually or with your team, use these questions to reflect on the information in this chapter.

1. What surprised you most about cooperative learning strategies?
2. Have you used cooperative learning pedagogies, and if so, do you believe they increased your students' academic achievement? How so?
3. How do cooperative learning pedagogies help with social cohesion in your classroom?
4. How can you better connect cooperative learning pedagogies to curriculum goals?
5. How does a cooperative versus a competitive classroom change the implicit curriculum?

CHAPTER 10

Developmentally Appropriate Practice

Developmentally appropriate practice (DAP) is a pedagogical movement started by early childhood educators. The proponents of DAP opposed what they felt was a developmentally inappropriate increase in academic expectations for students (National Association for the Education of Young Children [NAEYC], 2009). In their book *Developmentally Appropriate Practice in Early Childhood Programs*, editors Carol Copple and Sue Bredekamp (2008) write that DAP holds three central concepts.

1. There is a specific age at which it is developmentally appropriate for students to learn certain curricula.
2. Teachers possess expert knowledge in education and, therefore, should be able to make decisions about developmentally appropriate curriculum goals for students.
3. The younger the student is, the less direct instruction and the more inquiry-based learning a student should have.

I have some doubts and reservations regarding the efficacy of DAP. While I believe instruction should be moving more toward evidence-based practices (not only in education but in all fields), I am not convinced that DAP is entirely evidenced-based within its approach, as I have been unable to find any meta-studies examining its efficacy. It is also difficult to evaluate the quality of such an all-encompassing approach as DAP with scientific objectivity when it includes so many tenets, methods, and sub-theories. Some of the principles of DAP are inspired by scientifically validated principles, such as active learning approaches (Freeman et al., 2014). DAP, however, also places a heavy emphasis on lowering learning expectations, especially regarding early reading intervention (Copple & Bredekamp, 2008).

Potential Problems With Developmentally Appropriate Practice

The following sections examine and discuss some of the possible issues with DAP, including low expectations for reading intervention, bias in observational assessment, and use of an inquiry-based learning model.

Low Expectations for Reading Intervention

I often see DAP cited on social media as a reason to withhold early phonics instruction from prekindergarten and kindergarten students. This idea is deeply problematic and not supported by the literature. My own phonics meta-analysis shows that students who receive phonics instruction in kindergarten and prekindergarten outperform control group students on reading tests by an effect size of 0.33 (Joseph, King, & McGlynn, 2022). Similarly, the National Reading Panel (2000) phonics meta-analysis shows that students who receive phonics instruction in kindergarten outperform control group students on reading tests by an effect size of 0.56.

In college, my undergraduate textbook on DAP even went so far as to suggest that reading instruction that takes place too early could cognitively damage students. In an interview on the *Pedagogy Non-Grata* (2019a) podcast, I discussed this claim with Timothy Shanahan (2021), lead author on the 2000 NRP report and previous president of the International Literacy Association. He assured me that there is no scientific research to support the DAP claims regarding early literacy instruction (Shanahan, 2021).

This primary focus of DAP, then, does not appear to be strongly evidence based. While DAP advocates will cite studies supporting its pedagogical efficacy, these studies do not compare DAP to any alternative strategies, which is an indicator of a very weak evidence case. In 1997, Lorraine Dunn and Susan Kontos published a literature review on DAP, the results of which are in table 10.1.

The studies in table 10.1 are largely correlational and qualitative. The qualitative studies claimed that academics were unimportant in the earliest years of education and that play-based learning was more important. The correlational studies showed weak effect sizes in favor of schools that focused on play-based learning over academics. However, the schools that used more play-based learning were also wealthier. Therefore, these students might have done better because they came from wealthier homes and not because play-based learning was important. Moreover, only one of these studies was an efficacy study that was still publicly available, and it showed higher academic achievement for the group not using DAP.

TABLE 10.1: DAP Meta-Analysis Results

Study	Design	Type of Control Group	Results
National Association for the Education of Young Children (2009)	Position paper	N/A	Favorable
Burts, Hart, Charlesworth, DeWolf, Ray, & Manuel (1993)	Quasi-experimental	Play based versus explicit instruction	Less stress for play based
Burts, Hart, Charlesworth, & Kirk (1990)	Quasi-experimental	Appropriate classroom versus inappropriate	Not publicly available
Dunn, Beach, & Kontos (1994)	Correlational and qualitative	None	Less impoverished day cares used more developmentally appropriate practice
Elkind (1981)	Book, not a study	N/A	N/A
Frede & Barnett (1992)	Case study	N/A	Public schools can implement developmentally appropriate prekindergarten programs
Hirsh-Pasek, Hyson, & Rescorla (1990)	Correlational	Academic versus nonacademic settings in preschool	No academic benefit for nonacademic settings Social-emotional benefits for nonacademic settings
Hyson, Hirsch-Pasek, & Rescorla (1990)	Not a study	N/A	N/A
Mantzicopoulos, Neuharth-Pritchett, & Morelock (1994)	Unpublished	N/A	N/A
Marcon (1992)	Randomized controlled trial	Student-centered classroom versus teacher-centered classroom versus mixed classroom	Student-centered classrooms showed the highest results; mixed classrooms showed the lowest results. Full statistical results are not available, as the paper is no longer publicly available.
Sherman & Meuller (1996)	Correlational	Classrooms qualitatively rated for how developmentally appropriate they were and compared to their academic achievement	A small correlation of $r = 0.39$ was found for more developmentally appropriate classrooms.
Stipek, Feiler, Daniels, & Milburn (1995)	Randomized controlled trial	Less academic classrooms versus more academic classrooms	The more academic classrooms showed higher results for mathematics and reading. The less academic classrooms showed higher results for motivation. There was insufficient information published to find or calculate effect sizes.

Source: Dunn & Kontos, 1997.

Bias in Observation Assessment

Another potential problem with DAP research is its heavy emphasis on observational assessment. While I think it is possible to establish solid criteria for making observational assessments objective, I'm concerned about the overall efficacy of those assessments and their potential for fostering bias. The studies listed in table 10.1 (page 71) typically referred to classrooms as developmentally appropriate versus inappropriate. They defined *inappropriate classrooms* as being didactic (using explicit instruction), which ostensibly seems to refer to using explicit instruction (Dunn & Kontos, 1997). This is deeply problematic, as explicit instruction is one of the most evidence-based teaching pedagogies (Stockard, Wood, Coughlin, & Khoury, 2018).

When I first started teaching primary classes, I objected to product-based assessments, because I felt they lacked relevance to student development relative to what I could observe directly from them. However, after my principals encouraged me to use them, I was surprised to find that student achievement on my product-based assessments was radically different from my observational impressions of student development. There is a large body of research showing that all people harbor some level of social bias (Dee & Gershenson, 2017; Gershenson & Papageorge, 2018; Warikoo, Sinclair, Fei, & Jacoby-Senghor, 2016). Just as researchers can introduce bias into their studies (see Researcher Bias in chapter 1, page 9), teachers can be biased for or against students for many different reasons, either consciously or unconsciously. I would, therefore, hypothesize that the less observational the assessments and the more detailed the rubrics educators use, the less biased assessment data will be.

Inquiry-Based Learning Model

Another potential problem with DAP is its proposed model of inquiry-based learning. The DAP movement pushed the idea that the younger a student is, the less developmentally appropriate direct instruction is and, conversely, the more appropriate inquiry-based learning is. This idea is likely a response to the fact that students in kindergarten or the early primary grades have very short attention spans and little prior knowledge, making long periods of direct instruction virtually useless.

However, the fact that very young learners in the primary grades cannot handle long periods of direct instruction does not make inquiry-based learning any more effective as a pedagogical method. In fact, meta-studies and reviews on the topic (Friesen & Scott, 2013; Lazonder & Harmsen, 2016) suggest that the older the student, the more developmentally appropriate inquiry-based learning is. Conversely, the younger the student, the less appropriate inquiry-based learning is (Lazonder & Harmsen, 2016).

Ultimately, my most pressing concern with the DAP movement is that it advocates for teachers to be the final arbiters of reasonable expectations for students (Copple & Bredekamp, 2008). However, when we look at the Pygmalion effect (see Appropriately Challenging Curriculum in chapter 3, page 33), teachers lowering their expectations for students might be one of the most harmful practices in which a teacher can engage (Good et al., 2018). Furthermore, labeling theory research suggests that if we give a person a label, that the person will, over time, grow to fit the label. Ultimately, the result is to create a kind of self-fulfilling prophecy (Gold & Richard, 2012).

While not all teachers would use the philosophy of DAP to lower their expectations, some educators may lower academic expectations in an area negatively impacted by socioeconomic factors and social biases, such as schools affected by racialized populations. Therefore, I worry that DAP could negatively affect marginalized students at a disproportionate rate.

Summary Points to Remember

Following is a list of highlights and significant points outlined in this chapter.

- ☑ DAP is a pedagogical movement that focuses on greater teacher autonomy, less curriculum guidance, inquiry-based learning, and observational assessments over standardized ones.
- ☑ DAP pedagogy often focuses on lowering academic expectations, specifically for reading.
- ☑ There is no meaningful empirical evidence to support the use of DAP pedagogical frameworks and some evidence that it might even be harmful because it might lead to lower academic expectations.

Reflection Questions

Individually or with your team, use these questions to reflect on the information in this chapter.

1. Under the DAP framework, reading instruction is often very limited prior to first grade. When do you think reading instruction should start, and why?
2. What's better for assessing students, formal assessments or observational assessments?
3. What different factors might bias your understanding of a student's performance?
4. Should teachers be the final arbiters for curriculum in their classrooms? Why or why not?
5. The DAP approach suggests that teachers use more inquiry-based learning for younger students and less inquiry-based learning for older students. How do you think instruction should change as students get older?

CHAPTER 11

Action Research Frameworks

When I started writing this book, I wanted to dispel the idea that there are magical solutions in teaching. Education companies often market their products and strategies based on minute differences. To make these differences seem meaningful, the scientific importance of these products and strategies is often exaggerated. I think this has led many educators to believe that finding one special trick will solve all their educational problems. And while I still do not believe such a strategy exists, I must admit if there is one that does work, it would probably be action research. Action research helps educators be accountable to themselves as well as their students; it enables teachers to better individualize their instruction and continually improve their practice.

This chapter discusses action research frameworks, the different types of action research frameworks, and the available scientific evidence on action research frameworks.

A Definition of Action Research Teaching

Action research teaching is the idea that teachers should use formative assessments to create data as they teach. Within this model, teachers are then supposed to use this data collection to inform themselves on what to teach and how to teach (Clark, Porath, Thiele, & Jobe, 2020). For example, if a teacher attempts to teach students how to use commas, and the formative assessment data show that students are not making progress, the teacher should use the data to conclude there is a need to change the method of instruction. Similarly, with these methods, if teachers collect formative data that show students have mastered the material faster than expected, they should use the data to inform their instruction and move on to new material. These types of approaches transform regular classroom instruction into data- and evidence-driven instruction. Action research teaching usually relies on a set framework that prescribes a specific process for data collection and making changes to instruction according to data. There are a multitude of action research frameworks that exist. However, all action research frameworks have the following three fundamental principles.

1. The use of data collection
2. The use of formative assessment
3. Instruction informed by student progress on formative assessments

Action research teaching usually relies on a complex framework that guides the processes by which teachers use the approach.

Types of Action Research Frameworks

In this section, I discuss the following three action research frameworks.

1. Collaborative inquiry
2. The literacy assessment, planning, and instruction cycle (LAPIC)
3. Response to intervention (RTI)

Collaborative Inquiry

In Ontario, Canada, the *Building Capacity* series (Ontario Ministry of Education, 2008) specifically advocates for the collaborative inquiry action teaching framework (Kutsyuruba, Christou, Heggie, Murray, & Christophe, 2015). The collaborative inquiry framework suggests that teaching should be relevant, collaborative, reflective, iterative, reasoned, adaptive, and reciprocal.

The collaborative inquiry action research framework includes the following four steps.

1. Collect formative assessment work examples and data. This can be either test scores or student work artifacts, like writing examples or other projects.
2. Collectively assess students' work in teacher teams to see if students are meeting expectations or if they are struggling with specific subskills. For example, a student could fail to correctly identify the solution to a mathematics problem. However, you might identify the specific step in the problem they are struggling with.

3. Collectively plan lessons based on these data. Teachers should specifically try to identify either instruction that is not working or gaps in student learning that need to be addressed.
4. Repeat the first three steps.

However, many other action research frameworks exist that are built on the same foundational principles listed previously.

The Literacy Assessment, Planning, and Instruction Cycle

LAPIC is another popular action research framework from Ontario (Ontario Ministry of Education, 2006). The LAPIC framework includes the following six steps.

1. Select curriculum-based learning goals. These are connected curriculum targets you and your colleagues collectively try to teach.
2. Preassess students' current knowledge to see what percentage of students already meet the target goal.
3. Plan instructional activities based on curriculum goals aligned across grades. For example, the grade 8 teacher might teach students how to write a persuasive essay; the grade 7 teacher might teach students how to write a persuasive paragraph with quotes; and the grade 6 teacher might teach students how to write a persuasive paragraph without quotes.
4. Gather formative assessment data. Use these data to monitor student progress to ensure successful instruction and identify weaknesses in student learning to target.
5. Adjust the instruction based on formative data results. If students are not progressing, change your instructional method. If students have specific weaknesses, plan lessons to target those weaknesses.
6. Assess the total learning during the unit, adjusting for the next cycle. Think about what went well and what could be improved for future cycles or for the next time you use this cycle.

Response to Intervention

The most well-researched of these action research frameworks is RTI. This framework is extremely popular in the United States and Australia (Hattie, 2023h). According to my training in RTI, the RTI framework includes five key steps for each unit.

1. Collectively select your learning goals for the year using backward planning. Backward planning should start in grade 8, and each teacher should align their goal to scaffold with the teacher in the grade above them.
2. Gather formative assessment work to assess which students can already meet the learning target.

3. Collectively mark student work and plan lessons based on student progress. Use collective marking to measure if students are making progress and if they have specific weaknesses in their learning. If the class is not progressing, readjust your instruction. If students have specific weaknesses, change your instruction to address those weaknesses.
4. Collect the final data results for the unit. Measure what percentage of students achieved the target.
5. Meet as a staff to reflect and brainstorm on the unit. Think about what went well, what you could improve for future cycles, and what needs to change the next time you use this cycle.

Multitiered systems of support (MTSS) is another strategy that has risen in popularity. MTSS has a very similar purpose and approach to RTI, except it also applies the same principles of RTI to student behavior (Rosen, n.d.), although there are RTI frameworks, such as RTI at Work™ (Buffum, Mattos, & Malone, 2018) that include behavior in their scope.

RESEARCH ON RTI EFFICACY

These frameworks can appear ominous and daunting because they essentially force the teacher not only to completely change how they teach in their classrooms but to do this repeatedly on a continual basis. However, there is also a lot of research supporting the efficacy of these frameworks. Hattie (2023h) puts the effect size of RTI, for example, at 1.29. That said, this effect size is likely inflated, as many of the studies included in these meta-analyses were case studies that did not have control groups.

I went through each of the RTI meta-analyses cited by Hattie (2023h). All these meta-analyses had weak inclusion criteria, as they did not specifically exclude case studies (studies without control groups). This is important to note, as case studies typically show larger and more random effect sizes. That said, some of these meta-studies reported a mean effect for studies that had control groups versus no control groups, which adequately controls for this weakness. I calculated a new mean effect size for the meta-analyses cited by Hattie (2023h), using only the effect sizes for experimental studies. While my resulting effect size was lower than Hattie's (2023h), it was still quite high and, in my opinion, more accurate, as it better measures the magnitude of effect for RTI.

Note that most of these meta-analyses are now quite dated and research methodology has improved vastly in that time. They did not exclude case studies (studies without control groups), which although normal at the time for a meta-analysis, inflates the mean effect size when compared to more modern meta-analyses.

Figure 11.1 shows the mean effect sizes I used to represent each meta-analysis on RTI identified by Hattie (2023h).

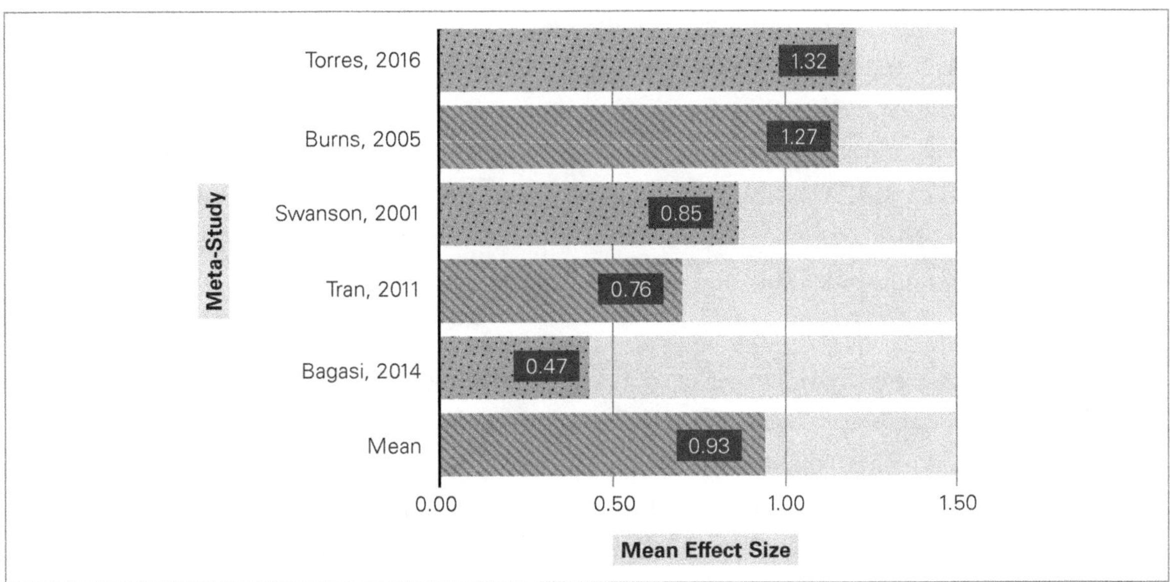

Source: Hansford, 2022d. Used with permission.

FIGURE 11.1: RTI meta-studies ranked by effect size.

Among these studies, the 2011 RTI meta-analysis conducted by Loan Tran and colleagues looked at thirteen studies and 107 different weighted effect sizes for RTI and still came up with a net positive effect size of 0.76 with a 95 percent confidence interval of 0.71 to 0.81. The confidence interval suggests that 95 percent of RTI studies examined showed an effect size of between 0.71 and 0.81.

Moreover, their effect sizes appeared to be lowered by the fact that they had large differences between high responders and low responders, as well as the fact that they were measuring multiple different outcomes. For example, their high responders on Reading Attack and Word Identification were 1.28 and 1.53, respectively, compared to 1.10 and 1.06, respectively, for low responders. More importantly, if you look at the low responders for reading comprehension, low responders had an effect size of 0.43 compared to the high responders, who had an effect size of 1.43. Obviously, the outliers in the effect size for reading comprehension are creating an artificially low overall mean effect size of 0.76 in this study. However, if you correct for this and average out all the effect sizes for just Reading Attack and Word Identification, you get an overall effect size of 1.24, which is comparable to Hattie's (2023h) 1.29 effect size (Tran et al., 2011).

PODDING

One of the most controversial elements of RTI is podding. With *podding*, teachers divide the class into groups during the literacy block based on the learning goals students are currently working on, not their grades. This is supposed to help with differentiation. If a student does not have the prerequisite skills for the unit, they work on building those skills in the next pod down. Conversely, if a student has already mastered the skills of a unit, they move to the next pod up. While not mutually exclusive with RTI, podding is often used within the RTI framework.

For example, let's say students in grade 1 and grade 2 classes are studying phonics during their podding time. The first pod is studying trigraphs, the second pod is studying digraphs, and the third pod is studying single-letter sounds. The teacher places students in pods, not based on their grades, but on their mastery of skills. Each week, the teacher assesses the students. If a student demonstrates mastery of all the letter-sound correspondences in their pod, they move to the next pod up. This approach is very different from, let's say, balanced literacy leveled groups, as they are completely fluid and not static. Students can move up at any time, and they are encouraged to keep a growth mindset.

In my experience, podding can be an extremely powerful tool for differentiating instruction and improving educational results. However, it is also often incorrectly applied. In podding, the groups are supposed to be fluid and based on skill. When the student masters the skill being worked on in a pod, they move to the next pod up (in skill level). Groups are supposed to be constantly changing. However, teachers can sometimes find it easier to group students based on a generalized perception of ability rather than specific skills. This leads to fixed groups and makes students in the lowest group feel incompetent.

VOLATILITY IN THE DATA

Nonetheless, there does appear to be a large amount of volatility in the data when looking at RTI research. When we consider the fact that the average mean effect size for RTI is so high, while many RTI studies show a net negative outcome, we must assume that in the studies where RTI was net positive, the results were even higher than the mean effect size would suggest. This statistical volatility might be caused by the following two things.

1. **The impact of executing a complex teaching intervention:** RTI requires a large degree of effort and training for teachers to effectively implement and ultimately, a lot of motivation. RTI is not an intervention that should be half-heartedly implemented, without serious intention.
2. **The impact of RTI on behavior:** RTI is often coupled with *podding*, which can be a useful tool, but often leads to increased behavior issues (Tran et al., 2011).

Action research and RTI have been most specifically focused on reading instruction. Many of the scholars who have promoted these frameworks have specifically envisioned them for the use of teaching reading (Ontario Ministry of Education, 2006, 2008; Tran et al., 2011). However, there are no logical reasons why these same principles cannot be applied to other subjects. I think action research may work better for mathematics than it does for literacy, due to the more concrete nature of mathematics. It is easy to track the concepts and procedures a student has learned in mathematics. For example, if the learning goal for students is to learn how to do long division, it's easy to find out which students have and have not mastered the desired skill. However, sometimes complex literacy skills like essay writing can be more difficult to track, because of the subjective components involved.

I have seen many teachers make the mistake of choosing literacy learning goals, which are too subjective to effectively monitor. For example, learning goals like "I can write with a sense of personal voice" or "I can write with more advanced vocabulary" are far too subjective to be effective. Similarly, choosing too many complex learning goals can also be a problem. For example, it would be problematic to expect students to learn how to write a persuasive, comparative, and narrative essay in one unit. The goal of a unit, within these frameworks, should be to bring students to a level of mastery for a specific learning goal, not to a level of cursory knowledge. If a student cannot be expected to independently demonstrate the targeted skills by the end of the unit, the learning goal is inappropriate. An example of effective unit learning goals would be: "I can write an effective thesis," "I can use quotations to evidence an argument," "I can write a literary essay," and "I can cite appropriately using a specific format." All these learning goals are connected and scaffolded, and moreover, there is only one challenging learning goal included.

My Experiences With Action Research Frameworks

In 2018, I received training on the RTI model while teaching in Quebec and have been using some form of action-based teaching ever since. Action-based teaching has not only completely changed how I teach but how I look at my teaching practice. In my experience as an educator, it is easy to assume I am doing a good job or at least think that I am doing the best I can—when I'm not collecting data. But if you start with the assumption that all students are capable of higher learning, and then collect data that show your students are not successfully learning something, you must assume the problem is not with students, it's with your methods. This means taking personal responsibility as a teacher for student outcomes. On one hand, this can be a very emotionally difficult task; on the other, it can make a dramatic difference in student achievement outcomes.

Over the years, I have developed my own action research teaching framework, which I believe improves the concept by taking a more global perspective. In my framework, I take all the learning goals from the curriculum for each year and enter them into tracking sheets. I then regularly monitor my students' learning with assessments. As soon as a student shows mastery of a learning goal, I allow them to start working on a new learning goal. I sometimes hear teachers say that teaching the entire mathematics curriculum is impossible, because there is too much content. However, by using my framework, I have been able to get all my students to mastery on the Ontario mathematics curriculum for multiple years in a row.

However, at the end of the day, I don't think it matters which action research teaching framework a teacher uses. Whether you use collaborative inquiry, LAPIC, RTI, or MTSS—these models all lift the veil of secrecy between you and your successes or failures as a teacher by requiring the monitoring of student learning via data tracking and formative assessment. Once you start tracking real, objective, formative data, you know who's learning and who's not; what students know and what they don't; and just as important, how fast students learn. Any teacher who uses one of these frameworks for a consistent period of time will vastly improve the academic achievement in their classrooms (Bagasi, 2018; Burns, Appleton, & Stehouwer, 2005; Swanson & Lussier, 2001; Tran et al., 2011).

Summary Points to Remember

Following is a list of highlights and significant points outlined in this chapter.

- ☑ Action research frameworks are models for tracking student achievement data and adapting instruction to fit students' needs.
- ☑ RTI specifically has a large body of experimental research showing that the framework for instruction vastly improves achievement outcomes.
- ☑ RTI works best when teachers choose specific and achievable learning goals and then monitor student progress via formative assessment.
- ☑ Central to action research frameworks is making instructional decisions based on data, not informal observations.
- ☑ Action research frameworks like RTI are complex and take time to implement effectively.
- ☑ Treatment groups should be fluid, not fixed. This means students change groups when they accomplish specific learning goals, as opposed to being put in one learning group for the entire year.

Reflection Questions

Individually or with your team, use these questions to reflect on the information in this chapter.

1. Why is tracking students' learning data valuable?
2. Can teachers accurately observe students' specific needs without relying on formal assessment? Why or why not?
3. How do you create learning groups in your classroom? Do you use static groupings or fluid groupings? What seems to work best?
4. Action research frameworks like RTI are difficult to implement; they should not be attempted before a school has established basic evidence-based routines. Do you think your educational setting is ready to manage implementing an action research framework? Why or why not?
5. Of the three action research frameworks reviewed, which do you think would work the best for your classroom, and why?

Multiple Intelligences Theory

Multiple intelligences theory was coined in 1983 by Howard Gardner, in his book *Frames of Mind*. This theory has been widely used as evidence for the practice of teaching to learning styles. However, as I discuss in this chapter, there is little scientific evidence in favor of multiple intelligences theory, as framed by Gardner (1983), or teaching to learning styles.

When I was in college (2008–2012), multiple intelligences theory and teaching to learning styles were taught as central concepts in most of my classes, and in the nine additional qualification courses I took between 2018 and 2021 after graduating. Indeed, the Ontario government has mandated teaching to learning styles as best practice in their policy document *Growing Success* (Ontario Ministry of Education, 2010). However, this same theory has been heavily criticized by proponents of evidence-based education and experts within the fields of pedagogical neurology and psychology (Wiliam, 2016; Willingham, 2018).

So why do current recommendations in teaching practice still cling to the idea (Ontario College of Teachers, 2023; Ontario Ministry of Education, 2010, 2022)? Arguably, it's because Gardner's (1983) theory, at face value, appears to make intuitive sense. Moreover, when teachers implement

Gardner's (1983) theory successfully, it can create a *confirmation bias*, which occurs when one notices evidence to support their hypotheses but fails to recognize the evidence that does not (Healy, 2016). What advocates fail to realize, however, is that just because something works does not mean it works better than something else. While Gardner's (1983) theory does hold some merits, it fails to hold up to scientific scrutiny and is not a time-efficient strategy for improving learning results, as is shown throughout this chapter.

The Neuroscience of Multiple Intelligences Theory

While it is an almost indisputable fact that there are multiple intelligences, the intelligences identified by Gardner (1983) may not all be completely different intelligences, and there are presumably many other intelligences he has not identified. When Gardner originally coined his theory in 1983, he identified seven specific types of intelligences.

1. Interpersonal (knowledge of how to build relationships)
2. Intrapersonal (knowledge of self)
3. Visual-spatial (knowledge related to art, design, and reading)
4. Verbal-linguistic (knowledge of spoken language)
5. Logical-mathematical (knowledge of mathematics)
6. Bodily-kinesthetic (physical capability)
7. Musical-rhythmic (knowledge of music)

He also later identified two other types of intelligences: naturalistic (knowledge of nature) and existential (one's ability to ask deep questions), only to later abandon the concept of existential intelligence (Cherry, 2023; Gardner, 2013).

While these identified intelligences correspond well with the subjects taught in the Western education system, they do not correspond specifically with the scientifically identified regions of the brain (Hines, 2018). Neurologists, for example, only identify six key regions of the brain (parietal lobe, occipital lobe, thalamus, amygdala, hippocampus, and temporal lobe); moreover, most of the intelligences Gardner (1983) lists are controlled by the same area of the brain, namely, the frontal lobe (Hines, 2018). Language and mathematics, for example, are both controlled by this region, which brings into doubt whether literary and mathematical intelligences are separate, especially when considering that both skill sets involve different forms of abstraction (Hines, 2018).

Furthermore, it was not by specifically neuroscientific methods that Gardner (1983) settled on his seven intelligences but rather through his own anecdotal experiences. Geneticists, on the other hand, have already uncovered 501 different genes associated with intelligence, which may suggest that there are far more than seven types (Deary, Spinath, & Bates, 2006; Goriounova & Mansvelder, 2019). There is no scientific evidence to suggest that there are specifically seven, eight, or nine different types of intelligence, as Gardner (1983) originally proposed.

Multiple Intelligences and Learning Styles

Gardner (1983) never intended his theory to be used as an instructional methodology; however, many have applied it as such and advocated that teachers instruct to students' individual learning styles. Gardner (2013) defines *learning styles theory* as the idea that all students learn differently, and teachers can improve student learning by teaching to their unique learning style. This theory predates Gardner's (1983) multiple intelligences theory, but learning styles were commonly adapted to fit the seven types of intelligences that Gardner (2013) suggested.

Even if the specifics of Gardner's (1983) theory are not neurologically accurate, it does not necessarily mean that teaching to learning styles is ineffective. After all, the minutiae of his science might be less important than the practical implications of the general concept. And, generally speaking, the broad application of his theory does demonstrate positive benefits in the classroom (Hattie, 2023e). However, there are still legitimate concerns with its implementation.

To be clear, even Gardner (2013) raised concerns with how his theory has been implemented, most specifically because it is often confused with the learning styles theory. While Gardner (1983) has argued that multiple intelligences exist and teachers should try to teach to a variety of intelligences within the classroom, the learning styles theory (which predates Gardner, 1983) argues that each student learns better when a teacher caters his or her instruction to the student's specific learning strengths (Gardner, 2013). For example, if a student has strong kinesthetic intelligence, a learning styles advocate might argue that the teacher should teach subjects like mathematics to that student kinesthetically.

While this idea sounds both constructive and engaging, in theory, it is incredibly impractical for a teacher to teach mathematics via kinesthetic activities on a consistent basis. This method also violates the principle of specificity, and there is little to no scientific evidence validating such an approach. Proponents of the learning styles theory will often use pseudoscientific personality tests to assess a student's learning style and then try to teach to the student based on the result (Nancekivell, 2019).

At the end of the day, if you want to take a research-validated approach to teaching, you should rely on quantitative evidence. And the quantitative evidence for the implementation of multiple intelligences theory has been meager. Within Hattie's (2023e) meta-x meta-analysis database, there are thirteen meta-analyses to date on teaching to learning styles, showing a mean effect size of 0.33. While the mean result was not negative, it should be remembered that due to the file drawer problem (see chapter 2, page 15), most education studies show a positive result (Wiliam, 2016). Moreover, teaching to learning styles is an incredibly time-intensive task, and the potential reward here does not match with level of effort required. It should also be noted that while some of the meta-analyses did show higher results, these meta-analyses were based on alternative learning styles theory created by Rita Dunn (1990; Hattie, 2023e), which is based on learner preferences and not perceived learning styles (Dunn, 1990). If we remove the Dunn (1990) meta-analyses from this secondary meta-analysis, we get a mean effect size of 0.26.

Multiple Intelligences, Learning Styles, and Growth Mindset

Some advocates might claim that a moderately effective pedagogy might still be worth the effort. However, many professional psychologists have started to question whether the prevalence of the learning styles theory could lead to more fixed mindsets (Nancekivell, 2019). As you learned in chapter 5 (page 41) on growth mindset, teachers should approach learning gaps with the question of *how* we can overcome them, not *whether* we can overcome them. The multiple intelligences theory, on the other hand, has led some educators to question whether we should consider catering to students' strengths by removing tasks or subjects that students struggle with (Boutelier & Smalligan, 2018).

Other proponents of the theory have given students and teachers pseudoscientific tests to determine students' natural strengths and weaknesses and their natural learning styles. The problem with these tests, however, is that they can create self-fulfilling prophecies for both the student and the teacher, in which both assume a student is doing poorly in a subject because of a hypothetical neurological weakness (Nancekivell, 2019).

However, learning is such a complicated process that it is almost impossible to determine if it is nature or nurture that is responsible for a student doing poorly in a subject. For example, growing up in Canada, I was required to take French classes. My parents did not believe French was an important subject and, therefore, did not mind if I passed or failed my French classes. Consequently, I used to read English novels under my desk during French class, and I grew up not being able to speak French. This was not a learning styles problem; this was a socially constructed problem. I was not applying myself because I did not value the subject, and now, consequently, I am a poor French speaker. And yet, as a child, I remember my father suggesting that I had a French learning disability, while my highest marks were in English. This anecdote is silly, of course, but it helps highlight the danger of automatically assuming learning deficits or gaps are neurological.

As a matter of equity, all students should learn how to read and do mathematics. I would hate to see learning styles theory or multiple intelligences theory be cited as a reason not to teach students either subject. Truthfully, in my professional career, I have seen some educators make this argument.

Summary Points to Remember

Following is a list of highlights and significant points outlined in this chapter.

- ☑ While there are undoubtedly multiple forms of intelligence, the multiple intelligences theory, as it was originally developed, lacks scientific validity.
- ☑ Multiple intelligences theory is often implemented by teaching to students' learning styles. This practice is both impractical and has not been empirically validated. It violates the principle of specificity and promotes a fixed mindset.

- ☑ Multiple intelligences and learning styles theories, while holding some valid concepts, ultimately do not yield enough results to be worth the time investment for teachers.
- ☑ Instead of focusing on teaching to students' learning styles, teachers should instead focus on making sure their instruction is explicit and specific to students' needs and that expectations for learning goals are clear.

Reflection Questions

Individually or with your team, use these questions to reflect on the information in this chapter.

1. What surprised you most about multiple intelligences or learning styles? Why?
2. Were you taught about multiple intelligences or learning styles in school, and what did you think of it at the time?
3. If you had to teach a lesson on long division, why would it be a challenge to incorporate musical and kinesthetic learning styles?
4. How do you think active versus passive learning might conflate with teaching to learning styles?
5. Why do you think teaching to learning styles became so popular?

CHAPTER 13

Constructivist Teaching Versus Traditional Teaching

Perhaps the most hotly debated topic in education research is constructivist teaching versus traditional (or transmission) teaching. These two overarching theories of how students best learn influence debates in mathematics, reading, and science. There are whole pedagogies and programs completely influenced by either theory. Indeed, two of these debates have been dubbed as the *reading wars* and the *math wars* (Barshay, 2023; Goldenberg, 2020). Both pedagogical arguments really come down to constructivist versus traditional teaching.

In this chapter, you will learn what these theories mean, the pedagogies that fall under each theory, the difficulty in examining these theories, and the empirical support for both sides of the argument. Because many different pedagogies fall under each branch of instruction, I reviewed the empirical research on the most popular pedagogies that fall under each theory.

Note that most of the material in this chapter comes from the article "What Is Constructivist Teaching and Why Is It Important?" (Hansford, 2022i). The material is used with permission.

Traditional Teaching

Traditional teaching, transmission teaching, explicit instruction, direct instruction, and *Direct Instruction* are often used as interchangeable terms. Some view these as opposite methods compared to more modern and constructivist methods. However, there are differences in the meanings associated with some of these terms. According to Chen Xie, Mingshuai Wang, and Huimin Hu (2018), in *traditional teaching* practices, teachers use the:

> transmission instructional model . . . a teacher-centered teaching and learning model in which the teacher's role is to design lessons aimed at predetermined goals and to present knowledge and skills in a predetermined order, and students' tasks are to passively acquire teacher specified knowledge and skills.

To put this in less academic language, transmission scholars believe that learning is linear. In a transmission (or traditional) classroom, a teacher presents curriculum to the students based on a carefully scaffolded curriculum. It is the teacher's job to teach and the student's job to learn. Teachers are the active providers of knowledge, whereas students are the passive recipients.

Traditional teaching often includes more explicit instruction than has been popularized by modern education theorists (Xie et al., 2018). It should be noted that *explicit instruction* is often also referred to as *direct instruction*. Within the scientific literature, two versions of direct instruction are often represented. *Direct Instruction* (capitalized) refers to scripted programs in which the teacher has an actual script to read from in their lessons. *Direct instruction* (not capitalized) is a strategy in which the teacher explicitly teaches the content but does not follow scripted lessons (National Institute for Direct Instruction, n.d.).

Differences between traditional teaching and modern or constructivist teaching extend beyond the differences between explicit and implicit instruction. However, it is within this difference where there is the greatest debate. To help build clarity around the differences between these interrelated terms, see table 13.1.

TABLE 13.1: Traditional Teaching Terms and Definitions

Term	Definition
Traditional teaching	Teaching methods popularized prior to the rise of constructivist teaching
Transmission theory	The theory of learning that informs both direct instruction and traditional teaching
Explicit instruction	Instruction in which the teacher explains concepts and information to students
Direct instruction	Another term for *explicit instruction*
Direct Instruction	Scripted programs based on the transmission theory that rely on direct instruction

One way to conceptualize these differences would be to view *transmission theory* as the underpinning belief; explicit instruction, direct instruction, and Direct Instruction as the teaching methods; and *traditional teaching* as a colloquial term for a collection of teaching practices that include explicit instruction.

Constructivist Teaching

According to Hattie (2022a), "Constructivist teaching involves providing students with learner-centered, active instruction, where students explore ideas, propositions, explanations, solutions and take subsequent actions." The theory originates from Jean Piaget (1964), who believed that learning happens through the scaffolding of understanding. This theory is especially prevalent in mathematics instruction (University of Buffalo, n.d.). According to the University of Buffalo (n.d.), there are four main principles to constructivist teaching.

1. **Create cognitive dissonance:** Assign problems and activities that will challenge students. Knowledge is built as learners encounter novel problems and revise existing schemas as they work through the challenging problem.
2. **Apply knowledge with feedback:** Encourage students to evaluate new information and modify existing knowledge. Activities should allow for students to compare preexisting schema to the novel situation. Activities might include presentations, small group or class discussions, and quizzes.
3. **Reflect on learning:** Provide students with an opportunity to show you (and themselves) what they have learned. Activities might include presentations, reflexive papers, or creating a step-by-step tutorial for another student.
4. **Elicit prior knowledge:** New knowledge is created in relation to learner's preexisting knowledge. Lessons, therefore, require eliciting relevant prior knowledge. Activities include pretests, informal interviews, and small-group warm-up activities that require recall of prior knowledge.

Ultimately, it is very challenging to evaluate the efficacy of constructivist teaching because it is not a singular pedagogical concept but rather both a philosophy and a theory of learning. Moreover, it is also closely connected with other pedagogies.

Constructivist Teaching Methods

There are many teaching methods that fall under the umbrella of constructivist teaching. However, the most common include inquiry-based learning, student-centered learning, problem-based learning, play-based learning, teaching to learning styles, and cooperative learning. For example, while constructivism is not inquiry-based learning, inquiry-based learning is inherently constructivist in style. Similarly, student-centered learning is also arguably a constructivist pedagogy, but constructivist teaching cannot be solely defined as student centered (Xie et al., 2018).

Constructivist teaching methodologies often focus on metacognition strategies to help students solve problems rather than explicit skill-based instruction. Constructivist teaching is popular, in part, because of the influence of Jean Piaget on learning theory (University of Buffalo, n.d.). However, it is undoubtedly also driven by a pedagogical movement that is against skill-based instruction because its proponents believe this type of instruction is inherently authoritarian and boring (Small, 2008).

For reading instruction, constructivists often argue for the use of three-cueing instruction over systematic phonics instruction, claiming that instruction that focuses too much on skill development will kill the love of reading (Bailey, 2023). With the three-cueing method, students are told that when they get stuck on an unfamiliar word, they should look at the picture, look at the first letter of the word, or consider the meaning of the sentence. Indeed, students are often told to do this before trying to sound out the word.

In Mathematics instruction, constructivists argue against skill-based instruction, claiming it causes mathematics anxiety. Instead, constructivists argue for the use of metacognition strategies, like the ones often used in number talks. In number talk, teachers and students brainstorm together different methods for solving a mathematics problem. For example, a constructivist might see a problem like 9 × 9 and suggest to students that they should solve the problem by multiplying 9 × 10 and then subtracting 9. Whereas in a traditional classroom, a teacher would likely expect the student to memorize that answer (Boaler, 2015).

Of course, it is important to recognize that constructivism and using strategies instead of skills instruction are not necessarily the same thing. While many constructivists might advocate for these ideas, constructivism is a philosophical approach to instruction that includes a host of ideas; it is not one singular concept (University of Buffalo, n.d.). This makes it very difficult to evaluate in terms of its efficacy.

In 2022, I conducted a meta-analysis comparing transmission-based literacy programs (structured literacy) to constructivist-based literacy programs (balanced literacy). I found that transmission-based literacy programs showed almost double the effect sizes as did constructivist ones. These results suggest that for reading instruction, a constructivist approach appears to be less effective. However, consider that balanced literacy programs represent only one version of constructivist teaching. Moreover, just because constructivist teaching does not work for one subject does not necessarily mean that it would not work for others.

While three cueing is often theorized to be the reason, balanced literacy programs show lower reading outcomes (Hanford, 2022). However, I wonder if it's the three-cueing instruction or if it's the lack of phonics instruction that is to blame for low reading outcomes. My hunch would be that it's the lack of phonics, not the three-cueing instruction. While three cueing is often highly debated and theorized about, there is a surprisingly small amount of experimental research specifically on the topic. When it comes to mathematics instruction, there are some theoretical criticisms of constructivist metacognition strategies (Ndlovu, 2013).

However, it's not the strategy instruction, like mathematics metacognition strategies or three-cueing, which concerns me most; it is the replacement of fluency instruction with strategy instruction. Within constructivist mathematics instruction, teachers are encouraged to spend less time on teaching procedures and mathematics facts (fluency instruction) and more time on problem solving. Students are then supposed to rely on metacognition strategies to reduce reliance on the memorization of procedures and facts (Boaler & Zoido, 2016). But I don't think one can replace the value of developing skills like multiplication or phonetic decoding to automaticity with just strategy instruction.

Constructivist Teaching and Learning Outcomes in Meta-Analysis

According to Hattie (2022a), there are two meta-analyses on the topic of constructivist teaching (Abrami et al., 2006; Erisen & Günay, 2017). Philip C. Abrami and colleagues' (2006) study found a mean effect size of 0.11, which is not statistically significant. Yavuz Erisen and Rafet Günay's (2017) study found a mean effect size of 1.10. However, only Abrami and colleagues' (2006) paper was peer reviewed. Conversely, the Erisen and Günay (2017) study was more recent and included far more studies. Both studies had a stringent inclusion criterion and excluded all case studies, which should increase confidence in the results.

I think it's even more problematic that even though Hattie (2022a) claims that the Abrami and colleagues' (2006) study is about constructivist teaching, the original authors did not use this term once. Moreover, the Abrami and colleagues' (2006) study was not on reading or mathematics instruction. For these reasons, I do not think this study can be used to determine the efficacy of constructivism, especially not for mathematics or reading instruction.

The Erisen and Günay (2017) study specifically looked at mathematics instruction; however, there were a few outlier studies within the data, and only two of the studies were specifically on mathematics. This is important to note because constructivist teaching methods are especially popular in mathematics. As Steve Graham pointed out, you cannot truly call something science if you don't have proper replication, which he defined as six or more studies (Pedagogy Non-Grata, 2022).

Figure 13.1 shows the results of the Erisen and Günay (2017) study, including the estimated mean effect sizes for constructivist teaching methods.

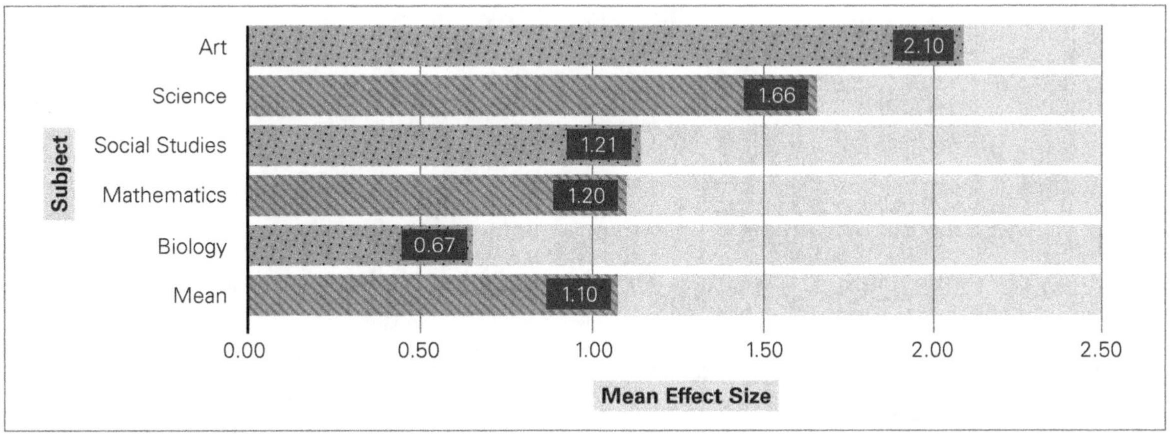

Source for data: Erisen & Günay, 2017.
Source: Hansford, 2022i. Used with permission.

FIGURE 13.1: Constructivism meta-analysis results.

While these results seem to suggest efficacy for constructivist teaching, most of the studies were not on English or mathematics. This means you cannot apply these findings to those subjects. In my own research, I was able to find another meta-analysis by Xie, Wang, and Hu (2018). This meta-analysis was specifically on constructivism instruction in mathematics within mainland China. The meta-analysis included eighty-nine experimental or quasi-experimental studies. All studies compared a constructivist approach to a traditional approach to teaching. The meta-analysis also looked at twenty-five studies that compared a nontraditional, nonconstructivist approach to traditional education (which they defined as *transmission instruction*). The inclusion criteria for this study were very rigorous. Figure 13.2 (page 94) shows the results of this study—the impact of constructivist teaching in mainland China.

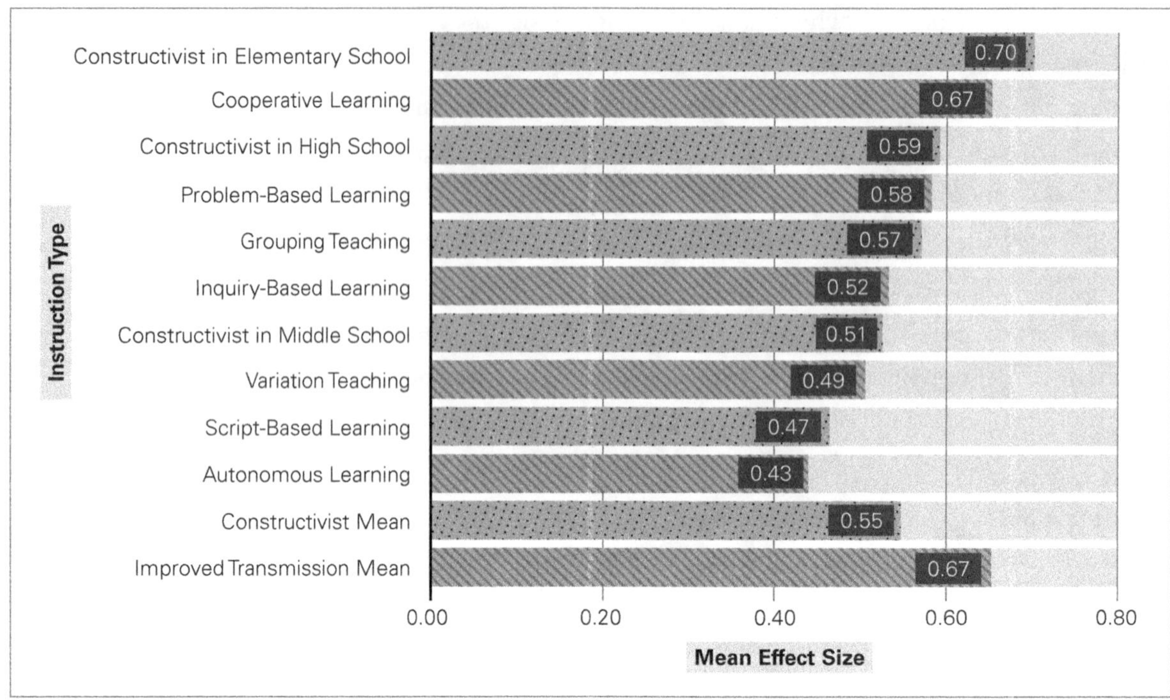

Source for data: Xie, Wang, & Hu, 2018.
Source: Hansford, 2022i. Used with permission.

FIGURE 13.2: Constructivist teaching meta-analysis results.

In their meta-analysis, Xie and colleagues (2018) used categories not normally referred to within Western education literature. To aid in understanding the results of this study, I have provided an explanation of some of these strategies, such as *variation teaching*, *grouping teaching (ability grouping)*, *script-based learning*, *autonomous learning*, and *improved transmission.*

- **Variation teaching:** This strategy involves providing multiple scaffolded examples of problems and how to solve them.
- **Grouping teaching (ability grouping):** This strategy involves grouping students according to their ability level.
- **Script-based learning:** This strategy is a direct instruction teaching methodology in which teachers follow a script for all lessons.
- **Autonomous Learning:** This strategy involves having students choose their own learning goals, monitor their own learning, and evaluate their own progress. In Western education, this might be referred to as *discovery-based learning.*
- **Improved transmission:** To distinguish between traditional and newly developed models of instruction, this meta-analysis names them *traditional transmission model* and *improved transmission model*, respectively. The former is the traditional method of teaching, as defined earlier in this chapter. The latter still satisfies the definition of the transmission instructional model and has some new characteristics. Within this label of improved transmission, one could include grouping teaching and variation teaching (Xie et al., 2018).

Normally, I would find the Xie and colleagues' (2018) meta-analysis quite compelling. However, this meta-analysis does have some unique limitations. First, the meta-analysis did not base its inclusion criteria on its definition of constructivist teaching but rather looked at studies on topics *related to* constructivist teaching. For this reason, I would argue that this is not actually a meta-analysis on constructivist teaching but rather on cooperative learning, inquiry-based learning, problem-based learning, variation teaching, and ability grouping. Of course, this is part of the problem with evaluating the efficacy of constructivist teaching; it's not one pedagogy but a philosophical approach that includes many different pedagogies and concepts.

Second, the fact that this meta-analysis was conducted on Chinese studies only is another convoluting factor. China consistently has the highest mathematics scores in the world as determined by the Programme for International Student Assessment (PISA) (OECD, 2018a; see more about this topic in chapter 16, page 129). And, as Xie and colleagues (2018) point out, the Chinese education system typically uses a more traditional mathematics education focusing on mathematics fluency taught via explicit and systematic instruction. Considering that China has the best student mathematics results in the world, it makes sense that some element of their transmission instruction model is working. Additionally, did the constructivist teaching work in this study (Xie et al., 2018) because it was better, because it was novel, or because the students already had strong mathematics fluency skills and could, therefore, benefit from the more open-ended curriculum?

The Limitations of Meta-Analyses on Constructivist Teaching Methods

While Xie and colleagues (2018) found strong improvement in academic success for constructivist teaching, the results are at odds with meta-analyses on individual types of constructivist methods. Moreover, constructivist teaching does not exist within a vacuum, so analyzing its efficacy requires examining opposing types of teaching methods. In order to better evaluate the efficacy of constructivist teaching methods, I reviewed the meta-analyses conducted on various pedagogies under this umbrella term. Moreover, I examined the efficacy of the competing pedagogy—direct instruction.

For the sake of clarity, I have broken down this research into the sub-categories of direct instruction, inquiry-based learning, problem-based learning, discovery-based learning, and cooperative learning. I also have conducted a secondary meta-analysis of all this research at the end of the chapter to better examine how constructivist versus transmission-based education differs in terms of research outcomes.

DIRECT INSTRUCTION

Hattie's (2022b) secondary meta-analysis of direct instruction found a mean effect size of 0.59. In 2018, Jean Stockard, Timothy Wood, Cristy Coughlin, and Caitlin Khoury published the largest of these meta-analyses, examining 328 direct instruction studies on language and mathematics. However, the inclusion criteria were not particularly stringent, as the authors did not specifically exclude nonexperimental studies, which is problematic as nonexperimental studies produce inflated and less accurate effect sizes.

Figure 13.3 shows the results of the Stockard and colleagues (2018) study.

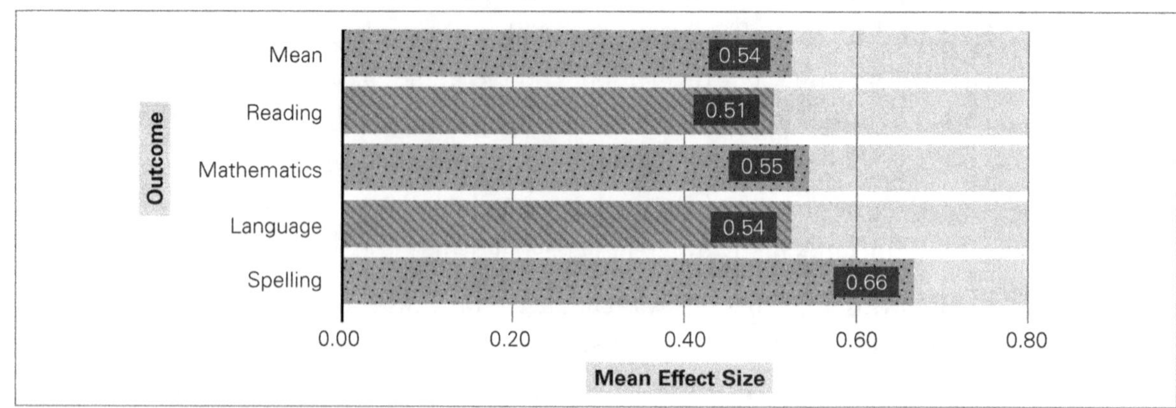

Source for data: Stockard et al., 2018.
Source: Hansford, 2022i. Used with permission.

FIGURE 13.3: Direct instruction meta-analysis results.

As you can see, Stockard and colleagues (2018) found comparable results to Xie and colleagues (2018). Both Xie and colleagues (2018) and Stockard and colleagues (2018) compared direct instruction to inquiry-based learning. However, the two findings should have been diametrically opposed, as the two pedagogies are opposite.

In 2005, Mathew Haas conducted a meta-analysis on the impact of direct instruction for secondary students studying algebra. His meta-analysis looked at thirty-five experimental studies and found a mean effect size of 0.55 for direct instruction and a mean effect size of 0.51 for problem-based learning.

In 2009, Russel Gersten, David Chard, Madhavi Jayanthi, and Scott Baker conducted a meta-analysis of mathematics interventions on learning-disabled students and found a mean result of 1.22 for direct instruction. Their meta-analysis was specifically on single case studies, which lowers the statistical reliability of their results, as the sample size for each study was extremely small. That said, the very large effect size found might be attributed to the fact that this meta-analysis was looking at students with learning disabilities. Therefore, the results might suggest that students with learning disabilities need more explicit instruction.

Gary Adams and Siegfried Engelmann (1996) conducted a meta-analysis on direct instruction in reading and found a mean effect size of 0.75. However, this meta-analysis was part of a book, and I was unable to evaluate the quality of their inclusion criteria. In 2000, a National Reading Panel meta-analysis looked at Lovett-style (Lovett is a popular Canadian author in the phonics movement) direct instruction programs and found a mean effect size of 0.41. The inclusion criteria were rigorous, and the meta-analysis was one of the most comprehensive reading meta-analyses ever conducted. Similarly, in 2001, Linnea Ehri and colleagues conducted a sub-analysis of the NRP report and found a mean effect size of 0.48 for direct instruction programs.

Across these six direct instruction meta-analyses, there is a mean effect size 0.77 for mathematics and 0.54 for reading. Admittedly, the Gersten and colleagues (2009) meta-analysis is likely inflationary, and if you correct for this effect size, you get a mean effect size of 0.55 for mathematics. These would suggest moderately positive results for direct instruction approaches over indirect instruction approaches in mathematics and English.

INQUIRY-BASED LEARNING

Inquiry-based learning is often referred to as the central pedagogy in constructivist teaching. Similarly, some view the interrelated pedagogies of problem-based learning and discovery-based learning as subtypes of inquiry-based learning pedagogies. Hattie (2022c) defines *inquiry-based learning* as:

> An educational practice in which students are called on to behave as scientists or philosophers, generating questions and seeking to develop answers through the accumulation of evidence. This could include asking questions and solving problems and often includes procedures such as small-scale investigations and practical projects.

He identifies eight meta-analyses on the topic with a mean effect size of 0.46. However, none of these meta-analyses were specifically on mathematics or language.

In 2016, Ard Lazonder and Ruth Harmsen conducted a meta-analysis on the topic of inquiry-based learning. While their study was not specifically on reading or mathematics, it was on mathematics and sciences. Their meta-analysis included seventy-two studies in total. However, their inclusion criteria did not specifically exclude nonexperimental studies, which might have inflated the results, as nonexperimental studies produce less accurate, more inflated effect sizes. Their meta-analysis found a mean effect size of 0.66. However, inquiry-based learning showed higher results when greater guidance was offered, possibly suggesting that more explicit instruction was better than less explicit instruction. In general, the current body of research shows no meaningful support for the use of inquiry-based learning in reading instruction and limited support for the use of inquiry-based learning in mathematics instruction.

PROBLEM-BASED LEARNING

Hattie (2022d) explains *problem-based learning* as follows:

> Students often act in groups and decide what they need to learn to resolve a particular problem or question, while teachers act as facilitators. It usually involves real-world problems to promote student learning of concepts and principles as opposed to direct presentation of facts and concepts. The aim is also to promote critical thinking skills, problem-solving abilities, and communication skills.

He identifies twenty meta-analyses on the topic, with a mean effect size of 0.35. However, most of these studies looked at adult learners studying medicine, which means these results are not applicable to school-aged students learning reading and mathematics.

Roslinda Rosli, Mary Margaret Capraro, and Robert Capraro (2014) conducted a meta-analysis on the effect of problem-based learning on mathematics outcomes. Figure 13.4 (page 98) shows the results of this meta-analysis. However, this meta-analysis only contains thirteen studies, which is a small number for a meta-analysis. While these studies examined grades 3 to 12, the inclusion criteria were strict, which improves confidence in their results, at least for these thirteen studies.

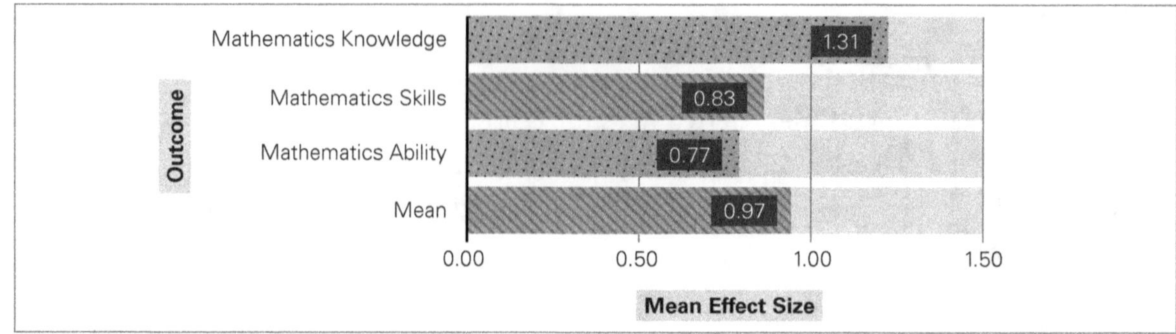

Source for data: Rosli et al., 2014.
Source: Hansford, 2022i. Used with permission.

FIGURE 13.4: Problem-based learning meta-analysis results.

In 2015, Kimberly Jensen conducted a meta-analysis of problem-based learning. However, only one of the studies looked at mathematics, and only one looked at reading. The reading effect size was 0.11 (statistically insignificant), and the mathematics effect size was 0.34. The meta-analysis was not peer reviewed and was, therefore, of lower reliability. Miray Dağyar and Melek Demirel (2105) also conducted a meta-analysis on problem-based learning and found a mean effect size of 0.86 for mathematics instruction across fifteen rigorously conducted studies.

One convoluting factor for this meta-analysis is the fact that most studies were conducted on high school and university students. This is problematic because problem-based learning makes more sense in these age brackets, as students should have already developed their basic procedural and computational fluency. Yet, one often sees problem-based learning recommended for students in primary or kindergarten classrooms.

Overall, these studies suggest that there is very strong evidence for the use of problem-based learning in mathematics instruction. However, most of this research is on secondary and university students. I think it might be problematic to use this evidence as justification for the extensive use of problem-based learning in elementary grades before students have developed their procedural and computational fluency.

DISCOVERY-BASED LEARNING

To the best of my knowledge, only one peer-reviewed meta-analysis exists on the topic of discovery-based learning. In 2011, Louis Alfieri, Patricia Brooks, Naomi Aldrich, and Harriet Tenenbaum conducted a meta-analysis on discovery-based learning. Their meta-analysis included 164 studies and used strict inclusion criteria. However, it did not specifically control for any subject. The study found a mean negative effect size of −0.30 for discovery-based learning and a mean effect size of 0.30 for combining discovery-based learning and direct instruction. To the best of my knowledge, the current evidence suggests that the use of discovery-based learning lowers academic achievement.

COOPERATIVE LEARNING

Hattie (2023a) defines *cooperative learning* as a pedagogical strategy in which students collaborate toward a common goal. Typically, cooperative learning programs try to increase face-to-face interactions and group accountability. Cooperative learning is supposed to engage students in complex learning material. Hattie (2023a) identifies twenty-seven meta-analyses on the topic with a mean effect size of 0.43. However, most of these meta-analyses did not look at mathematics or reading instruction.

In 2015, Gulfar Capar and Kamuran Tarim completed a meta-analysis of cooperative learning in mathematics. The inclusion criteria were rigorous and included a total of twenty-six studies. Figure 13.5 shows the results of this meta-analysis.

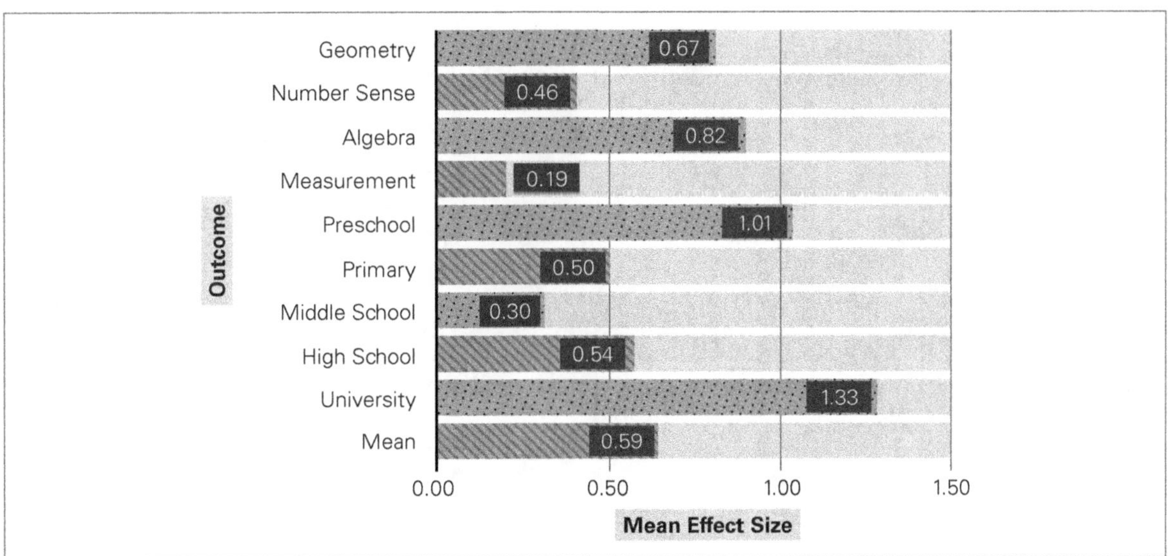

Source for data: Capar & Tarim, 2015
Source: Hansford, 2022i. Used with permission.

FIGURE 13.5: Cooperative learning in mathematics meta-analysis results.

In 1993, Francis Burton Spuler conducted a non-peer-reviewed meta-analysis on cooperative learning in mathematics for elementary students. He found a mean effect size of 0.59; however, the meta-analysis only included ten studies. The fact that this meta-analysis had only ten studies and was not peer reviewed makes it less reliable, as typically, ten studies within a meta-analysis is a very small sample.

In 2002, Kristen McMaster and Douglas Fuchs conducted a meta-analysis of cooperative learning for students in kindergarten through grade 12. It included fifteen studies total. Their study found a mean effect size of 0.29 for mathematics and reading outcomes. The inclusion criteria were high for the study, which increases my confidence in the results.

In 2013, Puzio and Colby conducted a meta-analysis of eighteen cooperative learning studies on literacy outcomes. Figure 13.6 (page 100) shows the results of this study. The study inclusion criteria were not rigorous, which should have inflated the effect sizes. However, the resulting effect sizes were low. This is important, as less rigorous studies show inflated effect sizes. This suggests that the impact of cooperative learning on literacy outcomes is likely small to insignificant.

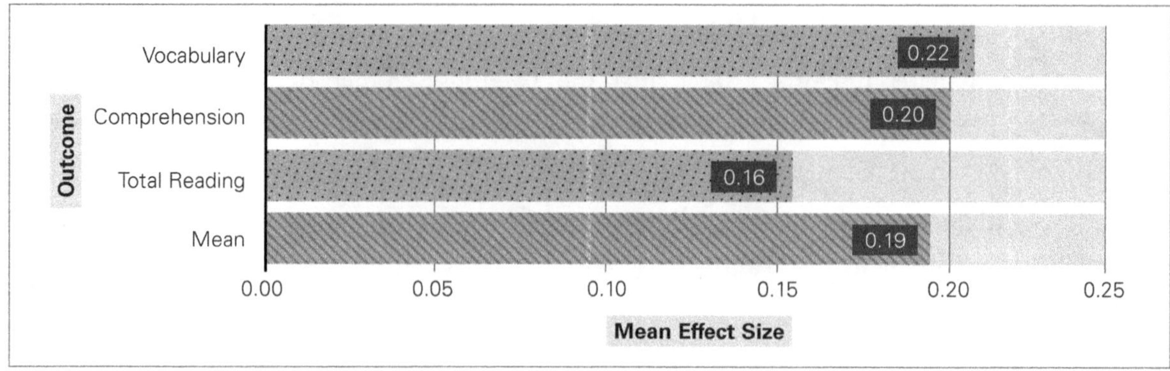

Source for data: Puzio & Colby, 2013.
Source: Hansford, 2022i. Used with permission.

FIGURE 13.6: Effects of cooperative learning on literacy outcomes meta-analysis results.

In 2018, Sedat Turgut and Ilknur Turgut conducted a meta-analysis of forty-seven experimental or quasi-experimental cooperative learning studies on mathematics. The inclusion criteria were rigorous, and there was a sufficiently high number of studies. The results of this meta-analysis are in figure 13.7. Overall, the results of this meta-analysis were high, and the studies experimental, which suggests that cooperative learning does benefit students in mathematics.

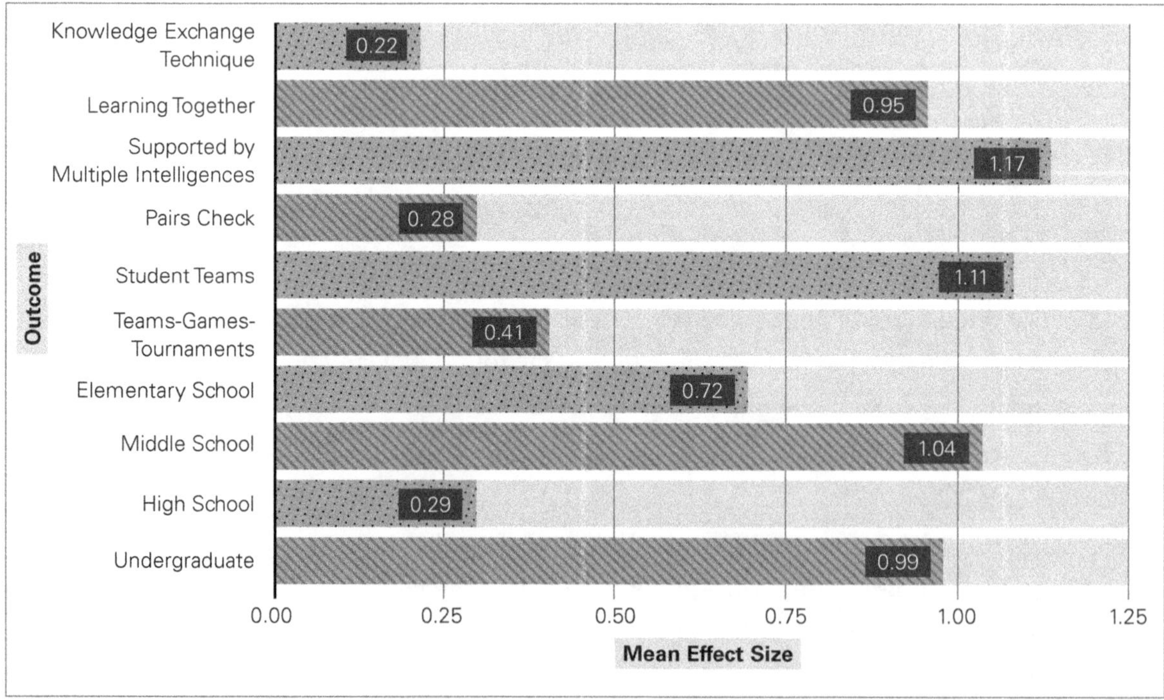

Source for data: Turgut & Turgut, 2018.
Source: Hansford, 2022i. Used with permission.

FIGURE 13.7: Effects of cooperative learning on mathematics meta-analysis results.

Overall, there is moderate evidence for the use of cooperative learning in mathematics. Across all these pedagogies and topics, there is weak evidence for the use of constructivist pedagogies in reading. There is strong evidence for the use of constructivist pedagogies in mathematics, but only for secondary and post-secondary schooling, as most of that research has been conducted on older students or students with more previous mathematics fluency instruction. Moreover, we also see greater impacts on direct instruction for learning disabled students, perhaps because they require less open-ended instruction.

BALANCED LITERACY

All the previous research is not really a collection of meta-analyses on constructivism but rather meta-analyses on various constructivist pedagogies. This is important because there is a big difference between implementing a single constructivist pedagogy into instruction and adopting only constructivist pedagogies. For this reason, I think it might make more sense to look at a meta-analysis of constructivist pedagogical programs that use exclusively constructivist pedagogies rather than one individual constructivist pedagogy at a time. Otherwise, how do we measure the impact of constructivist teaching in totality? To the best of my knowledge, no such meta-analysis exists for mathematics, which makes judging the efficacy of constructivist teaching in mathematics hard to do on a credible level. However, I have conducted a meta-analysis examining constructivist reading programs (Joseph, King, & McGlynn, 2022).

In my opinion, *balanced literacy* is a pedagogical approach to reading instruction that de-emphasizes skill instruction, uses metacognition strategies (three-cueing), implements ability grouping, and emphasizes the importance of enjoying reading over the importance of academic achievement. Balanced literacy is also different from structured literacy because it doesn't typically use decodable readers or phonics scope and sequences.

In 2022, Joshua King and I conducted a meta-analysis of phonics and balanced literacy programs (Hansford & King, 2022). This meta-analysis is not yet peer reviewed, and some of the studies included in the meta-analysis were also not peer reviewed. All sixty-three studies included were of an experimental or quasi-experimental design. We found a mean effect size of 0.25 for balanced literacy. Comparatively, we found a mean effect size of 0.45 for phonics (transmission or traditional) instruction. This suggests that a skill-based approach showed roughly double the impact of a constructivist approach for reading achievement. At the writing of this book, I updated this meta-analysis and submitted it for peer review. However, it is not yet published. There were no statistically significant differences between the currently published 2022 meta-analysis and the 2023 manuscript submitted for peer review.

A Synthesis of the Data

To better synthesize all these data, I have conducted a secondary meta-analysis of the pedagogies discussed in this chapter and graphed those results in figure 13.8 (page 102). I calculated each effect size across the mean of all meta-analyses discussed in this chapter, per category.

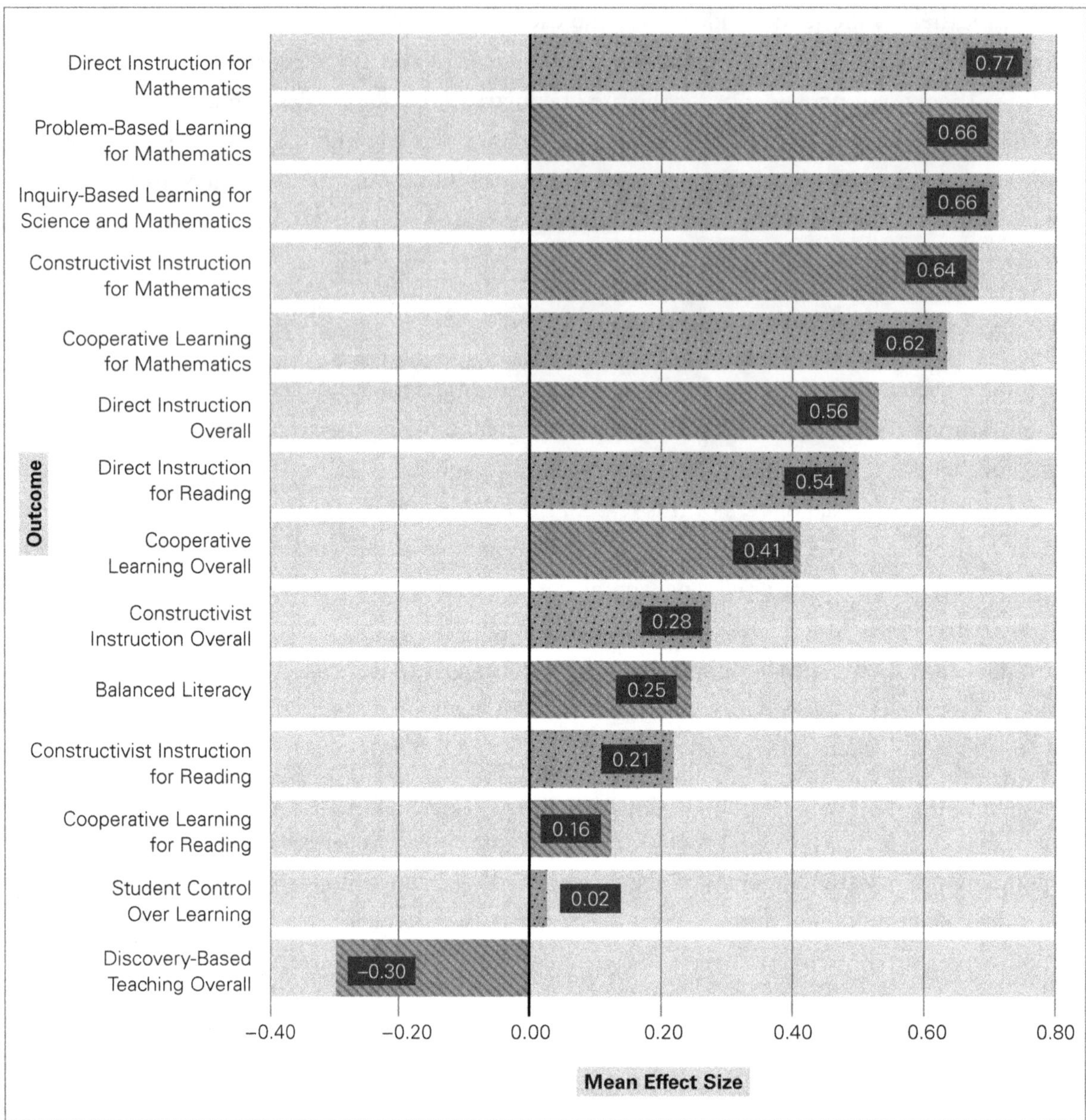

Source: Hansford, 2022i. Used with permission.

FIGURE 13.8: Secondary meta-analysis of constructivist teaching.

Secondary meta-analyses risk taking experimental research out of context and misapplying the results. However, they can be useful when comparing multiple pedagogies or when multiple high-quality meta-analyses produce seemingly contradictory results. As both of these factors applied to this chapter, I decided a secondary meta-analysis was necessary to best determine the efficacy of constructivist teaching.

At the risk of sounding repetitive, these data suggest that constructivist teaching works for mathematics instruction but not for reading instruction. However, I would caution against this interpretation for three reasons.

1. Most of the mathematics instruction data were for older students, which means that these results cannot be extrapolated to be meaningful for younger students. Moreover, it seems to contradict the reading research we have for younger students, as shown by the meta-analysis on balanced literacy.
2. All the meta-analyses on mathematics instruction were on individual constructivist pedagogies and not on constructivist teaching itself.
3. To the best of my knowledge, there have been no meta-analyses of constructivist mathematics programs in which all the principles are constructivist based. Therefore, there are no data regarding the efficacy of combining multiple constructivist pedagogies together.

To reiterate, constructivist teaching is not a pedagogy; it is a theory of learning and a philosophical viewpoint, which has inspired other pedagogies. It is always easier to evaluate the efficacy of a single pedagogical concept with an experimental model than it is to evaluate an encompassing idea like constructivist teaching. There likely exists a spectrum between traditional or transmission instruction and constructivist instruction. Moreover, the type of instruction that works best might not be on either end of that spectrum but in the middle. Research into individual constructivist pedagogies, therefore, cannot be easily translated into programming that is entirely constructivist.

Much of the debate around constructivist teaching is often focused on the metacognition strategies used to teach hard skills in a less explicit way. However, it is not these strategies that most concern me, but rather the extreme versions of applied constructivist teaching. For example, on many occasions, I have heard constructivist educators say that teachers should never teach mathematics formulas. This goes directly against the scientific consensus on mathematics research.

As Bethany Riddle and Michael Schneider demonstrated in their 2007 literature review, student mathematics achievement is highest when teachers instruct on both conceptual and procedural knowledge (Riddle-Johnson & Schneider, 2015). Moreover, research suggests that students with learning disabilities benefit from explicit instruction, which makes me believe that these types of approaches will be particularly harmful to our most vulnerable students (Gersten et al., 2009).

Similarly, I have seen constructivist educators promote a minimalist level of phonics instruction based on the claim that skill instruction kills the joy of reading. This goes directly against the findings of most of the scientific research on reading and, in particular, disadvantages our most vulnerable students (Hansford & King, 2022; National Reading Panel, 2000).

I would argue that discovery-based learning represents one of the most extreme interpretations of constructivist teaching, and within the scientific literature, we see on average statistically significant negative results. Comparatively, direct instruction research and inquiry-based learning research both show, on average, moderate to high results. This, on its surface, is seemingly illogical, as the two methods are opposing pedagogies. However, this fact is likely representative of how meta-analyses on the topic were completed.

Most education studies, in general, show a positive benefit, likely for two reasons (Pedagogy Non-Grata, 2019b).

1. Researchers are usually focused on proving the efficacy of an idea and likely unintentionally create bias in their experiment for success.
2. Experiments that do not find statistically significant results are sometimes not published—as previously discussed, this is referred to as the *file drawer problem*.

So, even though inquiry-based learning and direct instruction are opposing pedagogies, experiments on both typically show moderately high results. Given that most education research shows a positive benefit and that meta-analysis into discovery-based learning showed negative results, it seems reasonable to conclude that more explicit instruction produces better results than less explicit instruction.

Summary Points to Remember

Following is a list of highlights and significant points outlined in this chapter.

- ☑ Constructivism is both a theory of learning and a philosophical movement.
- ☑ Constructivists view learning as a nonlinear process centered on the student.
- ☑ The traditional view of learning sees instruction as a learning process led by an instructor.
- ☑ There is some moderate evidence that constructivist teaching strategies can be helpful, but most of that evidence only applies to older students.
- ☑ Most of the scientific evidence suggests that traditional teaching methods are more effective than constructivist ones.

Reflection Questions

Individually or with your team, use these questions to reflect on the information in this chapter.

1. What theory of learning makes more sense to you, transmission theory or constructivist theory? Why?
2. Could both the transmission and constructivist theory of learning be partially valid? Why or why not?
3. Could some constructivist pedagogies be better than others? Do you think there is a time and place for more constructivist approaches?
4. What are the potential benefits of a constructivist approach?
5. What are the potential detriments of a constructivist approach?

Differentiation

D*ifferentiation* is an umbrella term that applies to a variety of different pedagogies, or teaching methods. Studies on differentiation often include research on ability grouping, teaching to learning styles, streaming, podding, enrichment, and individualized instruction.

This chapter reviews the experimental research conducted on different methods for differentiation, contrasts the commonalities between effective and ineffective forms of differentiation, and provides practical recommendations for best practice.

The Research on Differentiation

Differentiation can be a difficult topic to study because there are so many diverse types of instruction that fit under this umbrella term, and they are not all connected. However, I would argue that there are four main types of differentiation, as outlined in table 14.1 (page 106).

TABLE 14.1: Types of Differentiation and Their Pedagogies

Type of Differentiation	Pedagogies Included
Student Preferences	• Increasing student choice • Teaching to learning styles • Teaching to learning preferences • Self-directed learning
Pace of Instruction	• Mastery teaching • Acceleration programs • Grade skipping
Curriculum and Instructional Intensity	• Individualized curriculum • Pullout instruction • RTI • MTSS • Adaptive technology
Grouping	• Ability groupings • Small groups • Within-class groupings

Differentiating instruction makes intuitive sense. Teachers know that students have varying needs and preferences. However, catering to individual students' needs can be difficult, especially in large classes. Not only is attempting to meet the individual needs of students a complex challenge, but it increases the planning burden for teachers, both in terms of instruction and assessment. Moreover, evaluating the effectiveness of differentiation is no easy task, as there are so many methods for differentiation. Nonetheless, there have been meta-analyses on the topic.

In 2018, Marjolein I. Deunk, Annemieke E. Smale-Jacobs, Hester de Boer, Simone Doolaard, and Roel J. Bosker conducted a meta-analysis, with rigorous inclusion criteria, on twenty-one mathematics instruction (experimental) studies related to the term *differentiation*. Rather than using one specific definition of differentiation, they searched for studies that included the terms *instruct*, *differentiate*, *individualize*, *teach*, *ability group*, *aptitude treatment*, *grouping*, *mastery learning*, and *streaming*. Figure 14.1 shows the results of this meta-analysis.

The graph in this figure displays the mean effect size found for each form of differentiation identified in the meta-analysis. The results were low to negative, suggesting little possible benefit of differentiation in mathematics. But as noted previously, *differentiation* is an umbrella term, and some types of differentiation might be more effective than others.

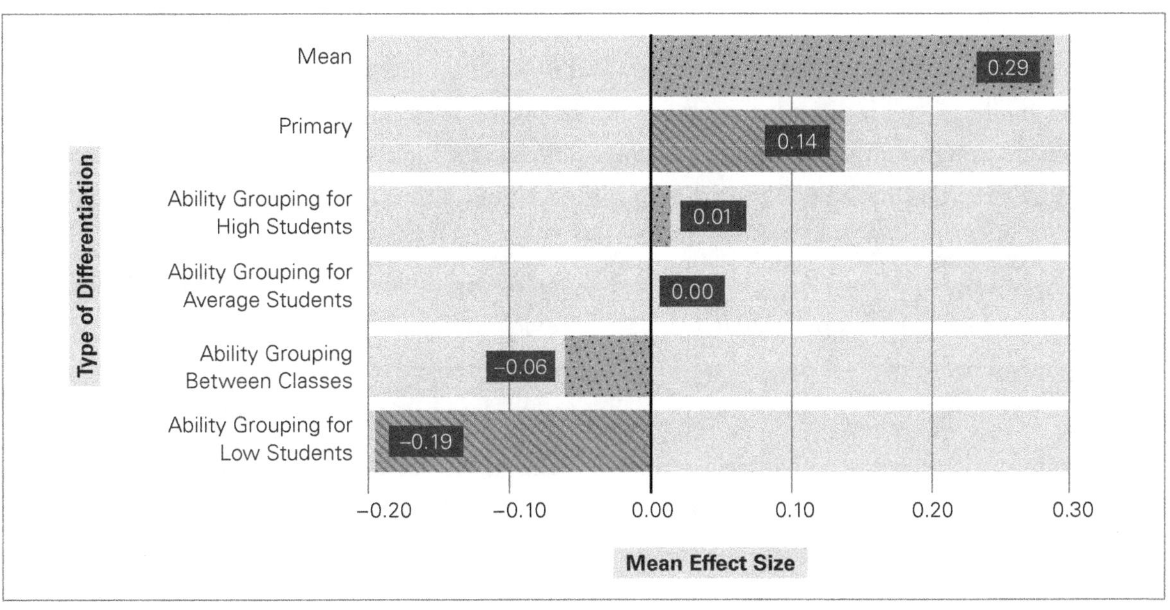

Source for data: Deunk et al., 2018.
Source: Hansford, 2022b. Used with permission.

FIGURE 14.1: Impact of differentiation in mathematics.

In 2020, Kelly Puzio, Glen T. Colby, and Dana Algeo-Nichols conducted a meta-analysis on differentiation in literacy instruction. They used a rigorous inclusion criterion and examined eighteen experimental and quasi-experimental studies. They found a mean effect size of 0.13 and concluded: "The most successful programs took very different approaches to differentiation, including individualization, choice, and an alternate curriculum" (Puzio et al., 2020).

In 2019, Annemieke E. Smale-Jacobse, Anna Meijer, Michelle Helms-Lorenz, and Ridwan Maulana conducted a meta-analysis of differentiation in secondary schools. This meta-analysis used a rigorous inclusion criterion and analyzed fourteen quasi-experimental and experimental studies on differentiation. They found a mean effect size of 0.50 (Smale-Jacobse et al., 2019).

These meta-analyses suggest that differentiation works for secondary education, but not for elementary. In the past, I have been a big proponent for differentiated instruction; however, I submitted two original, large-scale meta-analyses for peer review in 2023 that have shaken my confidence. The first was a large-scale meta-analysis on language programs, a summary of which you can find on my website (Hansford & King, 2022). In the first meta-analysis, we conducted a moderator analysis on the pace of instruction for phonics scopes and sequences (Hansford & King, 2022). We consistently found that phonics programs that allowed teachers the autonomy to individualize the pace of instruction for students' needs showed lower results. Instead, a set, mandated pace showed higher effect sizes.

In the second meta-analysis (Hansford, Reenstra, Aitchison, & McGlynn, 2022), we looked at computer programs that used adaptive technology to individualize literacy instruction to students' assessed learning needs. We found a mean effect size of 0.11, suggesting no statistically significant benefit. In other words, both of these meta-studies suggest that attempts by computers or humans to individualize instruction failed to increase learning outcomes and may even lower them.

I must admit, I am skeptical of the findings of these three reviewed meta-analyses (Deunk et al., 2018; Puzio et al., 2020; Smale-Jacobse et al., 2019) on differentiation, because they are trying to find a mean effect size for differentiation overall. However, there are so many ways to differentiate, it seems unreasonable to try and use one overall effect size for this teaching method. Instead, it seems more practical to look at the underlying pedagogies and evaluate them individually. To do this, I reviewed the meta-analyses in Hattie's (2023c) database for each individual pedagogy that could fit under the umbrella term *differentiation*. I also reviewed several meta-analyses in the Steenbergen-Hu and colleagues (2016) literature review on the topic of differentiation. Finally, I took my own related meta-analyses on the topic and synthesized all these studies into a secondary meta-analysis of fifty-six meta-analyses on pedagogies related to differentiation.

As previously discussed in chapter 2 (page 15), using Hattie's work runs the risk of comparing unlike findings, as he does not control for calculation method, research design, age, subject, or language (as cited in Pedagogy Non-Grata, 2019b). To increase the comparability of these findings, I screened out meta-analyses that were correlational, based on single case design, not on literacy or mathematics instruction, or on students in grades 9 or higher. Following are the results of secondary meta-analyses on the individual forms of differentiation, including ability grouping, RTI, grade skipping, mastery-based instruction, teaching to learning styles, intervention instruction, and individualized instruction.

Ability Grouping

Figure 14.2 shows the results of my secondary meta-analysis on the overall impact of ability grouping, which has mixed results.

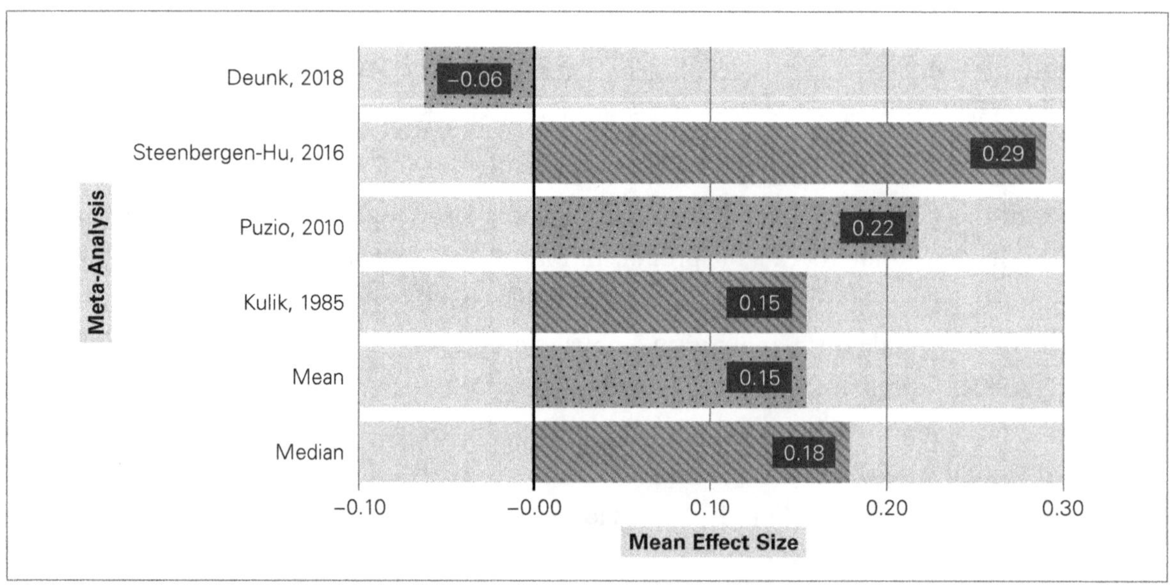

Source: Hattie, 2023c; Steenbergen-Hu et al., 2016.

FIGURE 14.2: Secondary meta-analysis on overall impact of ability grouping.

The data in figure 14.2 vary between high and low results. One study showed negative results, one study showed negligible benefits, and two studies showed small but meaningful benefits. Overall, it seems unlikely that ability grouping benefits the whole class. However, also consider how ability grouping might affect each ability level.

Figure 14.3 shows the results of my secondary meta-analysis on the impact of ability grouping on gifted and high-level learners.

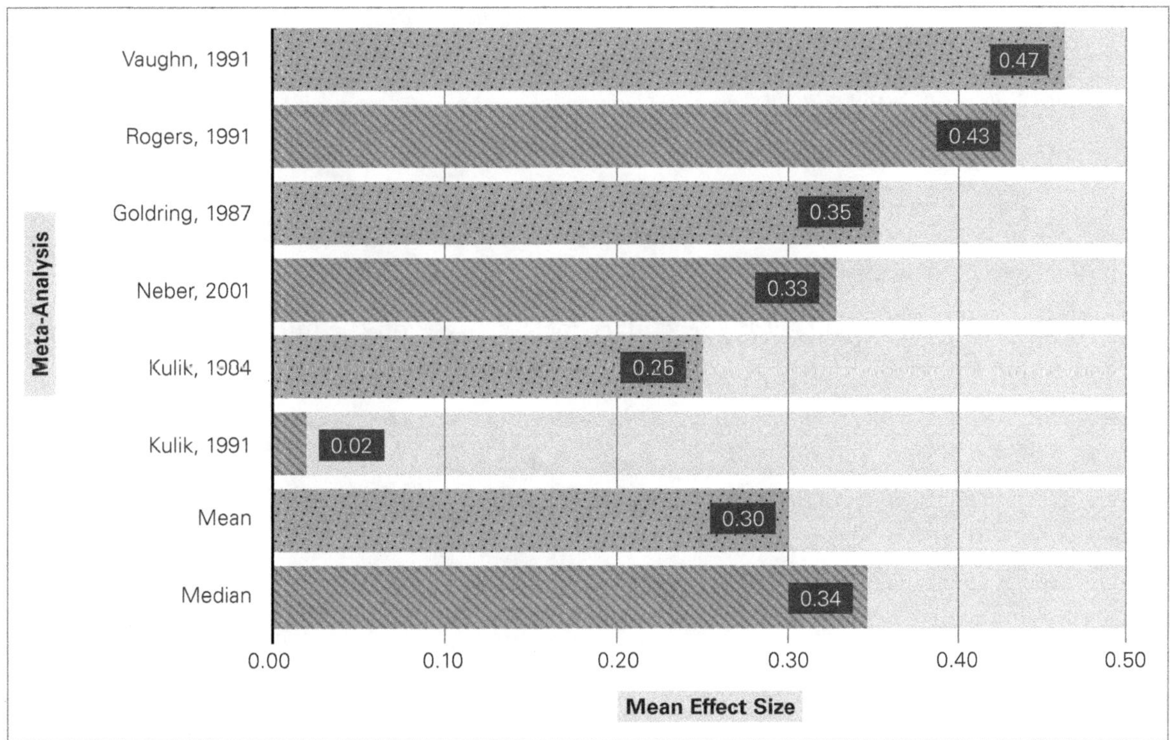

Source: Hattie, 2023c; Steenbergen-Hu et al., 2016.

FIGURE 14.3: Secondary meta-analysis on the effect of ability grouping on gifted learners.

The data in figure 14.3 show that ability grouping appears to provide a small but statistically significant benefit for gifted students, as only one study showed a negligible benefit. However, you might consider how removing gifted students from other student groups affects other students in the class. I hypothesize that learners who are struggling would benefit from having those students in their groups. I also wonder if grouping students by ability could lead to self-fulfilling prophecies, in which the gifted students challenge each other and learners who are struggling feel labeled.

Figure 14.4 (page 110) shows the results of my secondary meta-analysis on the impact of ability grouping on average learners.

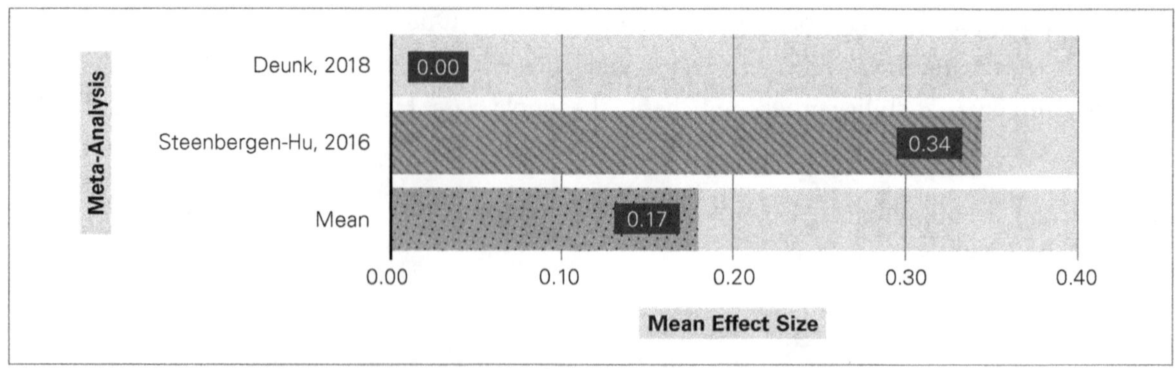

Source: Deunk et al., 2018; Steenbergen-Hu et al., 2016.

FIGURE 14.4: Secondary meta-analysis on the effect of ability grouping on average learners.

The data in figure 14.4 suggest that, on average, ability grouping shows a small to negligible benefit for average students.

Figure 14.5 shows the results of my secondary meta-analysis on the impact of ability grouping for learners who are struggling.

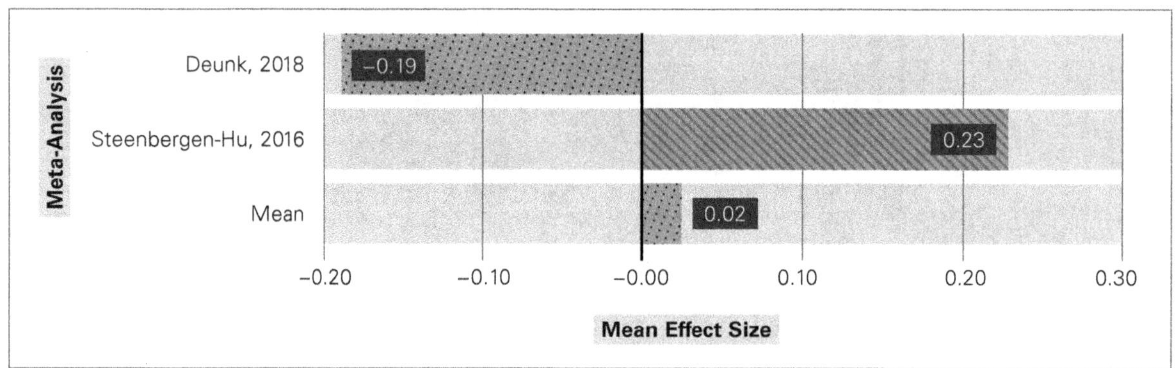

Source: Deunk et al., 2018; Steenbergen-Hu et al., 2016.

FIGURE 14.5: Secondary meta-analysis on the effect of ability grouping on learners who are struggling.

The data in figure 14.5 show a small to negative possible benefit of ability grouping for learners who are struggling. Overall, these meta-analyses on ability grouping suggest that the practice might benefit the most advantaged students and negatively impact the most disadvantaged students. This should constitute a moral dilemma for educators who might think they have to choose who most deserves greater learning opportunities—gifted learners or learners who are struggling.

Another form of ability grouping, often used with RTI, is called *podding*. As previously discussed, in this form of ability grouping, teachers group students across classes and not within a single class. Two meta-analyses examine the efficacy of this method, as shown in figure 14.6.

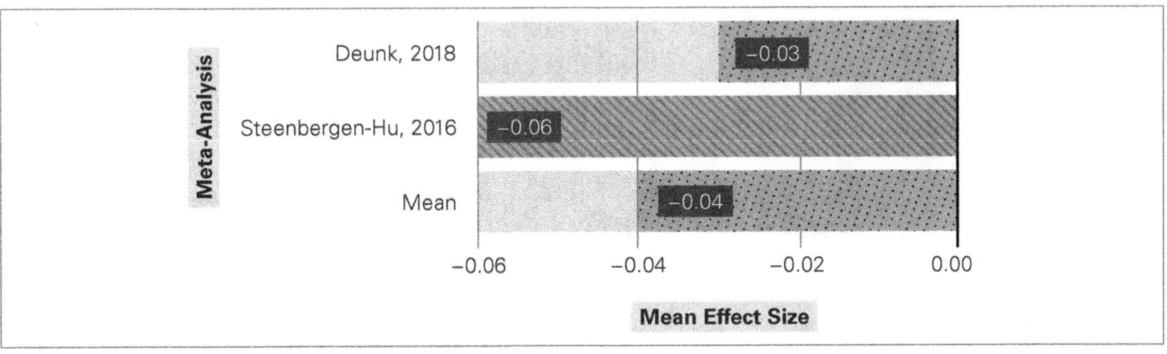

Source: Deunk et al., 2018; Steenbergen-Hu et al., 2016.

FIGURE 14.6: Secondary meta-analysis on the effect of podding on learning outcomes.

The data in figure 14.6 suggest that podding, on average, shows no meaningful benefits for students and may even diminish learning outcomes. This finding may be a result of the disruptions caused by mixing classes on a daily basis.

Response to Intervention

RTI involves like-ability grouping. However, the methodology is different in that the more students are struggling, the more explicit instruction they receive in smaller groups. Students in Tier 1 receive regular class instruction. Students in Tier 2 receive small-group instruction from the classroom teacher. Students in Tier 3 receive intensive support from a resource teacher. This model requires teachers to make instructional decisions based on frequent formative assessment.

As discussed in chapter 11 (page 75), there is strong evidence that RTI works. Figure 14.7 shows my secondary meta-analysis on the overall effectiveness of RTI for all ages, ability levels, and subjects.

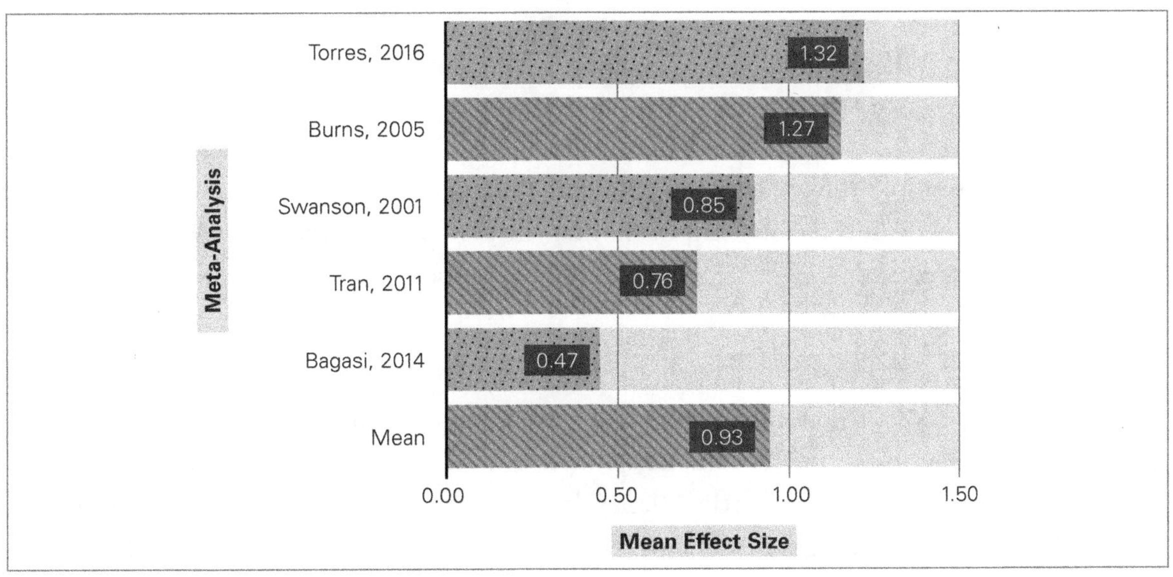

Source: Hansford, 2022d. Used with permission.

FIGURE 14.7: Secondary meta-analyses on RTI.

As previously discussed, some of the studies included in RTI meta-analyses use non-rigorous designs, which may inflate the results. However, overall, the results are still impressive and suggest substantial efficacy for RTI. Again, as discussed in chapter 11 (page 75), MTSS is a similar model of action research. However, within the MTSS framework, the RTI model is applied to both behavior and academics. In 2019, Colin Shepley and Jennifer Grisham-Brown conducted a meta-analysis on the MTSS framework, including fourteen rigorous studies, which showed a mean effect size of 0.31.

Grade Skipping

One form of differentiation that seems to have fallen out favor in recent years is grade skipping. Figure 14.8 shows my secondary meta-analyses on this topic.

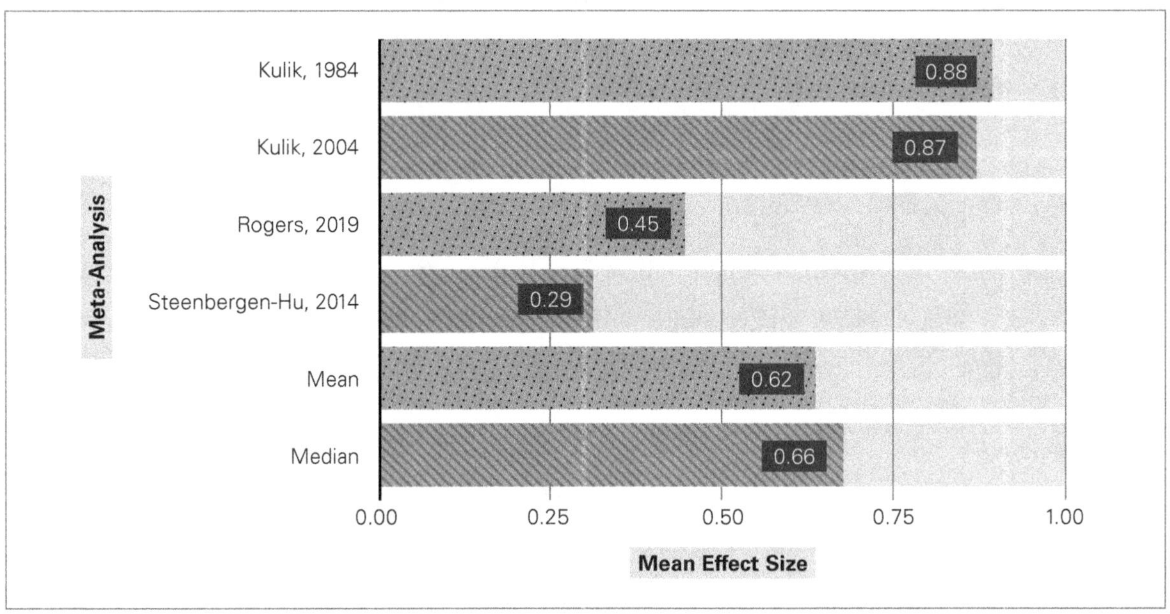

Source: Hattie, 2023c; Steenbergen-Hu et al., 2016.

FIGURE 14.8: Secondary meta-analysis on the effect of grade skipping.

The data in figure 14.8 show that having advanced students skip grades appears to have strong evidence of efficacy. It is, therefore, surprising that the practice has fallen out of favor. Mastery-based instruction is related to grade skipping in that they are both related to the pace of instruction.

Mastery-Based Instruction

In mastery-based instruction, the teacher teaches the curriculum until the student demonstrates mastery. The pace of instruction is completely dependent on student progress instead of a predetermined timeline. Within the (Hattie, 2023c) database, there are six relevant meta-analyses on mastery-based instruction. Figure 14.9 shows my secondary meta-analysis of these studies.

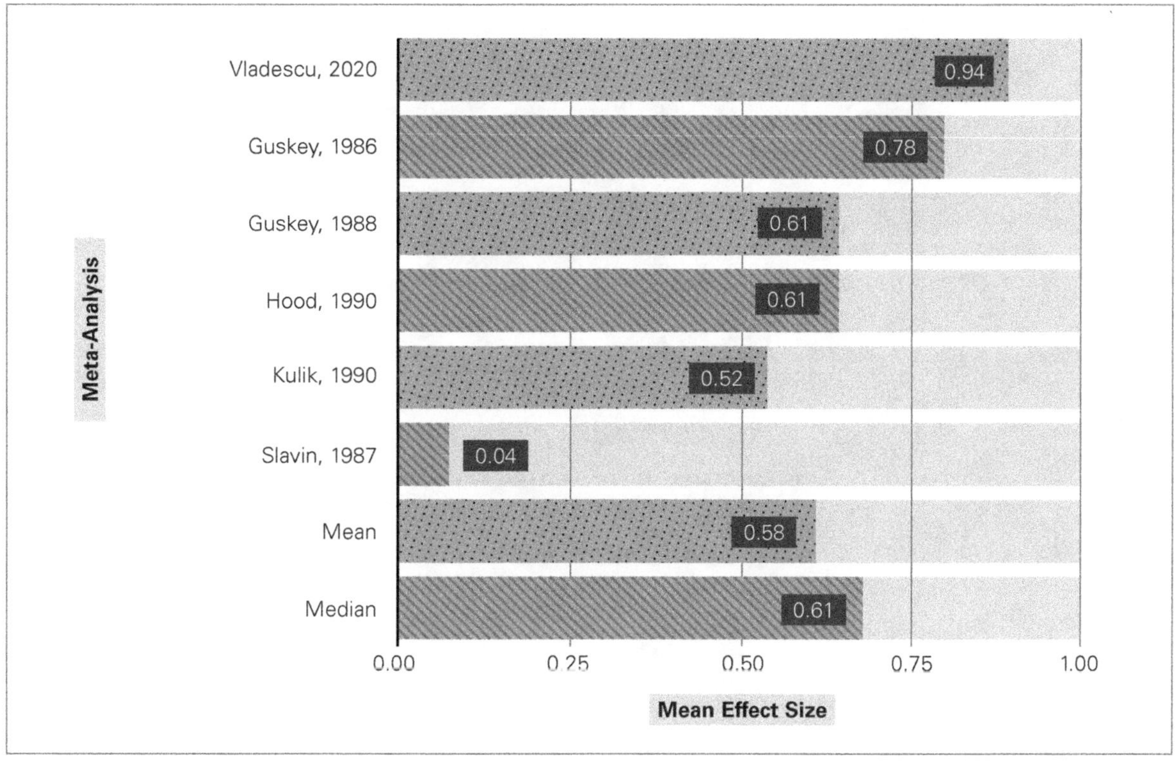

Source: Hattie, 2023c.

FIGURE 14.9: Secondary meta-analysis on the effect of mastery-based instruction.

In figure 14.9, only the 1987 Slavin meta-analysis shows a low effect size for mastery-based instruction. While it is interesting that Slavin's (1987) meta-analysis shows a low effect size, some of this is undoubtedly due to his strict inclusion criterion, which likely deflates effects (Slavin, 2018). Overall, there does seem to be strong evidence that mastery-based instruction is effective.

Teaching to Learning Styles

The most popular forms of differentiation often seem to include teaching to learning styles and increasing student choice. Figure 14.10 (page 114) shows the secondary meta-analyses on teaching to learning styles.

The data in figure 14.10 suggest strong effectiveness for teaching to learning styles. However, as previously noted in chapter 12 (page 83), most meta-analyses that showed a positive benefit for this teaching method were either very dated (and therefore, likely less rigorous) or based on the Dunn (1990) model and not the model often loosely based on Gardner's (1983) work. According to Hattie's (2023c) database, there was one relevant meta-analysis on increasing student choice. This was conducted in 2014 by Thomas F. Carolan, Shaun D. Hutchins, Christopher D. Wickens, and John M. Cumming. Their meta-analysis showed a mean effect size of 0.02, suggesting no meaningful benefit (Carolan et al., 2014).

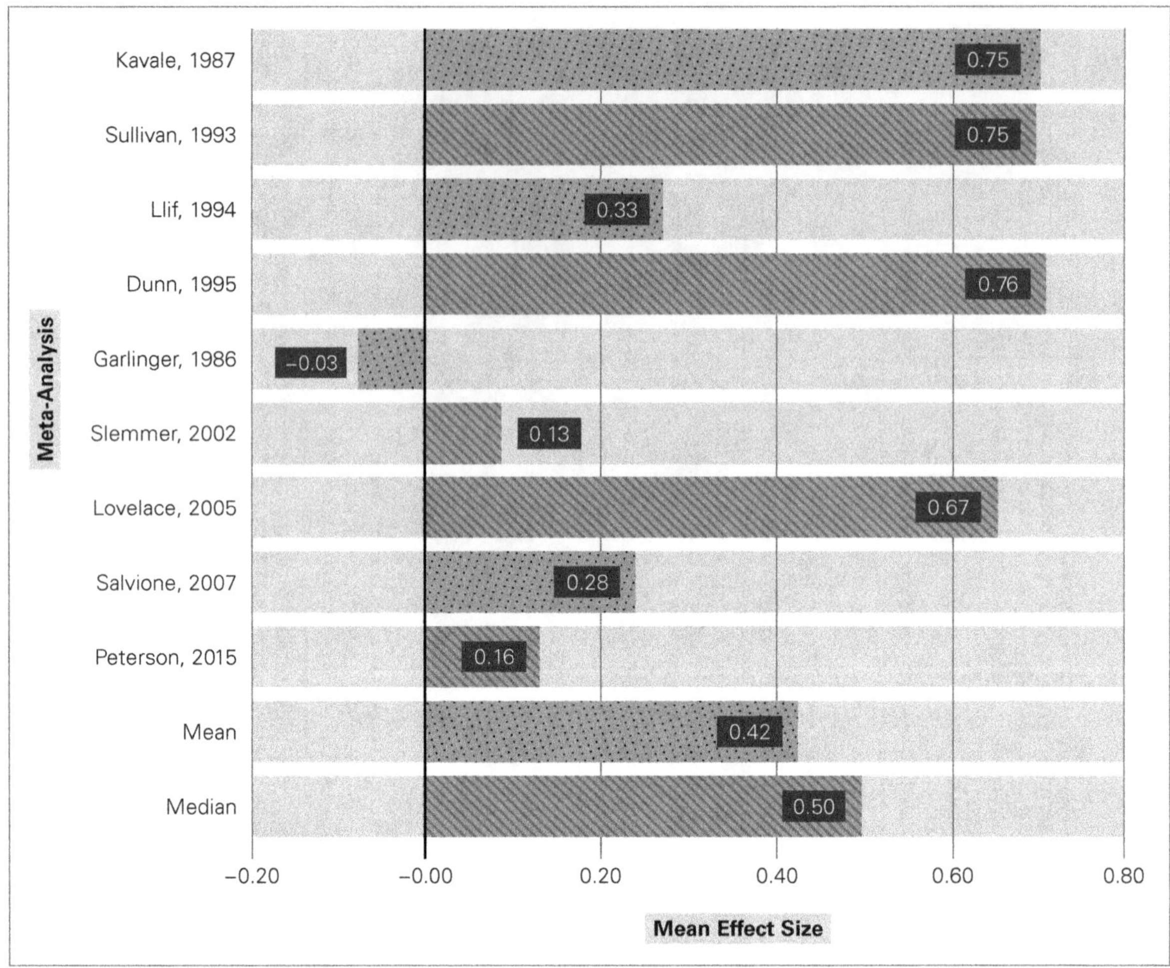

Source: Hattie, 2023c.

FIGURE 14.10: Secondary meta-analysis on the effect of teaching to learning styles.

Intervention Instruction

Providing intervention instruction to learners who are struggling is one form of differentiation that undoubtedly has evidence of efficacy. The Hattie (2023c) database identifies two meta-analyses on the general impact of tier 3 (or more intensive) reading interventions: one meta-analysis was conducted in 2021 by Amanda J. Neitzel, Cynthia Lake, Marta Pellegrini, and Robert E. Slavin, and the other was conducted in 2015 by Nancy K. Scammacca, Greg Roberts, Sharon Vaughn, and Karla K. Stuebing. However, Hattie (2023c) appears to have missed the 2022 meta-analysis by Colby Hall and colleagues on this topic.

Figure 14.11 shows the results of these three meta-analyses. The data in this figure show that, on average, Tier 3 reading interventions have small effect sizes for dyslexic students. However, it should be noted that both the Hall and colleagues (2022) and the Neitzel and colleagues (2021) studies used very rigorous inclusion criterion, which tend to deflate effect sizes.

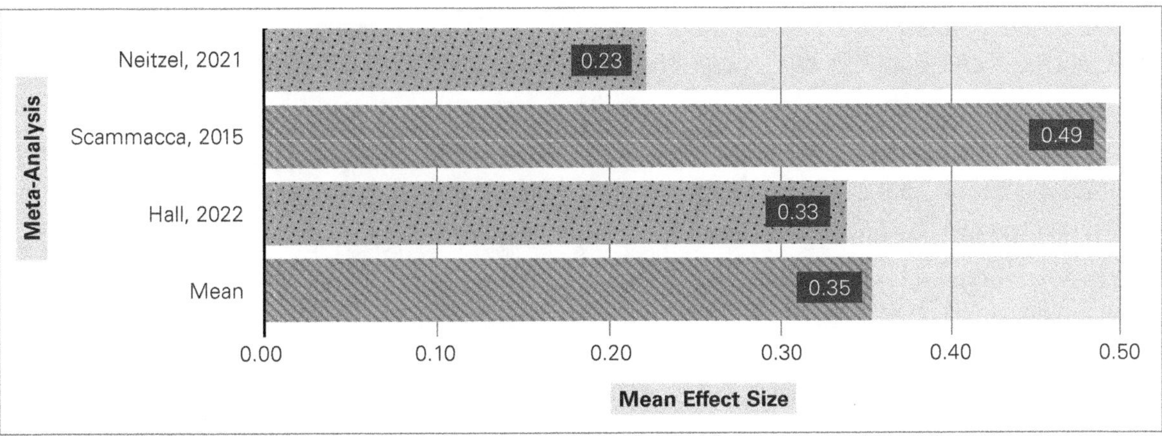

Source: Hall et al., 2022; Hattie, 2023c.

FIGURE 14.11: Secondary meta-analysis of the effects of Tier 3 reading interventions on students with dyslexia.

Robert E. Slavin was a coauthor for the study by Neitzel and colleagues (2021). He famously used very strict inclusion criteria for meta-analyses (Slavin, 2018). That said, I feel confident based on these results and the results of the (Torgesen, 2009) literature review, that reading interventions for dyslexic students are helpful for learning outcomes.

The results are similar for mathematics. According to the Hattie (2023c) database, there are six relevant meta-analyses for Tier 3 (more intensive) mathematics interventions. Figure 14.12 shows the results of my secondary meta-analysis of these six meta-analyses.

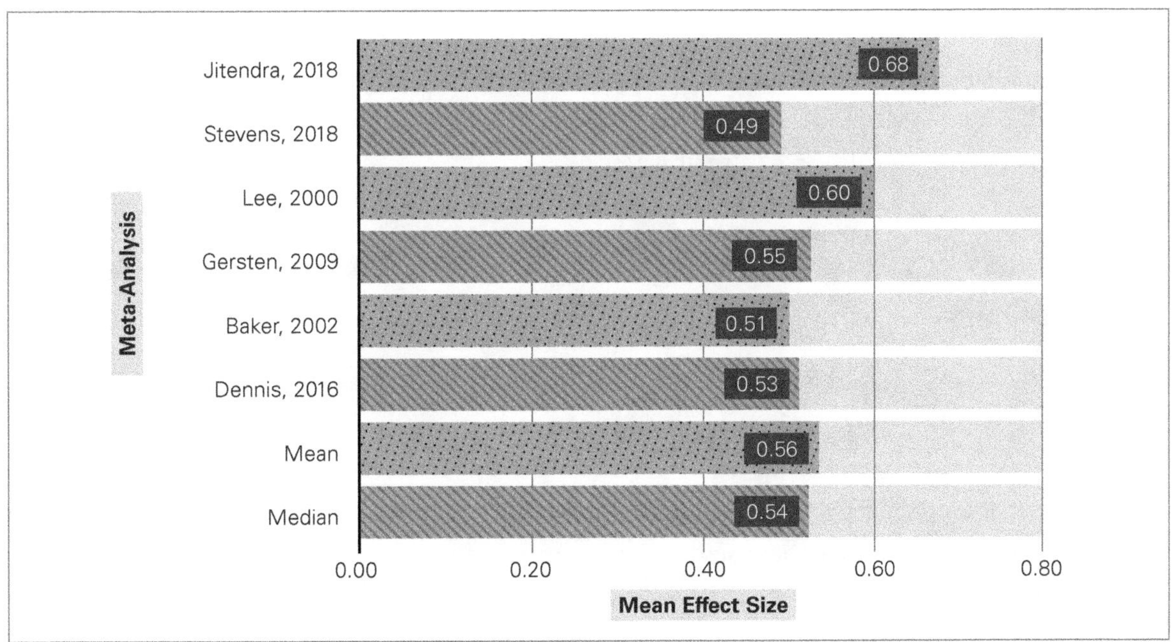

Source: Hattie, 2023c.

FIGURE 14.12: Secondary meta-analysis on the effects of Tier 3 mathematics interventions on students with learning disabilities.

The data in figure 14.12 (page 115) illustrate that every meta-analysis on Tier 3 mathematics intervention shows a strong effect, suggesting an incredibly positive benefit for students with learning disabilities. There is one meta-analysis on Tier 3 instruction in middle schools, specifically, for general academic achievement. In this meta-analysis, Tameeka Grant (2012) found a mean effect size of 0.18. Unfortunately, I was unable to view the full original study, only the summary found in Hattie (2023c). However, the effect size is very low, which might suggest that interventions for students in middle school or older are less effective. Of course, this provides even more reason for early intervention.

Individualized Instruction

One form of differentiated instruction I have always been enthusiastic about is individualized instruction, meaning that the curriculum was tailored to each student's individual pedagogical needs. To the best of my knowledge, only one meta-analysis has been published on this form of differentiation (Rogers, 2008). This meta-analysis showed an exceptionally large effect size of 2.35. This effect size has nagged at me, as rigorous studies rarely show effect sizes anywhere near close to that number. While I originally took this effect size as proof that individualization was amazing, the more I learned about meta-analysis, the more I questioned the effect size. I reviewed the meta-analysis and found four points of concern.

1. The paper was not published in a peer-reviewed journal.
2. There were only four studies behind this effect size.
3. The inclusion criteria for the meta-analysis were not clear.
4. It was specifically looking at gifted students.

While individualizing curriculum is still a practice I use in my classroom, I no longer feel that including this meta-analysis in my analysis of differentiation is a judicious choice. Instead, I hope to see more research on this topic in the future.

Secondary Meta-Analysis of Differentiation Pedagogies

To synthesize all these data into a logical and intuitive format, I conducted a secondary meta-analysis of all the pedagogies reviewed in this chapter. Figure 14.13 shows the results of this secondary meta-analysis, providing the mean effect size found across comparable meta-analyses for each differentiation pedagogy. In parentheses next to each pedagogy is the number of meta-analyses analyzed. Overall, the mean effect size for differentiation across these meta-analyses was small but meaningful.

However, as previously mentioned, this type of analysis might be too inaccurate, as there are such large differences between the various types of differentiation. To better compare these effects, I conducted a secondary meta-analysis of these results, according to the types of differentiation outlined in figure 14.1 (page 107). Figure 14.14 (page 118) shows the results of my analysis.

FIGURE 14.13: Secondary meta-analysis of differentiation pedagogies.

As figure 14.14 (page 118) shows, differentiation is most effective when it relates to curriculum or the pace of curriculum. However, differentiation related to student preferences or ability grouping is far less likely to be effective.

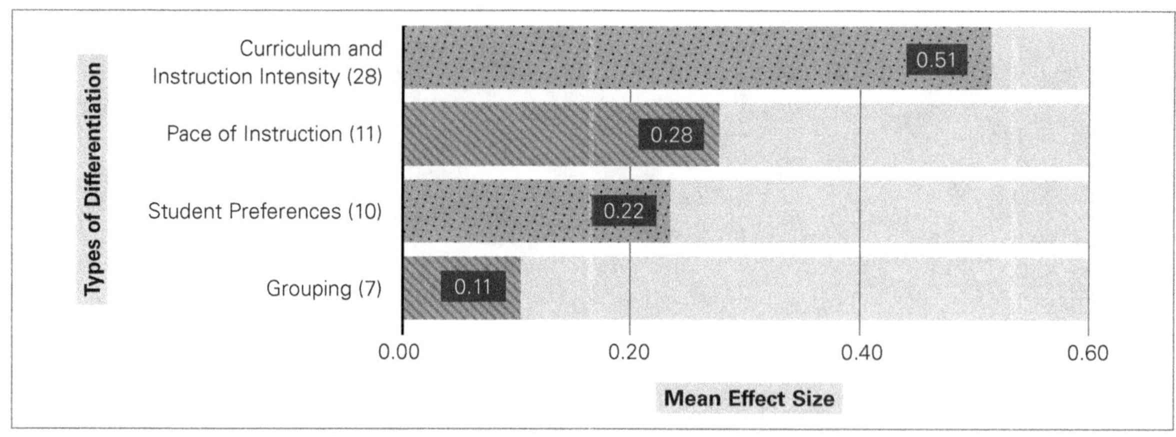

FIGURE 14.14: The effects of different classifications of differentiation.

Summary Points to Remember

Following is a list of highlights and significant points outlined in this chapter.

- ☑ Differentiation can take many different forms.
- ☑ Differentiation techniques that focus on students' individual learning needs show higher results.
- ☑ Differentiation techniques that focus on students' learning styles, preferences, or ability grouping tend to show lower results.

Reflection Questions

Individually or with your team, use these questions to reflect on the information in this chapter.

1. What are the potential downsides to increased differentiation in the classroom?
2. What are the potential benefits to increased differentiation in the classroom?
3. Do you differentiate your instruction? Why or why not?
4. What do you see as the most valuable differentiation techniques, and why?
5. What do you see as the least valuable differentiation techniques, and why?

CHAPTER 15

Secondary Meta-Analysis of Popular Teaching Pedagogies

Throughout this book, I discussed dozens of learning theories, pedagogies, and instructional methods. While each chapter presented various meta-analyses on these pedagogies, it's hard to understand the contextual meaning of data without comparing them. For example, a pedagogy or teaching method might have a statistically significant effect size of 0.22, but what does that mean? How does it compare to an alternative teaching method? Teachers have a limited time in the classroom and should focus on teaching strategies that work.

In this chapter, I rank teaching methods for literacy and mathematics using secondary meta-analysis. I conducted this analysis by combining the results of seventy different meta-analyses. I then ranked each pedagogy by effect size. By doing this, I hoped I could make it easy for teachers to quickly identify which pedagogies yielded the greatest results. I also ranked pedagogies by their difficulty to effectively implement in the classroom. Lastly, I also identified meta-analyses by subject, including mathematics, reading, and general teaching methods.

This type of research should not be taken in isolation, as it can only give you a general estimate of the efficacy of the pedagogy. It cannot tell you the context of the research, such as grade or study quality. However, it does provide a quick and easy resource for getting a general overview of the efficacy of the literature on a topic.

The Purpose of Secondary Meta-Analysis

In 2009, Hattie popularized using secondary meta-analysis to examine the efficacy of pedagogical factors. This analysis method has some advantages.

- It reviews thousands of studies with one easy-to-understand metric.
- It places a strong emphasis on study results and contextualizes results by comparing the results of different pedagogies with each other. Teachers only have so much time in a day, so it makes sense for teachers to consider the teaching interventions that are most likely to work.

However, there are also some flaws in this analysis.

- **It takes studies out of their original context:** Factors might have very different results in different grades and for different subjects. For example, a large body of empirical research shows that inquiry-based learning helps adults learn science. However, there is truly little evidence that inquiry-based learning is beneficial to younger students studying mathematics, as noted in Hattie's database of inquiry-based learning studies (Hattie, 2022c). Within Hattie's (2009) methodology, neither the students' age nor the subject matter is accounted for.
- **Hattie (2009) does not account for study quality:** Within his methodology, all meta-analyses are treated as equal. However, meta-analyses vary in study quality. A meta-analysis that only includes randomized control trials and quasi-experimental studies will produce a more accurate effect size than one that also includes case studies.
- **Hattie (2023c) includes meta-analyses that are correlational and thus not meant to examine efficacy:** A correlational study examines two sets of data to see if there is a correlation, whereas in an experimental study, the researchers provide a treatment to one group and not the other. The researchers then evaluate if the treatment caused a change in outcomes for the treatment group. Experimental studies examine causation, whereas correlation studies examine connection.

Hattie has taken a lot of heat over the years for these weaknesses and others (Pedagogy Non-Grata, 2019b). However, I defend Hattie's work, not because it is without weakness, but because he innovated a whole new way to examine education research. And while his methodology (as all methodologies) has flaws, it is helpful in providing an overly broad overview of what the scientific literature shows. Moreover, he has taken steps to address some of these flaws. His website now includes a transparent database of meta-analyses, which allows users to look up meta-analyses on almost any education topic (Hattie, 2023c).

My secondary meta-analysis in figure 15.1. In my analysis, I attempt to improve Hattie's methodology in the following ways.

- **I only included studies on reading and mathematics instruction:** Studies on mathematics are differentiated from reading by an asterisk, so you can immediately determine what subject this meta-analysis is examining.
- **I screened meta-analyses for quality:** Rather than take a mean across all meta-analyses, I attempted to use what I identified as the highest-quality overall mean effect size for each study. For example, with RTI, some of the meta-analyses identified a mean effect size based on only experimental studies and for both case studies and experimental studies. In these instances, I only used the experimental mean. This is important because nonexperimental studies show higher and less accurate effect sizes (Plonsky & Oswald, 2014). This means that my effect size is lower than the mean found by Hattie (2023h); however, it is also more accurate.
- **I removed all correlational, single-case design meta-analyses or meta-analyses that did not use either Cohen's *d* or Hedge's *g* effect sizes:** These effect sizes are analyzed in the same way and are, therefore, more generalizable with each other.
- **I used symbols to identify the different teaching methods based on how difficult or time intensive the method is to execute well:** Dashed lines indicate that the intervention is easy to implement. Dotted lines indicate that the intervention is either more time consuming or requires more expert knowledge. Gray lines indicate that the intervention is either very time consuming or requires a lot of expert knowledge.
- **I used moderator analysis:** As shown in figures 15.2–15.5 (pages 124–127), moderator analysis demonstrates how the results shifted across student ages and grades.

Figure 15.1 shows the results of the secondary meta-analysis of seventy meta-analyses on the topic of education.

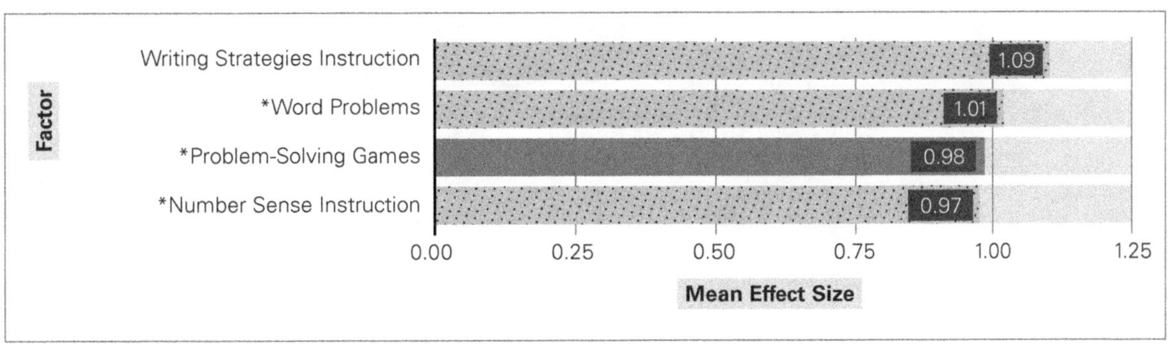

FIGURE 15.1: Teaching methods ranked by effect size.

continued ▶

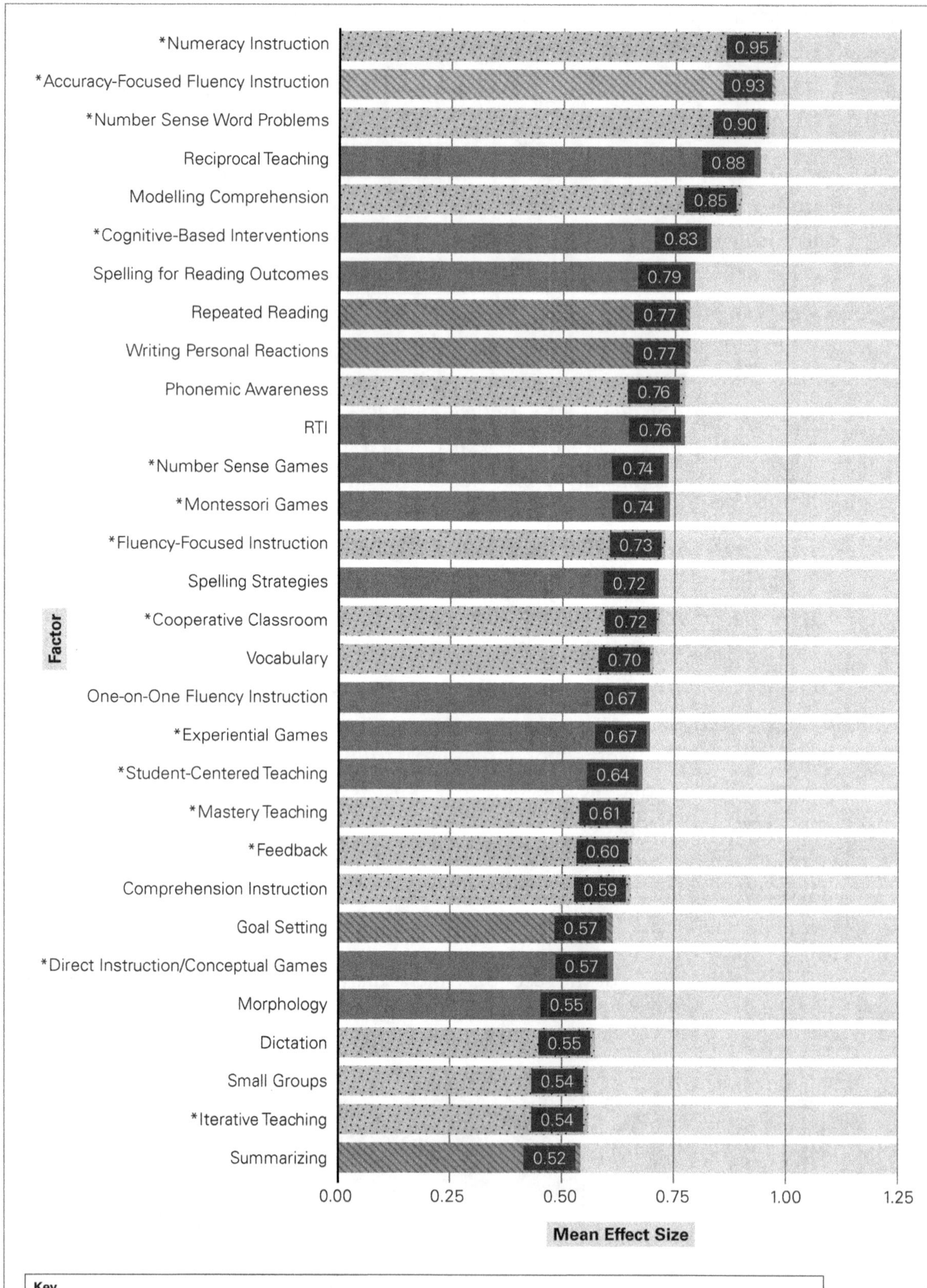
*Numeracy Instruction 0.95
*Accuracy-Focused Fluency Instruction 0.93
*Number Sense Word Problems 0.90
Reciprocal Teaching 0.88
Modelling Comprehension 0.85
*Cognitive-Based Interventions 0.83
Spelling for Reading Outcomes 0.79
Repeated Reading 0.77
Writing Personal Reactions 0.77
Phonemic Awareness 0.76
RTI 0.76
*Number Sense Games 0.74
*Montessori Games 0.74
*Fluency-Focused Instruction 0.73
Spelling Strategies 0.72
*Cooperative Classroom 0.72
Vocabulary 0.70
One-on-One Fluency Instruction 0.67
*Experiential Games 0.67
*Student-Centered Teaching 0.64
*Mastery Teaching 0.61
*Feedback 0.60
Comprehension Instruction 0.59
Goal Setting 0.57
*Direct Instruction/Conceptual Games 0.57
Morphology 0.55
Dictation 0.55
Small Groups 0.54
*Iterative Teaching 0.54
Summarizing 0.52
Factor
0.00
0.25
0.50
0.75
1.00
1.25
Mean Effect Size
Key
Indicates that the intervention is easy to implement.
Indicates that the intervention is either more time consuming or requires more expert knowledge.
Indicates that the intervention is either very time consuming or requires a lot of expert knowledge.
*Pedagogies with a star are for mathematics; pedagogies with no star are for reading.

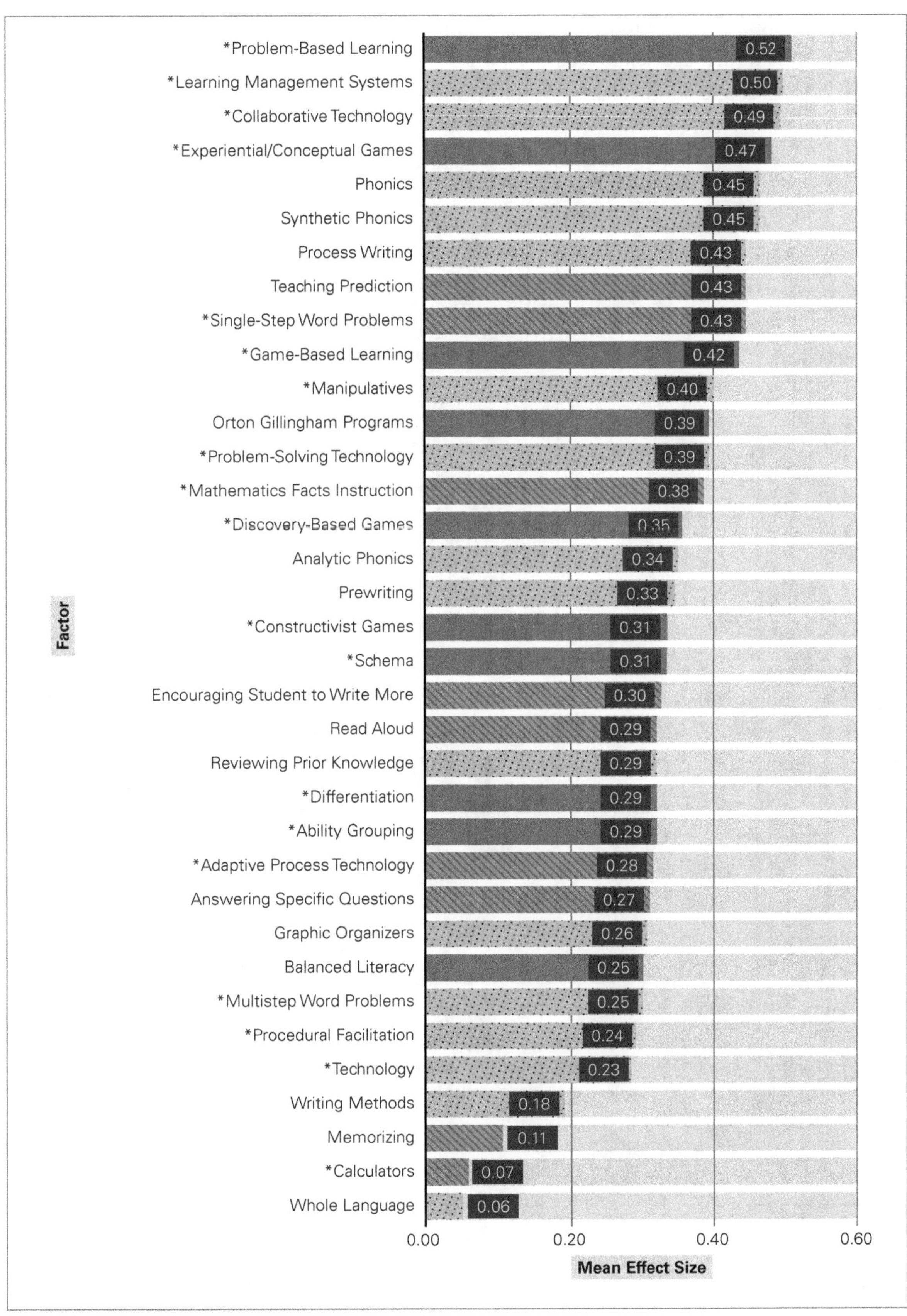

Source for data: Hansford, Garforth, & King, 2022.
Source: Hansford, 2022a. Used with permission.

As previously discussed, ideally, effect sizes should be taken in context, not just for their study rigor but also for their age demographic. Figure 15.2 breaks down the same research in figure 15.1 (page 121) as it applies to the context of studies on students in prekindergarten to grade 2.

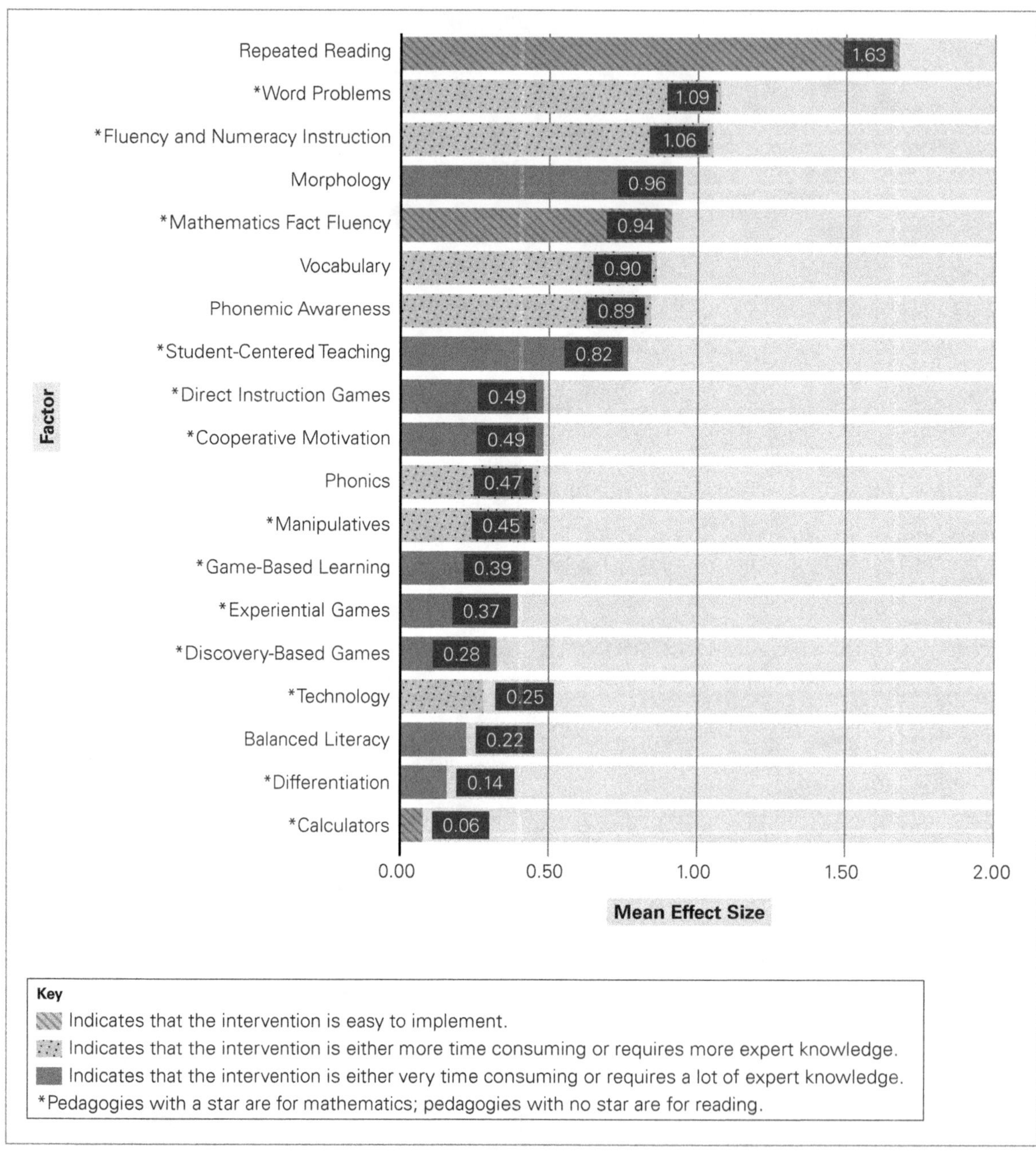

Source for data: Hansford, Garforth, & King, 2022.
Source: Hansford, 2022a. Used with permission.

FIGURE 15.2: Teaching methods ranked by effect size for grades preK–2.

The results in figure 15.2 suggest strong support for repeated reading, morphology, vocabulary, phonemic awareness, and phonics instruction for reading. In mathematics, the results show strong support for word problems, numeracy, mathematics facts, direct instruction, and manipulatives.

These results suggest the weakest support for game-based learning, technology, differentiation, and balanced literacy in both mathematics and reading instruction.

Figure 15.3 breaks down the meta-analyses in figure 15.1 (page 121) and shows how the results change when research is limited to students in grades 3–5.

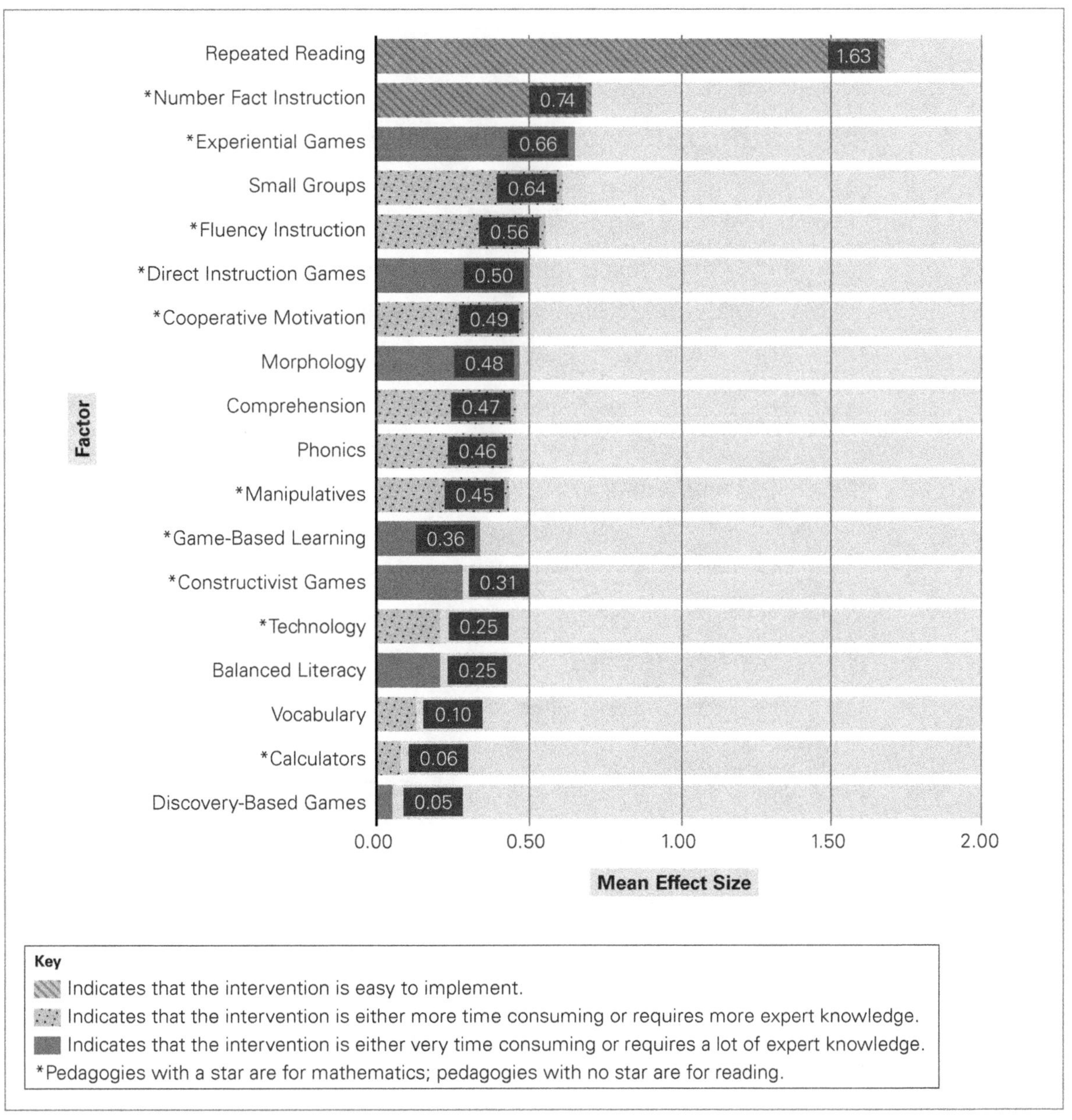

Source for data: Hansford, Garforth, & King, 2022.
Source: Hansford, 2022a. Used with permission.

FIGURE 15.3: Teaching methods ranked by effect size for grades 3–5.

The results in figure 15.3 suggest strong support for morphology, repeated reading and fluency, comprehension, and phonics for reading instruction. However, note that the phonics studies were only for struggling readers. For mathematics instruction, there is strong support for number facts, game-based learning, and manipulatives. These results suggest weak support for balanced literacy, vocabulary, and discovery-based learning in mathematics instructions.

Figure 15.4 shows how the meta-analysis results from figure 15.1 (page 121) changed when studies were limited to grades 6–8. Examining results in this way allows for interpretations specific to intermediate students.

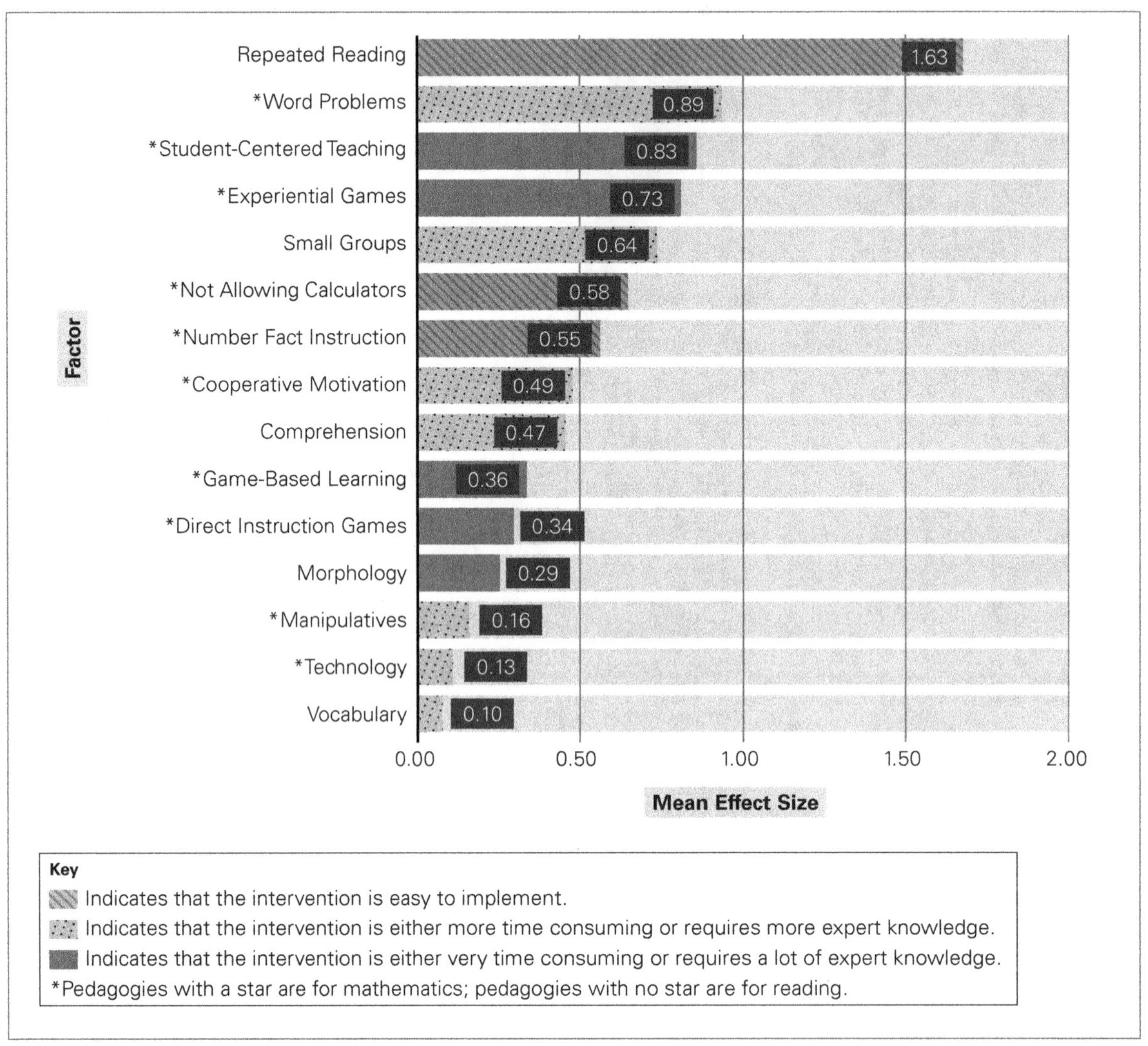

Source for data: Hansford, Garforth, & King, 2022.
Source: Hansford, 2022a. Used with permission.

FIGURE 15.4: Teaching methods ranked by effect size for grades 6–8.

The results in figure 15.4 suggest strong support for repeated reading, comprehension, and small-group instruction for reading. These results also suggest strong support for word problems, number fact instruction, experiential game-based learning, and not allowing calculators for mathematics instruction. These results suggest weak evidence for morphology and vocabulary in reading instruction and for manipulatives and technology in mathematics instruction.

Figure 15.5 breaks down the effect sizes in figure 15.1 (page 121), showing how they apply to secondary students only. You can use this chart to help make evidence-based recommendations for secondary education.

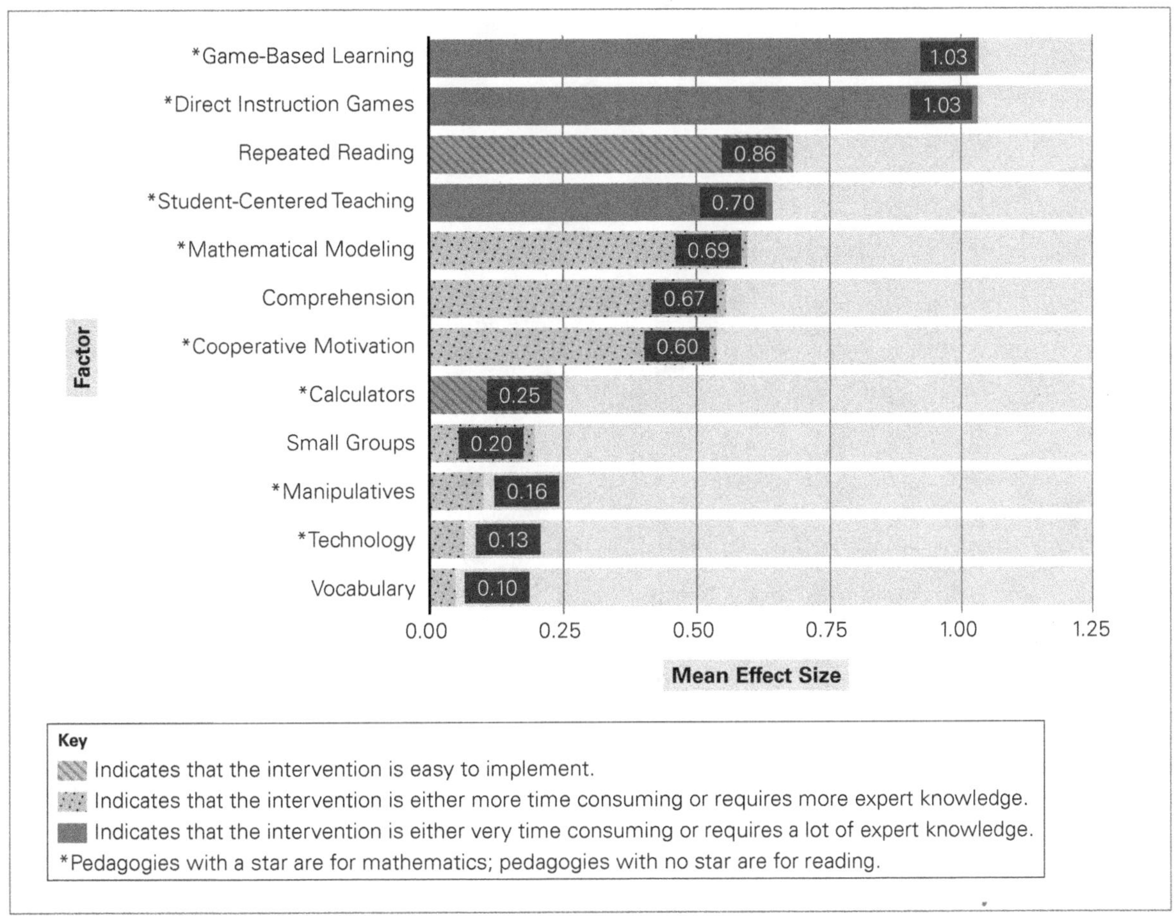

Source for data: Hansford, Garforth, & King, 2022.
Source: Hansford, 2022a. Used with permission.

FIGURE 15.5: Teaching methods ranked by effect size for grades 9–12.

The results in figure 15.5 suggest strong support for repeated reading and comprehension for reading instruction. The results also suggest strong support for direct instruction games and mathematical modeling instruction for mathematics instruction. These results suggest weak evidence for manipulatives and technology in mathematics instruction. They also suggest weak evidence for vocabulary in reading instruction.

Summary Points to Remember

Following is a list of highlights and significant points outlined in this chapter.

- ☑ Science is context specific. What works in one grade and for one subject will not necessarily be the same in other contexts or subjects.

☑ You must consider both the impact of a pedagogy and the ease with which it can be implemented.
☑ Pedagogies that are both easy to implement and have a large impact are likely the best.

Reflection Questions

Individually or with your team, use these questions to reflect on the information in this chapter.

1. What is your favorite pedagogy in figure 15.1 (page 121), and why?
2. What is your least favorite pedagogy on this list, and why?
3. What teaching methods or pedagogies seem to have the best cost-to-benefit ratios?
4. What teaching methods or pedagogies seem to have the worst cost-to-benefit ratios?
5. How do you think this research could best be used, and why?

The Best Education Systems in the World

The success of education systems is often cited as evidence that particular pedagogies are better or worse. Indeed, countries that use more constructivist approaches are often praised for their education systems, such as Norway and Sweden, whereas countries that use more transmission-based or traditional-based approaches, such as China, are often criticized for their education systems. Magazines, newspapers, and blogs often go so far as to rank education systems (Gao, 2023; Jackson, 2015; Yi, 2022). However, such rankings are usually qualitative and based on opinion.

Instead, I thought it would be valuable to rank education systems based on academic achievement, using standardized test scores. The Organisation for Economic Co-operation and Development (OECD; 2018b) PISA scores provided the perfect tool to do this. Originally, I intended to look at the top ten countries; however, for two of the rankings, there was a tie between countries. Consequently, I reviewed the top thirteen countries and then explored the education policies of each country to discover what I could learn from their success. In general, more transmission-heavy education systems showed higher academic achievement; however, there also appeared to be costs for students in terms of their social-emotional health and well-being.

In the following sections, I detail the challenges of comparing education systems, offer observations about the top thirteen PISA-ranked education systems, and give a final analysis of the findings and overall trends.

The Challenges of Comparing Education Systems

As soon as I began my research, I realized that this would be no easy feat. For starters, it is challenging to even evaluate the best education systems from an objective metric. Countless rankings and reviews of education systems already exist, which are broken down by multiple factors. However, once I began to dive into these rankings, I realized that most of them were entirely subjective.

Most reviews were based on educational philosophies, not academic results. They did not account for the level of investment countries provided and were often racially biased. Some describe European education systems as enlightened and progressive; whereas some describe Asian education systems as authoritarian and oppressive.

Pedagogies Versus Academic Results

Many reviews based their rankings not on the academic results of the education systems but on the pedagogies and factors that build those education systems. I wanted to look at the student achievement results of education systems first and then see what types of pedagogies and factors went into the making of these education systems.

Eventually, I came across the OECD PISA rankings, which provided me with exactly what I was looking for. The OECD works with international governments to promote evidence-based public policy. However, it also happens to collect standardized test scores in language, mathematics, and science and rank participating countries by these scores (OECD, 2018b). This metric gave me precisely what I was looking for—an independently verified metric purely based on achievement. Now, this is not to say an education system is only as good as its standardized test results; however, I wanted to explore the causality of achievement, not make subjective judgments about international education systems.

Unfortunately, there has not been a full PISA test conducted since 2018. So, the results of my analysis are from the era before COVID-19. The next set of PISA scores were released in December 2023 after the writing of this book (see www.oecd.org/pisa).

Objective Observations

Once I had my rankings, my next challenge was deciding what I could objectively say about an education system I had never worked in, based only on research. I wanted to look for correlations with the actual structure of education systems and their results. However, the scale of what I was looking at was intensely macro, and it became apparent that it would be hard to make any overarching judgments. Education systems might push certain pedagogical and philosophical beliefs, but that does not mean individual teachers follow those beliefs. Every education system is made up of thousands of schools and hundreds of thousands of individual educators. Additionally, the information I could find about international education systems was often sparse and focused on the institutional layouts, which was not wholly interesting to me. Ultimately, I tried to look for the most unique aspects of these education systems and get a broad, generalized understanding of some of the philosophical drivers behind each one.

Racial Bias

To make things even more challenging, I realized that there was a racial bias in how most authors tackled this topic. While most of the top-performing education systems were Asian, most authors tended to describe Asian education systems through pejorative and negative lenses while simultaneously describing most European education systems as enlightened and advanced. Part of this bias likely stems from the fact that I was doing my research in English, but part of this bias likely also stems from a major philosophical divide between European and Asian education systems.

Process Focus Versus Product Focus

While in my own analysis, most of the top-performing Asian education systems tended to be more product-focused and teacher-driven, European education systems tended to be very process-focused and less teacher-driven.

Figure 16.1 offers further clarification on these concepts.

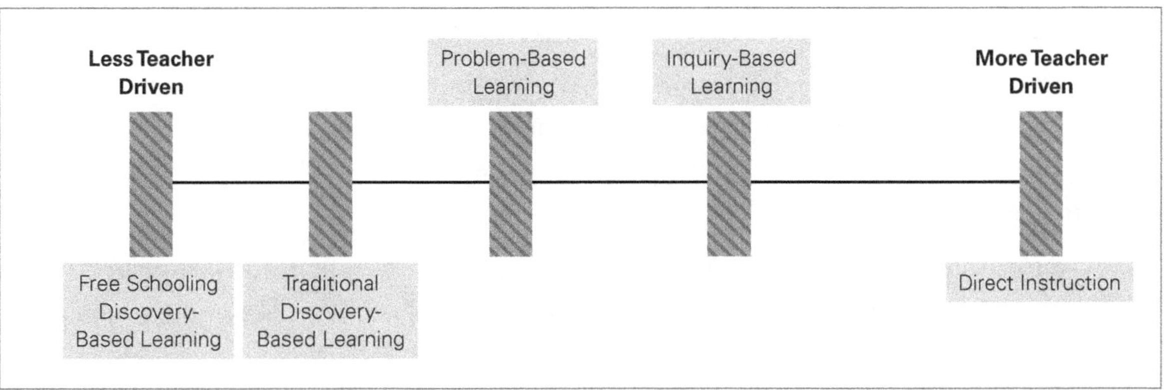

Source: Hansford, 2022h. Used with permission.

FIGURE 16.1: The product versus process teaching spectrum.

In many ways, the debate between Eastern and Western education philosophy is indicative of a larger debate between transmission and constructivist educational philosophies (see chapter 13, page 89). This said, I did not want to judge countries for their pedagogical philosophies; I wanted to look for the positives in each education system and see what lessons could be learned from these success stories. However, I also did not want to ignore the holistic result of these pedagogical differences and tried to include some reflection on these differences as I completed my analysis.

Economic Drivers for Achievement

One factor I was particularly interested in was the economic drivers of educational achievement. I wanted to know how much money successful education systems were investing in their schools, as it seems to reflect how much certain societies value education. Additionally, this research allowed me to explore the correlation between money spent on education versus education results. Finally, I also wanted to know how economically efficient these education systems were because, for an effective educational factor to be easily reproducible, it also needs to be economically viable. It would be easy, for example, to increase learning achievement simply by cutting class sizes in half, but that is also likely the most expensive education intervention, as schools would have to hire twice as many teachers. By examining the economic efficiency of an educational model, I hope to demonstrate how easy or challenging it would be to reproduce those results in other countries.

To describe the economic efficiency of these education systems, I hope to use a simplified metric as an easy way of understanding each country's overall economic efficiency in education spending. To the best of my knowledge, no such metric already existed, so I had to create one. I divided each country's average spending per student (rounded to the nearest ten thousand marker) by its averaged-out PISA score. The average OECD country spent 9,000 U.S. dollars per year, per student. The median OECD average score was 498. This resulted in an average efficiency number of 18. The higher the efficiency number, the less efficient the education system; inversely, the lower the efficiency number, the more efficient the education system.

Before you read the results of my study, I offer the disclaimer that almost all the information presented here is from secondary source material and, therefore, may be subject to errors. I apologize to anyone who might potentially find an error regarding their nation's education system.

As a result of my study, I created a series of charts that indicate the thirteen best education systems in the world organized by a variety of different metrics. As noted previously, originally, my intent was to look at the top ten countries; however, the result of ties for certain ranks changed this number to thirteen.

Figure 16.2 shows the OECD PISA score averages. This chart outlines the average overall academic performance of each country and provides the most basic ranking of education systems.

Country or Region	Average OECD Score
1. China	578
2. Singapore	556
3. Macau	542
4. Hong Kong	530
5. Estonia	525
6. Japan	520
7. Korea	519
8. Canada	516
8. Taiwan	516

8. Finland	516
9. Poland	513
10. Republic of Ireland	504
11. United Kingdom	503

Source for data: OECD, 2018b.
Source: Hansford, 2022h. Used with permission.

FIGURE 16.2: Top thirteen education systems in the world according to PISA score averages.

While figure 16.2 shows the average overall PISA outcomes, figure 16.3 shows all the PISA scores for each subject. This allows you to compare results across subjects.

Country or Region	Reading	Mathematics	Science
1. China	555	591	595
2. Singapore	549	569	551
3. Macau	525	558	544
4. Hong Kong	524	551	517
5. Estonia	523	523	530
6. Japan	504	527	529
7. Korea	514	526	519
8. Canada	520	512	518
8. Taiwan	503	531	516
9. Finland	520	507	522
10. Poland	512	516	511
11. Republic of Ireland	518	500	496
12. United Kingdom	504	502	505

Source for data: OECD, 2018b.
Source: Hansford, 2022h. Used with permission.

FIGURE 16.3: Top thirteen education systems in the world according to all PISA scores (across subjects).

As you can see in figure 16.3, while the ranking changes slightly between subjects, the scores are overall quite similar between subjects, in each country. This suggests two interesting things: (1) literacy scores and general academic achievement scores are correlated; (2) it challenges the modern understanding of multiple intelligences and learning styles as laid out by Gardner (2013). Gardner's (1983) theory suggests that students tend to be better in one subject than another. However, these results suggest that literacy and mathematics scores are interrelated (Gardner, 2013).

Figure 16.4 (page 134) shows the percentage of GDP spent on education. This allows you to assess how much each country prioritized education. For example, Hong Kong spends by far the most of its GDP on education, at 28 percent. This means Hong Kong, as a nation, must make great economic sacrifices for their education system.

Country or Region	Percentage of GDP
1. Hong Kong	28.0
2. Canada	17.0
3. Finland	5.7
4. United Kingdom	5.5
5. Estonia	5.2
6. Korea	5.0
7. Poland	4.6
8. China	4.0
9. Republic of Ireland	3.7
10. Japan	3.3
11. Singapore	2.5
Taiwan	Data not available
Macau	Data not available

Source for data: OECD, 2018a, 2018b.
Source: Hansford, 2022h. Used with permission.

FIGURE 16.4: Top thirteen education systems in the world according to the percentage of GDP spent on education.

While ranking countries by the percentage of GDP spent on education is useful in that it establishes how much individual nations value education, to a cost amount, it is not necessarily reflective of the actual dollar amounts spent per student. That's why I created an additional chart (see figure 16.5) ranking each country according to the actual dollar amount spent per student.

While looking at the percentage of GDP shows the proportionality of investment each country makes, it does not normalize the amount spent. For example, 1,000 U.S. dollars per student might be a relatively small amount for a wealthy country like the United States, but it would be relatively much larger for a poorer country.

Figure 16.5 shows the average U.S. dollars spent per student, rounded to the average $1,000 and ranked by money spent. This allows control for the actual dollars spent on education and better standardizes the interpretation of results.

After creating this chart, several things caught my attention. First, it was abundantly clear that ranking countries by percentage of GDP spent on education was almost useless, as it did not really give a clear picture of how much each country spent in terms of real dollars. The varying strengths of each economy made the percentage of GDP a very unreliable metric when measuring how much money is spent on education. Second, there seemed to be much less correlation between money spent and results than I would have expected.

Country or Region	USD Spent per Student
1. United Kingdom	26,000
2. Macau	Estimate: 19,667
3. Singapore	16,000
4. Canada	15,000
5. Finland	14,000
5. Hong Kong	14,000
6. Republic of Ireland	13,000
7. Estonia	12,000
8. Korea	10,000
8. Poland	10,000
9. Japan	8,000
Taiwan	Data not available
China	Data not available

Source for data: OECD, 2018a, 2018b.
Source: Hansford, 2022h. Used with permission.

FIGURE 16.5: Top thirteen education systems in the world according to the average U.S. dollar spent per student, rounded to the average $1,000 and ranked by money spent.

Because of this, I ran a Pearson correlation effect-size calculation, which is a tool used to calculate the statistical effect of two correlating sets of data. The result was −0.12, which suggests there is a negative but statistically insignificant effect of spending more money on education within the top thirteen OECD countries. While this effect size suggests there is no direct correlation between money spent and education results, these results are likely extremely biased by the fact that I was only looking at the top thirteen countries. It might be better to suggest that the lowest-spending countries on this list are examples of the minimum amount of money that could be spent on education for high results.

Ultimately, it seems logical to try to control the impact of money spent when comparing diverse education systems with varying amounts of money spent on education. Some countries could improve results simply by hiring more teachers without necessarily improving their pedagogical methods. However, such a strategy would be very expensive.

In order to account for the impact of money spent on individual education systems, I created economic efficiency ratios. I divided each country's average spending per student (rounded to the nearest ten thousand marker) by its averaged-out PISA score. The average OECD country spent 9,000 U.S. dollars per year, per student. The median OECD average score was 498. This resulted in an average efficiency number of 18. The higher the efficiency number, the less efficient the education system; inversely, the lower the efficiency number, the more efficient the education system.

Figure 16.6 (page 136) shows the PISA economic efficiency scores.

Country or Region	Efficiency Score
1. Japan	15
2. Korea	19
2. Poland	19
3. Estonia	22
4. China	25
4. Republic of Ireland	25
5. Hong Kong	26
6. Finland	27
7. Singapore	28
8. Canada	29
9. Macau	36
10. United Kingdom	51
Taiwan	Data not available

Source for data: OECD, 2018a, 2018b.
Source: Hansford, 2022h. Used with permission.

FIGURE 16.6: Top thirteen education systems in the world ranked by economic efficiency scores.

As stated, the lower the efficiency score, the more economically efficient the education system is. If you look at the rest of the OECD countries, the average efficiency is 18. This means that, on average, all countries in the top thirteen were spending more than their other OECD counterparts, per their results. Japan was the only country that spent less per their results than the OECD average. In some ways, this chart might give a better indication of the correlation between dollars spent and educational results than the charts that attempted to look at this correlation more directly.

Finally, I wanted to look for some kind of objective measure to examine how stressful each country's education system was, as many of the highest-performing education systems were criticized for being too stressful. So as morbid as it sounds, I decided to look up the youth suicide rate for each country.

The youth suicide rates might indicate stress levels of certain education systems. Most of the top education systems are Asian, transmission based, and often criticized for being too stressful for students (Geeraert, 2020). I wanted to find a statistical way to measure the stress of an education system. Of course, no such universal metric exists. However, I used youth suicide rates as a proxy to see if there was a correlation between high levels of achievement and increased suicide rates. One caveat about this research is that youth suicide rates are not routinely available every year for every country. Therefore, suicide rates research is based on varying years of reporting. Consequently, I am less confident in the implications of this research.

In figure 16.7, I ordered countries according to their suicide rates to examine whether there is a connection between high achievement and high stress.

Country or Region	Suicides per 100,000
1. Hong Kong	12.2
2. Singapore	7.0
3. Estonia	6.5
3. Korea	6.5
4. Finland	6.0
5. Taiwan	5.1
6. Canada	5.0
7. Japan	4.5
8. Poland	3.0
9. Republic of Ireland	2.0
10. China	1.5
10. United Kingdom	1.5
Macau	Data not available

Source: Chang, 2023; Hans, 2023; Lee et al., 2022; UNICEF, 2019.

FIGURE 16.7: Youth suicide rates, which might indicate stress levels of certain education systems.

If you average the youth suicide rates of all the product-based countries and regions listed in figure 16.7 (Hong Kong, Singapore, Korea, Taiwan, Japan, China, and United Kingdom), you get 5.47 per 100,000. Whereas, if you average the youth suicide rates of all the process-based countries (Canada, Estonia, Finland, Poland, and Republic of Ireland), you get 4.5 per 100,000 (Chang, 2023; Hans, 2023; Lee et al., 2022; UNICEF, 2019). On average, process-based education systems have a 17.75 percent lower suicide rate ($p = 0.3831$). However, this difference is not statistically significant.

These suicide trends correlate with other forms of academic research. For example, Tyler Black (2022) noted that suicide rates were far lower during nonschool days. Similarly, a 2022 study by Aqeel Khan and colleagues (2023) suggests that academic stress for students directly increases rates of suicidal ideation. Therefore, one would assume the process-driven school systems would correlate with lower suicide rates due to shorter hours of study. This is not to say that hours of study is the sole correlating factor for suicide rates but rather, it might be one correlating factor.

Observations for the Top Thirteen PISA-Ranked Education Systems

In this section, I qualitatively describe thirteen education systems. I hope to communicate the unique aspects of each of these systems and whether they are more constructivist or transmission-theory informed. However, my qualitative analysis of these countries was challenging for the following three reasons.

1. I have not studied or taught in most of these countries or regions.

2. There is very little peer-reviewed or even government-published information on the pedagogies used by different countries or regions.
3. The high-quality information that exists on various countries' and regions' education systems is often not focused on pedagogy, which makes analyzing the impact of pedagogy on a state level very difficult.

In the following sections, countries and regions are ordered according to their PISA test score rankings. I wanted to base the ranking on a quantitative metric to limit bias as much as possible. However, to learn from these education systems, it is important to consider the qualitative factors that might be leading to their success.

Thirteen: The United Kingdom

The United Kingdom is interesting in that it is the most tilted toward a product-focused education model of any Eurocentric education system in the top thirteen countries. The United Kingdom starts regular instruction of most common subjects in kindergarten. Moreover, unlike most other Eurocentric education systems, the United Kingdom starts with the direct instruction of basic academics, like phonics, in kindergarten. When students turn sixteen, they must take a national exit exam to be evaluated and placed into academic divisions, based on their scores. At the end of secondary schooling, students must take Government Certificate of Secondary Education exams or other national qualifications to graduate. However, students are also allowed to take these qualifications early, at the end of their junior year in secondary education (Study in the UK, n.d.).

I have taught in Korea, Canada, and the United Kingdom. Having personally taught in the United Kingdom, I can say that there is a very intense focus on teacher accountability within the education system. Schools and teachers are regularly graded based on teacher performance, which in my experience, both motivates teachers to work long and intense hours, but also leaves them feeling extremely stressed. While working in the United Kingdom, I routinely worked more than sixty hours per week. However, when I was working in Korea and Canada, I typically worked only forty hours per week. In the United Kingdom, there is also an intense focus on evidence-based teaching practices. I have always been shocked by how poorly the United Kingdom's students perform on standardized tests, despite its intense teacher work ethic and culture of evidence-based practice.

Twelve: Republic of Ireland

The Republic of Ireland's education model appears similar to the Canadian and American education models. (Note that the *Republic of Ireland* only refers to Southern Ireland, as Northern Ireland is part of the United Kingdom). The legal age to drop out of school is sixteen (Ireland Department of Education and Science, 2023). Secondary schooling begins in grade 6 and continues for five to six years, depending on the student. Academic streaming starts in secondary school, with a vocational, applied, and academic stream (Ireland Department of Education and Science, 2022). One point of interest is that the Republic of Ireland does allow students to take their national exit exams either at the end of their junior or senior year of secondary education, like the United Kingdom (Ireland Department of Education and Science, 2004). While in most schooling systems, grades have no consequences on postsecondary acceptance until grade 12, the Republic of Ireland's post-secondary schools look at grades as far back as grade 10.

The Republic of Ireland, like Canada, also has a systematic legal framework set up for special education, guaranteeing that support is put in place for all identified students. It also places a strong emphasis on equity within their education system, spending one billion Euros in 2023 on the establishment of programs aimed to help students affected by poverty (European Social Fund Plus, 2023).

Eleven: Poland

Since the 1990s, Poland has been attempting to make comprehensive changes to improve its education system (Wes & Bodewig, 2016). They have standardized expectations with national exams but transferred instructional authority to local governments. They created a curriculum that seeks to help the holistic well-being of the student by including cognitive and social-emotional skills (Wes & Bodewig, 2016). They have invested resources in providing teachers with further pedagogical training and given teachers more individual authority over their own classrooms and instructional resources (Wes & Bodewig, 2016). However, the largest change was the creation of a lower secondary program, which extends the general curriculum from the elementary years and delayed the period in which students are streamed by their academic levels (Wes & Bodewig, 2016).

Interestingly, like many other top-performing OECD countries, Poland seems to place a high cultural value on education. Indeed, Terry Ryan (2013) of the Fordham Institute, wrote an article on this specific topic. Unfortunately, Poland has been criticized for having too little equity in its results, as its PISA scores are not evenly divided among its different economic brackets, unlike Macau and Estonia (Wes & Bodewig, 2016).

Ten: Finland

Finland was once the only Western nation to make it into the top five education systems. However, their PISA scores have slipped in comparison to other countries since the 2010 PISA test (OECD, 2010). Finland is also an example of one of the most constructivist or process-driven education systems. While Finland offers very interesting and comprehensive education services to its students, it also is more economically efficient than Canada, Singapore, or the United Kingdom, and is as equally economically efficient as Korea. I point this out only to prove that Finland's educational success cannot be directly linked to financial input.

Finland gives the least amount of homework of any country in the world, and they have no standardized tests as a part of their regular schooling system (Colagrossi, 2018). They do not stress teacher accountability and do not have any kind of rigorous teacher grading or evaluation systems. Students don't start school until they are seven years old and only go to school for five hours per day (Colagrossi, 2018).

In short, Finland's school day is short, there is minimal stress, and there is minimal accountability for teachers. However, these might not actually be the reasons they are so successful

(Colagrossi, 2018). In the ranking of scientific principles of teaching (see chapter 2, page 15), I list *quality time under instruction* as the most important teaching method. While the time under instruction in Finland is lower, there are multiple factors that might make the quality higher. For example, as a driving educational philosophy, Finland's schools strive for equity over excellence (Colagrossi, 2018). By doing this, they might be placing a higher emphasis on helping underperforming students rather than their already high-performing students. They also place a large emphasis on cooperation over competition, which, according to (Hattie, 2023b), is a moderate-yield strategy with an effect size of 0.58.

Perhaps most interesting is that Finnish students have the same teacher for the first six years of their education, which might provide more continuity (Colagrossi, 2018). Every classroom also has one educator for every seven students, meaning they likely have one of the highest staff-to-student ratios of any education system in the world. Frankly, it's a bit surprising that Finnish schools can provide this level of support to students at such a low cost. Perhaps this indicates how much money in other countries' education systems gets spent on the bureaucracies that maintain them rather than on actually educating students.

Another interesting fact is that Finland's teachers are more educated than teachers in almost any other education system in the world. A teacher in Finland must have a master's degree (Colagrossi, 2018). Additionally, if a teacher wants to teach special education, they must complete an additional year of education.

This said, one confounding factor in evaluating Finland's education system is its extremely low poverty rate and strong social programming. While Finland's education system is obviously strong, its success could potentially be slightly inflated by more students having stable home lives. They also offer three years of postgraduate study in individual trades as an alternative for university, making it one of the best countries in the world for vocational education (Hancock, 2011).

Nine: Taiwan

Taiwan's education system is directly aimed toward helping students perform better on standardized tests. In other words, they are a product-based teaching model. However, Taiwan offers an exam-free stream in secondary school focused on the arts for students less interested in academics (Snyder, 2017). Students in Taiwan, like many other Asian countries, often study at a private school after the regular public-school day is finished, and then spend up to ten hours per day studying (Gottlieb, 2018). Schools in Taiwan also have been reported to have access to technology that would be considered less typical in Western schools, with science classrooms equipped with 3-D printers, laser cutters, and other top-of-the-line equipment. Finally, the Taiwan education system is often described as having high expectations and high stress (Gottlieb, 2018).

Eight: Canada

Canada is the only country I feel confident to discuss with any real authority on this list, as it is my country of residence. That said, as opposed to New Zealand or the United Kingdom, Canada has a *provincialized* education system (The Canadian Encyclopedia, 2022), which means education looks radically different depending on where you live. Canada is also one of the least economically efficient countries in terms of its education spending (see figure 16.6, page 136), which means its successes would likely be hard to replicate in other countries.

Like many countries on the list, Canada has three academic streams in secondary school: university bound, college bound, and vocational. However, unlike Belgium, students cannot switch back and forth between these streams without starting their secondary education over from scratch. Canada's education streams are much less organized and formalized than Australia's (Ontario Ministry of Education, 2020). For example, having worked in a secondary school in Quebec (a Canadian province), I know that it uses the same system as Norway to divide secondary school into two parts. In the Quebec secondary school model, students start lower secondary school in grade 7 and continue until grade 11. Then, if they want to complete postsecondary education, students must take two more years at an upper-secondary school (Quebec Ministry of Education, 2023). Ontario, which is right next to Quebec, does not have these additional years of secondary school, and yet, overall, it has significantly higher test scores (The Conference Board of Canada, n.d.).

Perhaps the most interesting aspect of Canada's education system is its litigious special education system. Most of its provinces have large amounts of special education legislation, designating students with identified special needs as protected classes, with specific educational rights. Indeed, Ontario alone has several hundred pages of legislation pertaining to special education (Ontario Ministry of Education, 2022). This special education system gives parents significant strength as advocates for their children and ensures that students identified with special needs receive significant support.

Having taught in Canada off and on since 2012, I can say with some degree of confidence that Canada's education systems have a strong bias toward process-driven pedagogies (Ontario Ministry of Education, 2008, 2010, 2022).

Seven: South Korea

Korea's education system is similar to Japan's: it is both economically efficient and has high test scores. As in Japan, Korean parents spend a large amount of personal money on education, sending their students to private tutors and after-school programs in addition to public school during the day (Yang, 2016). Many parents spend as much as 25 percent of their income on their children's education (Yang, 2016). Interestingly, Korea does not hold students back for failing grades. However, its universities are highly competitive and sought after, meaning that students need high grades to go to university (Yang, 2016). Having taught in Korea, I can say that it is very clear that Koreans place a high cultural value on education, and it is a product-driven education system.

Six: Japan

Japan has one of the most economically efficient models of education in the world. It has the highest efficiency score within the top thirteen OECD countries. However, some of this economic efficiency might stem from the fact that Japanese parents often spend large amounts of their income on tutoring and after-school private schools (Geeraert, 2020). Indeed, this is a practice that is popular in many Asian nations, where after the student is finished for the day at public school, they often attend a second school, which parents privately pay for (Geeraert, 2020).

However, this is not to say that Japan has no socialized practices within its education system. In fact, Japan is one of the only countries on this list to provide all their students with a free lunch. Not only do Japanese schools provide their students with free lunches, but the lunches are prepared by a professional nutritionist to ensure they are healthy. By providing free nutritious lunches to students, Japan makes sure their students are not hungry and ready to learn (Appel, 2019).

Interestingly, Japan, like the United Kingdom, has a very high-stress secondary school system. Students' acceptance is based entirely on one final exam at the end of secondary school. This system has received a lot of criticism for being too stressful for students (Geeraert, 2020); however, some of this criticism might be based in Western bias.

Five: Estonia

Finland was once the only Eurocentric nation in the top five OECD countries. However, since 2010, Finland's performance has dropped, and Estonia has taken its place. Estonia has several unique components to its education system. First, kindergarten in Estonia starts at age three (Jeffreys, 2019). Like Canada and Norway, Estonia begins primary education with a play-based model and slowly transitions to a more traditional education model. There are no tests in kindergarten; instead, students are graded qualitatively on their readiness for regular schooling (Jeffreys, 2019).

Most interestingly, in Estonia, there is only one stream in secondary school, and students are not divided according to academic ability. While some teachers would balk at this idea, many proponents of the Estonian education model claim that this is a strength of their education system. Like Norwegian teachers, Estonian teachers are generally trusted to manage the curriculum independently (Jeffreys, 2019). Estonia also prides itself on having education results that are not linked to economic demographics, like Macau (Jeffreys, 2019). Finally, Estonia has a formalized online learning system in which most homework is completed and graded online (Jeffreys, 2019). Despite being the highest-performing Eurocentric education system, Estonia has an average efficiency of 22 (as discussed earlier in this chapter; see page 136), making it far more economically efficient than Canada (Jeffreys, 2019).

Four: Hong Kong

The Hong Kong education system is pretty much the opposite of Finland's. It has a high focus on homework and is notoriously stressful. There is a heavy focus on repetition, textbooks, and exams, starting in the primary years. Like other Asian education systems, after-school private tutoring is very popular (Fung, 2019). While this model is clearly challenging for students, it does yield high results, as Hong Kong ranks fourth on the PISA rankings.

Like many other countries on this list, Hong Kong also places a high value on equity. Education funding in Hong Kong works opposite to the No Child Left Behind policy in the United States, so schools actually get *more* funding if their test scores are lower (National Center on Education and the Economy, 2020). This funding policy means Hong Kong's funding is needs based, not results based. Hong Kong has a very high dropout age of 19 and expects students to complete six years of secondary education (National Center on Education and the Economy, 2020). Finally, Hong Kong disproportionately funds secondary schools more than elementary schools. While this is normal for all education systems on this list, the margin by which Hong Kong does this is significantly higher. Hong Kong also places a very high emphasis on teacher accountability. Schools must do annual self-assessments, and an external review board randomly selects schools every year to audit (National Center on Education and the Economy, 2020).

Three: Macau

Like most of the top-performing countries, the Macau education system has faced criticism for its excessive homework and testing. Indeed, as of 2021, the system enacted policies to begin rolling back some of this schoolwork (Wong, 2021). Macau, like many top performers in the OECD, has six years of secondary school divided into junior and senior divisions (see www.studyinmacau.com). This system provides Macau students with one additional year of secondary education—more than most other countries in the world. Students in Macau who would like to go on to university must pass exams based on China's secondary school exams.

According to the OECD, Macau provides the most equitable test results in terms of how its education results are distributed across economic demographics (as cited in Macau Special Administrative Region, 2019). Macau does not have its own centralized education system, and participants must choose to attend a school that is either based on the United Kingdom, Portuguese, or Chinese school system (see www.studyinmacau.com). Please see the sections on the United Kingdom and Chinese education systems for more information about Macau.

Two: Singapore

In many ways, Singapore is like many other Asian nations' models of education, which are opposite to the Finnish model. In Singapore, 70 percent of parents sign up their students for additional private schooling on top of their public-school education (Rousseau, 2022). They have significantly shorter vacation periods than most other education systems (InterNations, n.d.a). The curriculum is highly scripted and based around exams. There is a heavy focus on memorizing, direct instruction, repetition, and homework. Mathematics teachers focus on a procedural view of mathematics. There is little emphasis placed on metacognition strategies or conceptual understandings of mathematics (Hogan, 2014). In many ways, Singapore is the perfect example of an education system at the furthest end of the teacher-driven, product-oriented perspective.

Singapore places a heavy cultural value on the importance of education. They have one of the most expensive education systems in the world, and yet parents still pay their public schools a small tuition fee and then send their students for additional private schooling after their regular school day is over (Rousseau, 2022). Both parents and the government are spending large amounts of capital on the education of Singapore's youth (Government Technology Agency of Singapore, 2022).

One: China

The fact that China was number one in the world in terms of test score results surprised me. I have never seen any rankings, aside from the OECD ones, that list China as even in the top ten. However, China's test scores do speak for themselves (OECD, 2018b). China's education results are by far the highest in the world, and their lack of international recognition for that success is likely a reflection of Western bias.

Personally, I found the high cultural value that China places on education the most interesting thing about its education system. China actually calls education the "true religion of the people" and has a strong cultural value of education dating all the way back to Confucius in the fifth century BCE (Watson & Ozanne, 2010). Chinese students also spend much more time in school than students in most other countries. Students go to school from 7:30 a.m. to 4:00 p.m. They also typically go to a private school after their regular public-school day is finished (Hao, 2021). When students get home from school, they usually do homework until it is time to go to bed. Chinese students essentially spend most of their time studying (Hao, 2021). In terms of educational philosophy, the Chinese system appears to place a strong emphasis on achievement. I think it would be fair to say China has a product- and transmission-driven education system.

Final Analysis and Trends

Ultimately, it is difficult to look at this information and find any definitive trends for how to improve education results, as defined by PISA test scores. All this information is very broad, generalized, and unspecific. However, I do have a couple of hypotheses and generalized extrapolations based on this research.

First, generally speaking, the more product focused an education system was, the more likely it was to appear toward the top of the OECD rankings. The only education systems that were significant exceptions to this were Finland and Estonia. However, Finland also provided the highest staff-to-student ratio of any country on this list, by a very significant margin. Even more important, Finland's position within the top three has since dropped to rank eight, tied with Canada and Taiwan (OECD, 2018a). There clearly is an important tradeoff between product-focused and process-focused education systems.

Second, I think it is fair to say that the more process focused an education system is, the less stressful the education system is for the students. Moreover, the more product focused an educational system is, the higher the PISA scores. Therefore, there is likely a balance that absolutely must be struck in an ideal education system, between being product based versus process based and, consequently, between stress and achievement. However, it also is important to note that some of this philosophical debate is divided across racial lines—Western nations tend to be more process focused, and Asian nations tend to be more product focused. Moreover, some of the claims that Asian education systems are too high stress are likely based in racial bias.

Tangential to the topic of racial bias is the Western interpretation of the overall value of process-based education regarding educational achievement. Many modern education scholars have tried to push the narrative that process-based pedagogies are superior for educational achievement. A 2021 report by the International Dyslexia Association (IDA) Ontario showed that 80 percent of teachers identified themselves as "balanced literacy" teachers (a constructivist approach). Similarly, a 2022 article by Tanya Evans and Heiko Dietrich showed that there has been a systematic shift in U.S. education policy and teacher training from a transmission approach to a constructivist approach. However, the trends within the meta-analyses discussed in this book do not support the validity of this shift. While the evidence regarding high-performing, transmission-based education systems in this chapter is by no means extensive or in-depth enough to disprove any individual hypothesis, this trend is also in line with large-scale quantitative research on the topic, as described in chapter 13 (page 89) and chapter 15 (page 119).

Again, this is not to say that process-based pedagogies don't have a place in education but rather that claims that process-based pedagogies, in general, increase educational achievement should be considered with some degree of greater skepticism by Western educators. Dozens of meta-analyses on education pedagogies seem to show little meaningful proof of efficacy for constructivist and process-driven pedagogies, as shown by the previous chapters of this book.

Many of the education systems on the 2013 PISA list (OECD, 2018b) placed a higher emphasis on equity. For example, Hong Kong used needs-based funding (National Center on Education and the Economy, 2020). This type of funding means that schools receive funding based on students' academic needs rather than property tax values (like in the United States). Similarly, Canada has an extremely sophisticated special education system, which ensures all students with learning challenges receive additional support. Multiple countries on this list ban private schooling outright. By banning private schools, all members of society are incentivized to support a strong education system. Almost every country that made this list had some kind of education policy that promoted greater equity, which leads me to hypothesize that greater educational equity leads to higher academic success.

The criticism of stress levels in product-focused schools might be exaggerated. I looked at suicide rates as a proxy for stress levels in research (Chang, 2023; Hans, 2023; Lee et al., 2022; UNICEF, 2019). As noted previously, the suicide rates for process-driven education systems were, on average, 17.75 percent lower than those in product-driven education systems (pooled SD = 2.94). However, the p value for this difference was very small ($p = 0.3831$), suggesting that the difference in youth suicides between process-driven and product-driven education systems is not statistically significant. While I am skeptical that more process-driven education systems might result in lower suicide rates, I feel somewhat confident in saying that the evidence for product-based education systems being more stressful is weak, albeit existent.

Most high-performing education systems involved students spending more time in school, whether it was additional years of elementary school, secondary school, after-school tutoring, or additional homework. Countries or regions at the top of the list tended to require students to study more hours in the day than countries at the bottom of the list, as demonstrated with Hong Kong, China, Singapore, Korea, Japan, and Macau (Fung, 2019; Hao, 2021; Wong, 2021; Yang, 2016).

Indeed, to this point, the country with the highest test scores—China—was one in which students spent the most time studying. While there were notable exceptions to this hypothesis, such as Finland, overall, this trend seemed strong. This leads me to make the somewhat obvious claim that more education equals higher test scores!

While there was no direct correlation between education spending and test scores, most countries or regions on this list spent more money per student on average than others in the OECD. This leads me to believe that while money spent on education does not directly result in higher test scores, a strong educational system is almost always expensive.

The countries and regions that made this list, especially the top of this list, placed a high cultural value on education. As noted previously, China, which was the highest-performing country on the list, refers to education as "the one true religion of the people." Unfortunately, this is also likely the hardest idea to replicate in another country. While cultural values do seem to have a direct impact on test scores, they are also hard to systematically build, especially from the perspective of any individual teacher.

Summary Points to Remember

Following is a list of highlights and significant points outlined in this chapter.

- ☑ Product-driven education systems tend to outperform process-driven education systems.
- ☑ There is some level of correlation between high test scores and more student stress and suicides. While this does not directly prove that transmission-based education systems are more stressful, it does suggest that there could be a connection between high levels of achievement and youth stress.
- ☑ Schools need to strike a balance between achievement and student well-being.
- ☑ Money spent on education does not directly correlate with higher test scores. However, a high-quality education system does seem to require a higher education budget.
- ☑ While heavily constructivist education systems like Norway are often cited as the best, heavily transmission-based education systems like China tend to perform the best on standardized tests.

Reflection Questions

Individually or with your team, use these questions to reflect on the information in this chapter.

1. What factors do you think most impact student achievement?
2. How do we strike an ideal balance between student achievement and well-being?
3. How does bias affect how you might interpret these results?
4. What lessons could you take from this chapter for your own classroom?
5. Which country do you feel has the most compelling education system?

CHAPTER 17

Unique Education Systems Around the World

This chapter examines some of the most unique education systems from around the world that didn't quite make the cut for the previous chapter. All these countries had education systems that were radically unique in some way and were still high performers. These countries tended to be more constructivist or process focused in their approaches. By doing this review, I hope to compare and contrast some of the possible benefits and drawbacks for more progressive education systems.

Why These Countries Are Unique

The countries detailed in this section—Norway, Belgium, Netherlands, and Australia—are often cited as having the most idealized education systems. While none of these countries were top performers in the last round of PISA testing (OECD, 2018b), they represent models of education focused on increasing student enjoyment over achievement. Ultimately, I think there is something to learn from most of these education models of education, whether it is China or Norway. Both types of education systems represent opposite approaches. However, it is my belief that developing a high-quality education system requires a balance of attending to both students' academic and social-emotional needs.

Norway

Norway has an average PISA score of 496, with a reading score of 499, a mathematics score of 501, and a science score of 490. Norway ranked twenty-third in the world on the 2018 PISA list (OECD, 2018b). Norway spends on average 13,000 U.S. dollars per student, or what equates to 30 percent of their GDP, and has an efficiency score of 26 (OECD, 2018a). Initially, I was surprised that Norway did not perform higher on the PISA test. I have read many education systems rankings that place Norway as the number-one education system in the world. One reason that Norway might be so often cited as the best education system is the fact that it is so unique.

The Norway education system appears to teach radically differently across its various divisions. In the early primary division, which includes prekindergarten, kindergarten, and grade 1, teachers only instruct students in language arts, mathematics, physical education, and social skills (Just Landed, n.d.). Moreover, during primary education, teachers mostly teach through games and activities, and they do not assign formal grades (Just Landed, n.d.).

During grades 2–7, Norwegian students are introduced to more subjects; however, they are given no formal grades, no standardized tests, and minimal homework. It is this aspect of their education system that likely makes it so popular. During grades 8–10, students not only begin to receive grades, but they must get good grades to go to the upper secondary schools of their choice (Just Landed, n.d.). While Norway's low-stress elementary school system is often cited as the reason their students do so well on standardized tests, I do not think you can ignore the fact that their lower secondary school level is much more demanding than most other countries'.

It is also important to note that students must start taking standardized tests in lower-secondary school. It is entirely possible that the more demanding secondary school system is the cause of Norway's high performance on standardized tests. During grades 11–13, participation is no longer mandatory. However, teachers who want to teach at this level must have a minimum of a master's degree.

Interestingly, Norway has almost completely banned private schools. Until 2003, they were not allowed at all, whereas now private schools are allowed for specific philosophical or religious reasons (Just Landed, n.d.). This suggests that there is less economic interest for the wealthiest individuals of the country to defund public education. Because students who come from more privilege and wealth must attend the same schools as everyone else, they are directly incentivized to campaign for a well-funded public education system.

If you examine the Norwegian education system from a cost-benefit analysis, they clearly do not have a cost-effective education system. However, that does not mean there is nothing positive to be gleaned from it. At the end of the day, Norway has one of the least stressful and highest performing education systems. Their model suggests that primary education does not have to be high stress for students to attain high levels of achievement in secondary school.

Belgium

Belgium had an average PISA score of 500, ranking twentieth in the world, with a reading score of 493, a mathematics score of 508, and a science score of 499. Belgium spends 5.8 percent of their GDP on education, which works out to an average of 13,000 U.S. dollars per student (OECD, 2018a). Belgium has an efficiency metric of 26. Belgium has a slightly more cost-effective education system than Norway, while providing higher test scores.

Belgium also provides some interesting socialized programming that would make most other Western nations jealous, including federally funded daycare and postsecondary education (InterNations, n.d.b). One point of particular interest in Belgium is that school is mandatory until the age of eighteen (InterNations, n.d.b). This is much higher than the average OECD country, let alone the average country overall. Belgium also presents a model of education that seems focused on economic equity. There are no mandatory education zones (InterNations, n.d.b). Students can attend any school they like. This is particularly important when you consider some countries fund their education systems partially through municipal taxes, meaning that poor neighborhoods get lower-quality schools than wealthy ones.

Belgium also has one of the most interesting trade school systems in the world. Students can take trade-oriented courses from the age of twelve until they are eighteen, and unlike most other education systems, students who take vocational-level courses in secondary are still eligible for post-secondary education (InterNations, n.d.b). While the Belgium education system is not the most economically efficient or highest performing, it is one of the most democratic.

Netherlands

The Netherlands has an average 2018 PISA score of 502, ranking them sixteenth in the world. They have a reading score of 487, a mathematics score of 519, and a science score of 503 (OECD, 2018a). The Netherlands spends 5.47 percent of their GDP on education, which equates to about 9,000 U.S. dollars per student (Trading Economics, 2023). These spending amounts and PISA scores give the Netherlands an efficiency metric of 17.9, meaning they are fairly economically efficient with education spending.

The Netherlands, like Belgium, has a very democratic model of education; however, it is both economically more efficient and has higher academic results. Like Norway, private schools in the Netherlands are banned, unless they have a specific philosophical or religious reason for existing (I Am Expat, n.d.). However, even if a student goes to a private school, their education is still 100 percent publicly funded. This means that there is less economic incentive to defund public education in the Netherlands.

Interestingly, the Netherlands also allows students to change academic streams in secondary school at any time, meaning that a student could take vocational-level courses until their final year of secondary school, switch to the academic stream, and graduate in that stream (I Am Expat, 2023). This is in sharp contrast to most education systems, which would force students to go back to the beginning of secondary school if they wanted to switch streams. This makes it much less punishing if a student decides to alter their career plans partway through secondary school. The Netherlands also allows students to enter any stream, regardless of their grades; however, teachers must recommend students to a specific grade (I Am Expat, 2023). Interestingly, the practice of teachers recommending students has come under scrutiny with the realization that many gifted students end up in the vocational stream.

Australia

Australia is ranked twenty-first in the world and has an average PISA score of 498, with a reading score of 503, a mathematics score of 491, and a science score of 503 (OECD, 2018a). Australia spends 5.1 percent of its GDP on education, or an average of 30,000 U.S. dollars per student (Edwards, Rice, & McMillan, 2019). These metrics give Australia an efficiency score of 60, making it the least economically efficient model of education that I examined. Australia has one of the most expensive education systems in the world; however, it is an interesting model of education.

Australia's secondary and postsecondary education is paired together and highly organized. Students can choose specific course routes in secondary school, which are linked to specific careers (Edwards et al., 2019). In fact, these routes are often developed in coordination with industry leaders, allowing students to do career-related co-op placements that match in-school coursework. With this system, students are allowed to earn specific accreditations in a variety of trades and industries starting in secondary school and extending into their postsecondary education, with up to six different accreditation levels in total (Edwards et al., 2019).

While Australia's education system is very expensive, it might be the most integrated with the workforce. This allows students to prepare for careers, regardless of the career path they choose. Moreover, like Belgium, it might have one of the best trade or vocational schooling systems in the world (Edwards et al., 2019).

Conclusions From the Data

As with the last chapter, it is difficult to make significantly meaningful conclusions from these types of data. All I can attempt to do is generate hypotheses and extrapolations. That said, the education systems featured in this chapter represent some of the most low-demand, process-based education systems in the world.

While advocates of these types of education systems would argue that these pedagogies increase learning, it's important to note that they are not competitive with the most product-based systems in the world in terms of their PISA ranking. Moreover, all these countries have slipped quite a bit in terms of their PISA rankings since 2010 (OECD, 2018a). In fact, in 2010, all these countries were in the top twelve PISA-ranked countries. All these countries have relatively strong education systems within the top twenty-three education systems of the world, according to international standardized testing (OECD, 2018a). While these countries might not be models of the highest-performing education systems, they might be potential models of how to balance the holistic needs of students with academic achievement.

Summary Points to Remember

Following is a list of highlights and significant points outlined in this chapter.

- ☑ Education systems that are more process or constructivist focused might produce lower academic achievement.
- ☑ These types of education systems tend to be less cost efficient.
- ☑ These types of education systems tend to be less demanding for students.
- ☑ These types of education systems may be less stressful.
- ☑ Policymakers might have to balance the holistic well-being of students and academic achievement.

Reflection Questions

Individually or with your team, use these questions to reflect on the information in this chapter.

1. What do you find the most surprising about the education systems featured in this chapter?
2. Which education system did you like best, and why?
3. Which education system did you like the least, and why?
4. Based on what you learned in this chapter, what changes would you like to see in your own education system?
5. What do you think your education system is doing well?

EPILOGUE
Putting It All Together

The journey for this book was years in the making. There were topics I was familiar with before writing, in which my understanding changed very little. However, after concluding my research, there were other topics about which I had to completely change my understanding. This is what being evidence based is truly all about. You cannot call yourself evidence based if you are not willing to change your viewpoint. Ultimately, *evidence based* means being willing to change your understanding based on the current best evidence.

When I first wrote and self-published this material on Amazon, I intended to update it every few years. While writing this edition with Solution Tree, most of the book remained the same, but I added research to some chapters and completely rewrote others based on new research, as some of the content was already outdated. Of course, this is necessary for any science book, as science is fluid.

When I first started this project, a colleague asked me, "What if a large part of this evidence is wrong?" The truth is some of this evidence will be wrong. Some pedagogies appear evidence based, but they may not be as evidence based as they seem. It's important to remember that the scientific method is fluid and not a static process. While this might not be a perfect process that always provides unquestionable truths, it is the only truly valid option for attempting to evaluate the validity of different teaching strategies and methods. The alternatives to using the scientific method are either using our personal instincts or blindly following the advice of individuals we trust. And as much as the scientific process might sometimes lead us astray, I think it is unlikely that we, as educators, can instinctively decipher the complex nuances of what pedagogical methods work best.

I have put a lot of my efforts into trying to simplify and communicate the pedagogical methods I feel hold the most value according to the evidence. I think the education industry has overcomplicated education in many ways, mainly for marketing purposes. However, being a good teacher does not require having an in-depth understanding of dozens of teaching methods. Rather, I think it would be better if teachers just focused on implementing a few high-yield but simple teaching methods.

My main goal is not to teach teachers how to teach but to help teachers learn how to evaluate for themselves what teaching methods are effective and ineffective and, in turn, help them discover a greater sense of self-efficacy and agency. If you were to take one thing away from this book, it would not be any single teaching strategy but instead, how to determine if a teaching strategy is evidence based for yourself.

After years of researching and writing this book, I determined there are a few generalized truths and recommendations I would like to synthesize from the material.

1. ***Time under quality instruction* is the most important principle:** The scientific principles listed in chapter 3 (page 27) provide an excellent set of priorities to focus on, with *time under quality instruction* as the most important principle. Make sure students have enough time to learn the material, as all students are capable of learning. If you have a student who is struggling to learn a specific learning goal, try to find the time somewhere else in your schedule to help them. While teachers often feel they do not have enough prep time, every student takes a certain amount of educational stimulus to learn a new curriculum, and you cannot expect all students to learn within the same time span. This does not mean you need to give up every prep period. Sometimes, you just need to find creative ways to carve out time for students.

   In the early 2020s, I had two students in an intermediate grade reading at a primary level. I would purposely give my class a task twice per day, which they could quietly work on for twenty minutes at a time while I worked one on one with these struggling students. Both students increased their reading levels by several grades. There was nothing special about what I was doing with these students; I just gave them the extra one-on-one attention they required.
2. **Teach specifically to established learning goals and expectations:** Once students receive enough time to learn, it is important to teach with a level of specificity and clarity that makes your instructional time valuable. Make sure to effectively communicate expectations and learning goals to students. Also, teach students in a manner similar to how you plan to assess them. For example, don't have students study only through reading for a test that is mostly assessed via writing. In my opinion, students are sometimes not successful on assessments not for a lack of desire or capability, but because they do not truly understand what you want them to learn, do, and demonstrate. The clearer you are with your goals and expectations, the more likely students are to be successful. I believe this is why pedagogies associated with clearer expectations are often associated with high effect sizes, as demonstrated in chapter 3 (page 27).

You should both be clear in how you express expectations to students *and* hold high expectations that empower students to learn. There is a plethora of research that shows holding high expectations for students significantly increases student learning. As discussed in chapter 3 (page 27), a teacher's high expectations can form a self-fulfilling prophecy. When teachers believe in students, students are more willing to believe in themselves and try harder. Also, teachers are more likely to provide students with the support they need.

3. **Keep a reflective mindset:** An evidence-based teacher should be willing to question the pedagogies of others as well as themselves. They should constantly reflect on what is working and what is not working in the classroom. The evidence-based teacher needs to remember that they are ultimately a part of their very own scientific process, and part of the scientific process is peer review. This means you should find teachers you trust to reflect on your teaching practices, with the intent of mutual growth and collaboration.
4. **In terms of pedagogy, I recommend a few specific pedagogical methods:** All these pedagogies are well supported by meta-analysis. Most of them have multiple meta-analyses showing strong levels of efficacy. All teachers use some type of assessment for learning and as part of the learning process. These assessments can include self-assessment, formative assessment, and peer assessment. I recommend that all teachers use some form of data-informed action research teaching, such as RTI. There have been multiple meta-analyses on this topic, all showing very large effect sizes, the most rigorous of which was done by Tran and colleagues (2011), as discussed in chapter 11 (page 75). However, I understand that not all teachers are willing to take on this type of program due to time constraints.
5. **In terms of reading instruction, all emergent students require a large amount of phonemic awareness, phonics, and spelling-based instruction:** There have been more than a dozen meta-analyses confirming the efficacy of systematic phonics instruction, most famously the National Reading Panel (2000) meta-analysis. Similarly, the National Reading Panel (2000) and David M. Rehfeld, Marie Kirkpatrick, Nicole O'Guinn, and Rachel Renbarger (2022) meta-analyses showed strong efficacy for phonemic awareness. Lastly, the Graham and Hebert (2011) meta-analysis showed strong support for the efficacy of spelling instruction. As students get older and become more proficient at reading, their instruction should become more focused on fluency (Lee & Yoon, 2017), comprehension (Filderman, Austin, Boucher, O'Donnell, & Swanson, 2022), and writing (Gillespie & Graham, 2014).
6. **A strong mathematics program should include multiple heuristics, in which teachers provide instruction on multiple procedures instead of one; some skill and drill (Methe, Kilgus, Neiman, & Riley-Tillman, 2012); and direct instruction on both procedural and conceptual mathematics knowledge (Rittle-Johnson & Schneider, 2015):** Research shows that these three strategies greatly benefit students' mathematics learning.

Since the early 2000s, there has been a rise of several constructivist teaching methods that, while popular, do not appear to be evidence based. I think these methods rose in popularity because they felt more democratic, not because they were better for helping students to learn (Powell, Hughes, & Peltier, 2022). These teaching methods de-emphasized the role of the teacher and limited skill instruction and rote learning. The goal of teaching was less about achieving specific learning objectives and more about making the processes by which students achieve their learning more democratic, creative, and engaging (Powell et al., 2022). In many ways, these methods were about escaping the characterized narrative of the schoolhouse teacher—a strict instructor standing at the front of the class, dictating knowledge.

I refer to these types of methodologies as *process-based pedagogies*. However, they are often associated with the educational theory of learning and philosophy, constructivism. While process-based pedagogies may not be the most effective way for students to learn, they can be the most engaging. In my opinion, the rise of these pedagogies was more of a response to the more authoritarian and product-based teaching systems of old, which were associated with negative memories for many adults today (Prawat, 1996). As educators, we should strive to create a balance between these types of pedagogies, so we can get the best benefits of both types of instruction. The first step is to establish the purpose and utility of both types.

Within evidence-based education, certain influencers and teachers fall into individual pedagogical camps. This can be a potential philosophical trap. Once teachers entrench themselves in a pedagogical camp, they risk not being open to new viewpoints. As I stated at the start of this epilogue, if you are never willing to change your viewpoint, you cannot be evidence based. I have been a strong advocate of phonics and action research; however, if over the next five years, I see a new strong trend of evidence against the efficacy of these pedagogies, I will happily abandon them. My goal is not to change the practices of teachers but to change the culture of the education community.

Question everything. Hold nothing sacred. And be willing to change your own mind.

GLOSSARY

Attrition: To weaken in effect or strength over time; usually refers to participants dropping out of a study. A study with a large degree of attrition can be a sign that data were manipulated.

Cohen's *d*: The most used effect size calculation in education research; also referred to as *d*.

Confirmation bias: The phenomenon in which researchers look for evidence that supports their viewpoint, while ignoring evidence that does not.

Control conditions: The design of a control group and the instruction students receive within the control group.

Control group (or comparison group): The group in a study that does not receive the experimental treatment; the magnitude of the treatment effect is found by subtracting the mean test scores of the control group.

Controls: Design choices researchers use to isolate the impact of an experimental variable.

Correlational effect size: Effect size that measures the magnitude of correlation between two sets of data (for example, a correlation effect size might be used to measure the impact of the number of books in a home and the student's literacy level).

Covariance calculations: Calculations that attempt to control the effect of multiple variables at the same time, such as study design, sample size, type of control group, and treatment received.

Effect size: Also referred to as a *standardized baseline difference*, this is a type of calculation used to standardize the results of different studies into one metric, so one can more easily interpret study results. There are many types of effect size calculations; however, most are interpreted as follows: below 0.20 is negligible, between 0.20 and 0.39 is small, between 0.40 and 0.79 is moderate, and above 0.79 is large. On average, education studies have a mean effect size of 0.40; however, study quality should impact how one interprets effect sizes.

Efficacy: The degree to which something, such as a teaching method, has the desired effect.

Experimental conditions: The design of a treatment group and the instruction that students receive within the experimental group.

Experimental group: Also referred to as *treatment group*, this is the group in an experiment that receives the treatment or instruction being tested.

Fidelity: *Fidelity* usually refers to the rigidity at which a teacher applies an intervention. Not all studies track fidelity. You can be less confident in the results of a study that does not track, because you do not know if the experimental conditions were properly applied.

File drawer problem: The well-recorded phenomenon of researchers not publishing studies when the results are negligible or negative. Some journals even discourage researchers from publishing such papers, as they are viewed as uninteresting. This phenomenon inflates the collective understanding of research, as all results are biased to the affirmative.

Fixed effect: All instruction and variables are the same in both the treatment and control group, except for the teaching method or factor being studied.

Funnel plot analysis: This plot is used to detect bias in study samples. Symmetrical funnel plots indicate less bias, while asymmetrical funnel plots suggest bias. Additionally, when a funnel plot has data points clustered in the bottom-right quadrant, this suggests that the studies in a meta-analysis were manipulated to increase the effect size.

Glass's Delta: An effect size calculation used when the range of results is dramatically different between the control group and the treatment group.

Hedge's *g*: An effect size calculation used to correct for smaller sample sizes (below fifty).

High yield: Showing high effect sizes in research.

Impact-to-time ratio: The ratio of effect size versus time cost of achieving an effect size.

Incremental cost-effectiveness ratio: A mathematical formula for calculating the impact-to-time ratio.

Magnitude: The degree, size, or scale of a finding.

Mean difference: The average difference between either two groups or the pre- and posttest of an experiment.

Mean effect size: The average effect size found.

Meta-analysis: A systematic study of studies in which the authors calculate the mean effect size for an intervention.

Moderator analysis: A sub-analysis within a meta-analysis of more specific questions, such as factors that increase or decrease the effectiveness of a treatment (for example, the impact of phonics instruction in each grade).

Moderator data: These are results of a moderator analysis.

Moderator variables results: The results of a moderator analysis commonly used to answer specific sub-questions of a study, such as those relating to demographics, dosage, or alternative forms of a treatment.

Multilevel modeling: A statistical method for controlling multiple factors simultaneously when modeling study results.

Nonexperimental studies: Studies that do not use control groups.

Opportunity cost: All teaching methodologies require time. Using one teaching methodology often means not using other teaching methodologies. The opportunity cost is the lost benefit of the teaching methodologies not used.

Outcome measure: Refers to the specific type of learning measured in a study (for example, a literacy study might test fluency, decoding, and comprehension; each of these terms refers to a specific outcome measure).

Outlier: A statistical anomaly, which can distort the data or understanding in a study.

Pearson effect size: An effect size used to calculate the level of correlation between two data sets (for example, the number of hours spent doing mathematics fluency work and the students' mathematics ability).

P-hacking: The malicious practice of unethical researchers to inflate results by using multiple assessments and then only publishing the results for assessments with significant results.

***p* value:** The percentage of chance that a dataset is random versus meaningful (for example, a *p* value of 0.04 indicates that there is a 4 percent chance the data are random). Any *p* values above 0.05 are supposed to indicate statistical insignificance. However, some dispute this cutoff point as being too arbitrary and small.

Qualitative research: Research based on researcher observations, not statistical measurement.

Quantitative research: Research based on trying to scientifically measure either the causality or correlation of factors.

Random effect: When there are multiple experimental variables in a study, one cannot be sure that the study results are due to any single variable. Therefore, the effect is random. Random effects are not meaningful in isolation. For example, if a study tests the impacts of more explicit instruction and more homework at the same time, the results will show a random effect, because it is impossible to know if the results should be attributed to the instruction, the homework, or a synergistic effect.

Randomization: The process for randomly selecting participants in a study. In theory, studies that randomly select participants are supposed to be more valid.

Randomized controlled trial (RCT): Also referred to as an *experimental study*, a study in which participants are randomly sorted into either a treatment group or control group to test the impact of an intervention or treatment.

Researcher bias: A study shows researcher bias when the author accidentally designs their study in a way that biases the result (for example, providing more instructional time to the treatment group than the control group).

Sample: The participants in a study.

Sample size: The number of participants in a study.

Scientific consensus: The most agreed-on answer to a question within the scientific community.

Secondary meta-analysis: A study that calculates the mean effect size from multiple meta-analyses, popularized by Hattie (2009).

Standard deviation (SD): A standard deviation shows how dispersed a set of data is in relation to the mean. This statistical measurement is primarily a representation of data variance. The higher the SD is in comparison to the mean difference, the less likely it is that the study results are meaningful.

Statistical significance: Researchers usually accept statistical significance as indicating a *p* value below 0.05. However, psychologist and statistician Jacob Cohen argued against this perspective and, instead, suggested that effect sizes above 0.20 proved significance (Sullivan & Feinn, 2012).

Structure factor: The idea that providing a more structured instructional approach improves academic outcomes when compared to a less structured approach. This can bias the results of a study, as the treatment group usually has more structured instruction.

Synthesis research: Research that synthesizes the results of many studies into one paper (for example, literature reviews, meta-analyses, or secondary meta-analyses).

Treatment: Something a treatment or experiment group receives that the control group does not. In medicine, this would likely be a medication. In education, this would likely be a form of instruction, such as phonics.

Treatment group: Also referred to as an *experimental group* or *intervention group*, a treatment group is the group that receives treatment in an experimental study.

White paper: A paper that lays out the theoretical argument for a new pedagogy or product.

REFERENCES AND RESOURCES

Abrami, P. C., Bernard, R. M., Wade, A., Schmid, R. F., Borokhovski, E., Tamim, R., et al. (2006). A review of e-learning in Canada: A rough sketch of the evidence, gaps and promising directions. *Canadian Journal of Learning and Technology, 32*(3), 1–14. Accessed at https://files.eric.ed.gov/fulltext/EJ1073702.pdf on June 26, 2023.

Abrami, P. C., Lysenko, L., & Borokhovski, E. (2020). The effects of ABRACADABRA on reading outcomes: An updated meta-analysis and landscape review of applied field research. *Journal of Computer Assisted Learning, 36*(3), 260–279. https://doi.org/10.1111/jcal.12417

Adams, G. L., & Engelmann, S. (1996). *Research on direct instruction: 25 years beyond DISTAR.* Seattle, WA: Educational Achievement Systems. Accessed at www.nifdi.org/docman/suggested-reading/book-excerpts/research-on-direct-instruction-25-years-beyond-distar-engelmann-adams-1996 on June 27, 2023.

Alfieri, L., Brooks, P. J., Aldrich, N. J., & Tenenbaum, H. R. (2011). Does discovery-based instruction enhance learning? *Journal of Educational Psychology, 103*(1), 1–18. https://doi.org/10.1037/a0021017

American Psychiatric Association. (2013). *Diagnostic and statistical manual of mental disorders: DSM-5* (5th ed.). Washington, DC: Author.

American Psychiatric Association. (2021, September). *What are disruptive, impulse control and conduct disorders?* Accessed at www.psychiatry.org/patients-families/disruptive-impulse-control-and-conduct-disorders/what-are-disruptive-impulse-control-and-conduct on April 18, 2023.

American Psychological Association. (2019, May 30). *Belief in learning styles myth may be detrimental* [Press release]. Accessed at www.apa.org/news/press/releases/2019/05/learning-styles-myth on May 8, 2023.

Appel, D. (2019, November 18). *Japan's school lunch program serves nutritious meals with food education.* Accessed at www.nycfoodpolicy.org/food-policy-snapshot-japans-school-lunch-program on June 17, 2023.

Australian Trade and Investment Commission. (n.d.). *Australia's education system.* Accessed at https://studyaustralia.gov.au/en/plan-your-studies/australias-education-system on December 11, 2023.

Bagasi, M. A. (2018). Meta analysis of the effectiveness of response to intervention models in special education and implications for international implementations. *Multi-Knowledge Electronic Comprehensive Journal for Education and Science Publications* (MECSJ), *14*. Accessed at www.mecsj.com/uplode/images/photo/META_ANALYSIS_OF_THE_EFFECTIVNESS_OF_RESPONSE_TO_INTERVENTION_MODELS.pdf on August 6, 2023.

Bailey, N. (2023, March 26). *The science of reading and the rejection of picture books.* Accessed at https://nancyebailey.com/2023/03/26/the-science-of-reading-and-the-rejection-of-picture-books on May 9, 2023.

Barquero, L. A., Davis, N., & Cutting, L. E. (2014). Neuroimaging of reading intervention: A systematic review and activation likelihood estimate meta-analysis. *PLoS ONE*, *9*(1), e83668. https://doi.org/10.1371/journal.pone.0083668

Barrett, C. A., Gadke, D. L., & VanDerHeyden, A. M. (2020). At what cost? Introduction to the special issue "Return on investment for academic and behavioral assessment and intervention." *School Psychology Review*, *49*(4), 347–358.

Barshay, J. (2023, May 8). *Proof points: How a debate over the science of math could reignite the math wars.* Accessed at https://hechingerreport.org/proof-points-how-a-debate-over-the-science-of-math-could-reignite-the-math-wars on August 7, 2023.

Batdi, V. (2014). Determining the effect of jigsaw technique on students' academic achievements through meta-analysis method. *EKEV Akademi Dergisi*, *58*, 699–714.

Bauer, C. C. C., Caballero, C., Scherer, E., West, M. R., Mrazek, M. D., Phillips, D. T., et al. (2019). Mindfulness training reduces stress and amygdala reactivity to fearful faces in middle-school children. *Behavioral Neuroscience*, *133*(6), 569–585. https://doi.org/10.1037/bne0000337

Bennett, S., Dworet, D., & Weber, K. (2013). *Special education in Ontario schools* (7th ed.). St. Catherines, Ontario, Canada: Highland Press.

Bernburg, J. G. (2009). Labeling theory. In M. D. Krohn, A. J. Lizotte, & G. P. Hall (Eds.), *Handbook on crime and deviance* (pp. 187–207). New York: Springer.

Black, T. (2022, August 22). *Children's risk of suicide increases on school days.* Accessed at www.scientificamerican.com/article/childrens-risk-of-suicide-increases-on-school-days on June 27, 2023.

Boaler, J. (2015). *The elephant in the classroom: Helping children learn and love maths* (Rev. ed.). Chicago: Souvenir Press.

Boaler, J., & Zoido, P. (2016, November 1). *Why math education in the U.S. doesn't add up.* Accessed at www.scientificamerican.com/article/why-math-education-in-the-u-s-doesn-t-add-up on June 27, 2023.

Boutelier, S., & Smalligan, N. (2018, November 13). *Playing to students' strengths: A framework for giving students choice in demonstrating their understanding of course content.* Accessed at www.edutopia.org/article/playing-students-strengths on June 27, 2023.

Boyer, N., & Ehri, L. C. (2011). Contribution of phonemic segmentation instruction with letters and articulation pictures to word reading and spelling in beginners. *Scientific Studies of Reading, 15*(5), 440–470. https://doi.org/10.1080/10888438.2010.520778

Brewe, E., Bartley, J. E., Riedel, M. C., Sawtelle, V., Salo, T., Boeving, E. R., et al. (2018). Toward a neurobiological basis for understanding learning in university modeling instruction physics courses. *Frontiers in ICT, 5*(10). https://doi.org/10.3389/fict.2018.00010

Brydges, C. R. (2019). Effect size guidelines, sample size calculations, and statistical power in gerontology. *Innovation in Aging, 3*(4). https://doi.org/10.1093/geroni/igz036

Buffum, A., Mattos, M., & Malone, J. (2018). *Taking action: A handbook for RTI at Work™.* Bloomington, IN: Solution Tree Press.

Burnette, J. L., Billingsley, J., Banks, G. C., Knouse, L. E., Hoyt, C. L., Pollack, J. M., et al. (2023). A systematic review and meta-analysis of growth mindset interventions: For whom, how, and why might such interventions work? *Psychological Bulletin* [Advance online publication], *149*(3–4), 174–205. https://doi.org/10.1037/bul0000368

Burns, M. K., Appleton, J. J., & Stehouwer, J. D. (2005). Meta-analytic review of responsiveness-to -intervention research: Examining field-based and research-implemented models. *Journal of Psychoeducational Assessment, 23*(4), 381–394. https://doi.org/10.1177/073428290502300406

Burts, D. C., Hart, C. H., Charlesworth, R., DeWolf, D. M., Ray, J., Manuel, K., et al. (1993). Developmental appropriateness of kindergarten programs and academic outcomes in first grade. *Journal of Research in Childhood Education, 8*(1), 23–31.

Burts, D. C., Hart, C. H., Charlesworth, R., & Kirk, L. (1990). A comparison of frequencies of stress behaviors observed in kindergarten children in classrooms with developmentally appropriate versus developmentally inappropriate instructional practices. *Early Childhood Research Quarterly, 5*(3), 407–423.

Camilli, G., Vargas, S., & Yurecko, M. (2003). Teaching children to read: The fragile link between science and federal education policy. *Education Policy Analysis Archive, 11*(15). Accessed at www.researchgate.net/publication/49610142_Teaching_Children_to_Read_The_Fragile_Link_Between_Science_Education_Policy on November 9, 2023.

Canadian Education Centre Network. (2003). *The education system in Canada*. Accessed at https://studycanada.ca/english/education_system_canada.htm on April 18, 2023.

The Canadian Encyclopedia. (2022, March 15). *Constitution of Canada (plain-language summary)*. Accessed at www.thecanadianencyclopedia.ca/en/article/constitution-of-canada-plain-language-summary on August 15, 2023.

Capar, G., & Tarim, K. (2015). Efficacy of the cooperative learning method on mathematics achievement and attitude: A meta-analysis research. *Educational Sciences: Theory and Practice, 15*(2), 553–559.

Carbonneau, K. J., Marley, S. C., & Selig, J. P. (2013). A meta-analysis of the efficacy of teaching mathematics with concrete manipulatives. *Journal of Educational Psychology, 105*(2), 380–400. https://doi.org/10.1037/a0031084

Carolan, T. F., Hutchins, S. D., Wickens, C. D., & Cumming, J. M. (2014). Costs and benefits of more learner freedom: Meta-analyses of exploratory and learner control training methods. *Human Factors, 56*(5), 999–1014. https://doi.org/10.1177/0018720813517710

Cason, M., Young, J., & Kuehnert, E. (2019). A meta-analysis of the effects of numerical competency development on achievement: Recommendations for mathematics educators. *Investigations in Mathematics Learning, 11*(2), 134–147.

Castiglioni-Spalten, M. L., & Ehri, L. C. (2003). Phonemic awareness instruction: Contribution of articulatory segmentation to novice beginners' reading and spelling. *Scientific Studies of Reading, 7*(1), 25–52.

Chang, S. (2023). *Protecting Taiwan's youth from suicide*. Accessed at www.taipeitimes.com/News/editorials/archives/2023/08/02/2003804096 on February 27, 2024.

Chappell, S., & Nunnery, J. (2013). A meta-analysis of a cooperative learning models effects on student achievement in mathematics. *Cypriot Journal of Educational Sciences, 8*(1). Accessed at www.researchgate.net/publication/264274116_A_Meta-analysis_of_a_Cooperative_Learning_Models_Effects_on_Student_Achievement_in_Mathematics on August 5, 2023.

Cherry, K. (2023, March 11). *Gardner's theory of multiple intelligences*. Accessed at www.verywellmind.com/gardners-theory-of-multiple-intelligences-2795161 on April 18, 2023.

Clark, J. S., Porath, S., Thiele, J., & Jobe, M. (2020). *Action research*. New York: New Prairie Press. Accessed at https://newprairiepress.org/ebooks/34 on June 27, 2023.

Colagrossi, M. (2018, September 9). *Ten reasons why Finland's education system is the best*. Accessed at https://bigthink.com/the-present/finland-education-system-2 on April 18, 2023.

The Conference Board of Canada. (n.d.). *Education and skills*. Accessed at www.conferenceboard.ca/hcp/provincial/education.aspx on April 19, 2023.

Copple, C., & Bredekamp, S. (Eds.). (2008). *Developmentally appropriate practice in early childhood programs: Serving children from birth through age 8* (3rd ed.). Washington, DC: National Association for the Education of Young Children.

Crossman, A. (2020, February 3). *An overview of labeling theory.* Accessed at www.thoughtco.com /labeling-theory-3026627 on April 18, 2023.

Cunningham, W. A., Johnson, M. K., Raye, C. L., Gatenby, J. C., Gore, J. C., & Banaji, M. R. (2004). Separable neural components in the processing of Black and White faces. *Psychological Science, 15*(12), 806–813.

Dağyar, M., & Demirel, M. (2015). Effects of problem-based learning on academic achievement: A meta-analysis study. *Eğitim ve Bilim, 40*(181). Accessed at www.researchgate.net /publication/284224370_Effects_of_Problem-Based_Learning_on_Academic _Achievement_A_Meta-analysis_Study on June 26, 2023.

Dahiru, T. (2008). P-value, a true test of statistical significance? A cautionary note. *Annals of Ibadan Postgraduate Medicine, 6*(1), 21–26. https://doi.org/10.4314/aipm.v6i1.64038

Deary, I. J., Spinath, F. M., & Bates, T. C. (2006). Genetics of intelligence. *European Journal of Human Genetics, 14*, 690–700. https://doi.org/10.1038/sj.ejhg.5201588

Dee, T., & Gershenson, S. (2017). Unconscious bias in the classroom: Evidence and opportunities. *Google's Computer Science Education Research.* Accessed at https://cepa.stanford.edu/content /unconscious-bias-classroom-evidence-and-opportunities on June 27, 2023.

Delagran, L., & Haley, A. (2023). *What is mindfulness?* Accessed at www.takingcharge.csh.umn.edu /what-mindfulness on April 26, 2023.

Deunk, M. I., Smale-Jacobse, A. E., de Boer, H., Doolaard, S., & Bosker, R. J. (2018). Effective differentiation practices: A systematic review and meta-analysis of studies on the cognitive effects of differentiation practices in primary education. *Educational Research Review, 24*, 31–54.

Dunn, L., Beach, S. A., & Kontos, S. (1994). Quality of the literacy environment in day care and children's development. *Journal of Research in Childhood Education, 9*(1), 24–34. https://doi.org/10.1080/02568549409594950

Dunn, L., & Kontos, S. (1997). *Developmentally appropriate practice: What does research tell us?* (ED413106 1197-10-00). Accessed at https://files.eric.ed.gov/fulltext/ED413106.pdf on July 13, 2023.

Dunn, R. (1990). Understanding the Dunn and Dunn Learning Styles Model and the need for individual diagnosis and prescription. *Journal of Reading, Writing, and Learning Disabilities International, 6*(3), 223–247.

Dweck, C. S. (2016). *Mindset: The new psychology of success* (Updated ed.). New York: Ballantine Books.

EAB. (2019). *Narrowing the third-grade reading gap: Embracing the science of reading to improve student outcomes.* Washington, DC: Author. Accessed at https://attachment.eab.com /wp-content/uploads/2019/01/Embracing-the-Science-of-Reading-1.pdf?fbclid=Iw AR32kRlLKC28pdMm80hOOTizznf_SAAI5JUIAEwMvD5NI0lZwy-5hpb-POU on December 8, 2023.

Edutopia. (2016, July 20). *Multiple intelligences: What does the research say?* Accessed at https://edutopia.org/multiple-intelligences-research on April 21, 2023.

Edwards, D., Rice, J. M., & McMillan, J. (2019, July 23). *Three charts on: How much Australia spends on all levels of education.* Accessed at https://theconversation.com/three-charts-on-how-much-australia-spends-on-all-levels-of-education-120076 on April 18, 2023.

Ehri, L. C., Nunes, S. R., Stahl, S. A., & Willows, D. M. (2001). Systematic phonics instruction helps students learn to read: Evidence from the National Reading Panel's meta-analysis. *Review of Educational Research, 71*(3), 393–447. https://doi.org/10.3102/00346543071003393

Elkind, D. (1981). *The hurried child: Growing up too fast too soon.* Reading, MA: Addison-Wesley.

Ellington, A. J. (2003). A meta-analysis of the effects of calculators on students' achievement and attitude levels in precollege mathematics classes. *Journal for Research in Mathematics Education, 34*(5), 433–463.

Elmaghraby, R., & Garayalde, S. (2021, September). *What are disruptive, impulse control and conduct disorders?* Accessed at www.psychiatry.org/patients-families/disruptive-impulse-control-and-conduct-disorders/what-are-disruptive-impulse-control-and-conduct on August 4, 2023.

Erisen, Y., & Günay, R. (2017). A meta-analysis into the effectiveness of doctoral dissertations on constructivist learning. *The Anthropologist, 21*(1–2), 202–212. Accessed at www.tandfonline.com/doi/abs/10.1080/09720073.2015.11891809 on August 14, 2023.

European Social Fund Plus. (2023, March 23). *Ireland launches €1 billion ESF+ programme.* Accessed at https://ec.europa.eu/european-social-fund-plus/en/news/ireland-launches-esf-programmes-2021-2027 on June 27, 2023.

Evans, T., & Dietrich, H. (2022). Inquiry-based mathematics education: A call for reform in tertiary education seems unjustified. *STEM Education, 2*(3), 221–244.

FactsMaps. (2018). *PISA 2018 worldwide ranking: Average score of mathematics, science and reading.* Accessed at https://factsmaps.com/pisa-2018-worldwide-ranking-average-score-of-mathematics-science-reading on April 18, 2023.

Fan, H., Xu, J., Cai, Z., He, J., & Fan, X. (2016). Homework and students' achievement in math and science: A 30-year meta-analysis, 1986–2015. *Educational Research Review, 20*(6), 35–54.

Filderman, M. J., Austin, C. R., Boucher, A. N., O'Donnell, K., & Swanson, E. A. (2022). A meta-analysis of the effects of reading comprehension interventions on the reading comprehension outcomes of struggling readers in third through 12th grades. *Exceptional Children, 88*(2), 163–184.

Flynn, J. R. (1987). Massive IQ gains in 14 nations: What IQ tests really measure. *Psychological Bulletin, 101*(2), 171–191. https://doi.org/10.1037/0033-2909.101.2.171

Frede, E., & Barnett, W. S. (1992). Developmentally appropriate public school preschool: A study of implementation of the high/scope curriculum and its effects on disadvantaged children's skills at first grade. *Early Childhood Research Quarterly, 7*(4), 483–499.

Freeman, S., Eddy, S. L., McDonough, M., Smith, M. K., Okoroafor, N., Jordt, H., et al. (2014). Active learning increases student performance in science, engineering, and mathematics. *Proceedings of the National Academy of Sciences, 111*(23), 8410–8415.

Friesen, S., & Scott, D. (2013, June). *Inquiry-based learning: A review of the research literature.* Edmonton, Alberta, Canada: Alberta Ministry of Education. Accessed at https://galileo.org/focus-on-inquiry-lit-review.pdf on April 18, 2023.

Fung, M. (2019, August 16). *Hong Kong's high-pressure education system has failed us all, but there's still hope.* Accessed at https://hongkongfp.com/2019/08/16/hong-kongs-high-pressure-education-system-failed-us-theres-still-hope on August 8, 2023.

Gao, H. (2023, June 22). *How China's education system trapped a generation.* Accessed at https://foreignpolicy.com/2023/06/22/china-education-system-lying-flat-state-control-xi-jinping on October 30, 2023.

Gardner, H. (1983). *Frames of mind: The theory of multiple intelligences.* New York: Basic Books.

Gardner, H. (2013). *Frequently asked questions: Multiple intelligences and related educational topics.* Accessed at https://howardgardner01.files.wordpress.com/2012/06/faq_march2013.pdf on May 8, 2023.

Geeraert, A. (2020). *Japanese cram schools are not what you think—An interview with Takahiro Goto.* Accessed at https://kokoro-jp.com/interviews/1541 on August 8, 2023.

Genius Tests. (n.d.). *Can you study for an IQ test?* Accessed at https://geniustests.com/frequently-asked-questions/can-you-study-for-iq-test on April 17, 2023.

Gershenson, S., & Papageorge, N. (2018). The power of teacher expectations: How racial bias hinders student attainment. *Education Next, 18*(1). Accessed at https://link.gale.com/apps/doc/A520581893/AONE?u=anon~4368c109&sid=googleScholar&xid=5ab60035 on August 14, 2023.

Gersten, R., Chard, D. J., Jayanthi, M., Baker, S. K., Morphy, P., & Flojo, J. (2009, January). *A meta-analysis of mathematics instructional interventions for students with learning disabilities: A technical report.* Los Alamitos, CA: Instructional Research Group.

Gillespie, A., & Graham, S. (2014). A meta-analysis of writing interventions for students with learning disabilities. *Exceptional Children, 80*(4), 454–473.

The Global Economy. (n.d.). *Macao: Education spending, percent of GDP.* Accessed at www.theglobaleconomy.com/Macao/Education_spending on April 18, 2023.

Go! Go! Nihon Staff. (2018, July 4). *The Japanese education system: Similarities and unique differences to the Western world* [Blog post]. Accessed at https://gogonihon.com/en/blog/learn-about-the-japanese-education-system on June 17, 2023.

Goddard, H. H. (1946). What is intelligence? *Journal of Social Psychology, 24*(1), 51–69. https://doi.org/10.1080/00224545.1946.9918858

Gold, M. E., & Richards, H. (2012). To label or not to label: The special education question for African Americans. *The Journal of Educational Foundations, Ann Arbor, 26*(1–2), 143–156.

Goldenberg, C. (2020). Reading wars, reading science, and English learners. *Reading Research Quarterly, 55*(S1), S131–S144. https://doi.org/10.1002/rrq.340

Good, T. L., Sterzinger, N., & Lavigne, A. (2018). Expectation effects: Pygmalion and the initial 20 years of research. *Educational Research and Evaluation, 24*(3-5), 99–123. https://doi.org/10.1080/13803611.2018.1548817

Gopalan, M., Rosinger, K., & Ahn, J. B. (2020). Use of quasi-experimental research designs in education research: Growth, promise, and challenges. *Review of Research in Education, 44*(1), 218–243.

Goriounova, N. A., & Mansvelder, H. D. (2019). Genes, cells and brain areas of intelligence. *Frontiers in Human Neuroscience, 13*, 44. https://doi.org/10.3389/fnhum.2019.00044

Gottlieb, A. (2018, January 11). *I just got back from Taiwan. U.S. schools have so much to learn.* Accessed at https://educationpost.org/i-just-got-back-from-taiwan-u-s-schools-have-so-much-to-learn on April 19, 2023.

Government of Québec. (2023, May 10). *Québec education system.* Accessed at www.quebec.ca/en/education/study-quebec/education-system on August 15, 2023.

Government Technology Agency of Singapore. (2022, December 29). *Government recurrent expenditure on education per student.* Accessed at https://beta.data.gov.sg/datasets/d_d1c04ad1a201a76b0ab7753a498b3bfb/view on December 18, 2023.

Graham, S., & Hebert, M. (2011). Writing to read: A meta-analysis of the impact of writing and writing instruction on reading. *Harvard Educational Review, 81*(4), 710–744.

Graham, S., Liu, X., Aitken, A., Ng, C., Bartlett, B., Harris, K. R., et al. (2018). Effectiveness of literacy programs balancing reading and writing instruction: A meta-analysis. *Reading Research Quarterly, 53*(3), 279–304.

Grant, T. (2012). *A meta-analysis of school-based interventions for middle schoolers: Academic, behavioral, and social outcomes* [Doctoral dissertation, Fordham University]. Fordham Research Commons. Accessed at https://research.library.fordham.edu/dissertations/AAI3542750 on February 5, 2024.

Günay, R. (2015, October). *A meta-analysis into the effectiveness of doctoral dissertations on constructivist learning.* Accessed at www.researchgate.net/publication/283008790_A_Meta-analysis_into_the_Effectiveness_of_Doctoral_Dissertations_on_Constructivist_Learning on July 5, 2022.

Haas, M. (2005). Teaching methods for secondary algebra: A meta-analysis of findings. *NASSP Bulletin, 89*(642), 24–46.

Hall, C., Dahl-Leonard, K., Cho, E., Solari, E. J., Capin, P., Conner, C., et al. (2022). Forty years of reading intervention research for elementary students with or at risk for dyslexia: A systematic review and meta-analysis. *Reading Research Quarterly, 58*(2), 285–312. https://doi.org/10.1002/rrq.477

Hall, M. S., & Burns, M. K. (2018). Meta-analysis of targeted small-group reading interventions. *Journal of School Psychology, 66*, 54–66.

Hancock, L. (2011, September). *Why are Finland's schools successful?* Accessed at www.smithsonianmag.com/innovation/why-are-finlands-schools-successful-49859555 on April 19, 2023.

Hanford, E. (Host). (2022). Sold a story: How teaching kids to read went so wrong [Audio podcast]. In *APM Reports*. Accessed at https://features.apmreports.org/sold-a-story on July 13, 2023.

Hansford, N. (2020, December 24). *Ability grouping? Does it matter?* Accessed at www.pedagogy nongrata.com/ability-grouping on June 25, 2023.

Hansford, N. (2022a, April 7). *Commonly used math pedagogies and factors ranked by effect sizes found in meta-analysis*. Accessed at www.teachingbyscience.com/2022-png-math-list on June 23, 2023.

Hansford, N. (2022b, February 27). *Differentiation*. Accessed at_www.teachingbyscience.com /differentiation on July 10, 2023.

Hansford, N. (2022c, December 11). *Feedback*. Accessed at www.teachingbyscience.com/feedback on November 20, 2023.

Hansford, N. (2022d, June 5). *Is RTI an evidence-based concept?* Accessed at www.teachingbyscience .com/rti on June 10, 2023.

Hansford, N. (2022e, July 28). *Letterland*. Accessed at www.teachingbyscience.com/letterland on June 25, 2023.

Hansford, N. (2022f, June 18). *Morphology instruction: A secondary meta-analysis*. Accessed at www.pedagogynongrata.com/morphology on June 25, 2023.

Hansford, N. (2022g, May 20). *Repeated reading is part of the science of reading*. Accessed at www.teachingbyscience.com/repeated-reading on June 25, 2023.

Hansford, N. (2022h). *The scientific principles of teaching*. United States: Author.

Hansford, N. (2022i, July 5). *What is constructivist teaching and why is it important?* Accessed at www.teachingbyscience.com/constructivist-teaching on July 10, 2023.

Hansford, N., Garforth, K., & King, J. (2022, September 14). *A road map to evidence-based instruction in reading and writing education: A secondary meta-analysis on the science of reading and writing instruction*. Accessed at www.teachingbyscience.com/sor-recommendations on June 23, 2023.

Hansford, N., & King, J. (2018). *The scientific principles of teaching*. Website no longer available.

Hansford, N., & King, J. (2022, December 31). *A meta-analysis and literature review of language programs*. Accessed at www.teachingbyscience.com/a-meta-analysis-of-language-programs on June 25, 2023.

Hansford, N., McGlynn, S., & King, J. (2023). *What's better for reading comprehension: Strategy or content knowledge instruction?* Accessed at www.pedagogynongrata.com/_files/ugd /237d54_6b9ad66d9e694a8c977aa3848fdd3747.pdf on June 10, 2023.

Hansford, N., Reenstra, E., Aitchison, P., & McGlynn, S. (2022). *Computer-based reading interventions*. Accessed at www.pedagogynongrata.com/_files/ugd/237d54 _62011c91c716487781f3126193a09b0f.pdf on November 9, 2023.

Hansford, N., & Schechter, R. (2021). *Is this _____ evidence-based? Rethinking how we evaluate evidence.* Accessed at www.pedagogynongrata.com/evidence-framework on February 23, 2024.

Hansford, N., & Schechter, R. I. (2023). Challenges and opportunities of meta-analysis in education research. *International Journal of Modern Education Studies*, *7*(1), 218–231.

Hao, T. (2021). *Chinese parents' complicated relationship with after-school tutoring* [Blog post]. Accessed at https://radii.co/article/chinese-parents-need-cram-schools-more-than-their-kids on December 19, 2023.

Hattie, J. (2009). *Visible learning: A synthesis of over 800 meta-analyses relating to achievement.* New York: Routledge.

Hattie, J. (2022a, June). *Constructivist teaching.* Accessed at www.visiblelearningmetax.com /influences/view/constructivist_teaching on July 5, 2023.

Hattie, J. (2022b). *Direct instruction.* Accessed at www.visiblelearningmetax.com/influences/view /direct_instruction on July 5, 2023.

Hattie, J. (2022c). *Inquiry-based teaching.* Accessed at www.visiblelearningmetax.com/influences /view/inquiry-based_teaching on July 5, 2022.

Hattie, J. (2022d). *Problem-based learning.* Accessed at www.visiblelearningmetax.com/influences /view/problem-based_learning on July 5, 2022.

Hattie, J. (2022e). *Whole language approach.* Accessed at www.visiblelearningmetax.com/influences /view/whole_language_approach on December 31, 2022.

Hattie, J. (2023a). *Cooperative learning.* Accessed at www.visiblelearningmetax.com/influences/view /cooperative_learning on June 25, 2023.

Hattie, J. (2023b). *Cooperative vs. competitive learning.* Accessed at www.visiblelearningmetax.com /influences/view/cooperative_vs._competitive_learning on June 26, 2023.

Hattie, J. (2023c). *Global research database.* Accessed at www.visiblelearningmetax.com/Influences on June 24, 2023.

Hattie, J. (2023d). *Mainstreaming/inclusion.* Accessed at www.visiblelearningmetax.com/influences /view/mainstreaming-inclusion on June 24, 2023.

Hattie, J. (2023e). *Matching teaching to style of learning.* Accessed at www.visiblelearningmetax.com /influences/view/matching_teaching_to_style_of_learning on June 25, 2023.

Hattie, J. (2023f). *Mathematics programs for LD.* Accessed at www.visiblelearningmetax.com /influences/view/mathematics_programs_for_ld on June 24, 2023.

Hattie, J. (2023g). *Phonics instruction.* Accessed at www.visiblelearningmetax.com/influences/view /phonics_instruction on June 24, 2023.

Hattie, J. (2023h). *Response to intervention.* Accessed at www.visiblelearningmetax.com/influences /view/response_to_intervention on June 26, 2023.

Hattie, J. (2023i) *Teacher estimates of achievement.* Accessed at www.visiblelearningmetax.com /influences/view/teacher_estimates_of_achievement on August 4, 2023.

Healy, P. (2016, August 18). *Confirmation bias: How it affects your organization and how to overcome it* [Blog post]. Accessed at https://online.hbs.edu/blog/post/confirmation-bias-how-it-affects-your-organization-and-how-to-overcome-it on June 27, 2023.

Hiermeier, U. M., & Verity, S. J. (2022). "Race" and racism in intelligence testing. *Clinical Psychology Forum, 1*(352), 19–23. https://doi.org/10.53841/bpscpf.2022.1.352.30

Hines, T. (2018, April). *Anatomy of the brain.* Accessed at https://mayfieldclinic.com/pe-anatbrain.htm on May 12, 2020.

Hirsh-Pasek, K., Hyson, M. C., & Rescorla, L. (1990). Academic environments in preschool: Do they pressure or challenge young children. *Early Education and Development, 1*(6), 401–423.

Hogan, D. (2014, February 11). *Why is Singapore's school system so successful, and is it a model for the West?* Accessed at https://theconversation.com/why-is-singapores-school-system-so-successful-and-is-it-a-model-for-the-west-22917 on April 19, 2023.

Hoge, R. D., & Coladarci, T. (1989). Teacher-based judgments of academic achievement: A review of literature. *Review of Educational Research, 59*(3), 297–313.

Hollingsworth, H. (2023, April 20). *Why more U.S. schools are embracing a new "science of reading."* Accessed at www.pbs.org/newshour/education/why-more-u-s-schools-are-embracing-a-new-science-of-reading on April 26, 2023.

Hudson, A., Koh, P. W., Moore, K. A., & Binks-Cantrell, E. (2020). Fluency interventions for elementary students with reading difficulties: A synthesis of research from 2000–2019. *Education Sciences, 10*(52), 1–28. Accessed at https://files.eric.ed.gov/fulltext/EJ1250532.pdf on July 13, 2023.

Hyson, M. C., Hirsh-Pasek, K., & Rescorla, L. (1990). The classroom practices inventory: An observation instrument based on NAEYC's guidelines for developmentally appropriate practices for 4- and 5-year-old children. *Early Childhood Research Quarterly, 5*(4), 475–494.

I Am Expat. (n.d.). *Primary and secondary education in the Netherlands.* Accessed at www.iamexpat.nl/education/primary-secondary-education-netherlands on April 21, 2023.

Inlay, L. T. (2016). Creating a culture of respect through the implicit curriculum. *Middle School Journal, 47*(2), 23–31. https://doi.org/10.1080/00940771.2016.1102600

Institute of Education Sciences. (n.d.). *About IES: Connecting research, policy and practice.* Accessed at https://ies.ed.gov/aboutus on April 20, 2023.

The International Dyslexia Association Ontario. (2021, September). *Lifting the curtain on EQAO scores.* Accessed at https://idaontario.com/wp-content/uploads/2023/08/LiftingTheCurtainOnEQAO69747.pdf on December 11, 2023.

InterNations. (n.d.a). *A guide to education and international schools in Singapore.* Accessed at www.internations.org/go/moving-to-singapore/education on April 20, 2023.

InterNations. (n.d.b). *A practical guide to the way of life in Belgium.* Accessed at www.internations.org/go/moving-to-belgium/living on April 20, 2023.

Ireland Department of Education and Science. (2004, January). *A brief description of the Irish education system*. Accessed at https://assets.gov.ie/24755/dd437da6d2084a49b0ddb316523aa5d2.pdf on April 19, 2023.

Ireland Department of Education and Science. (2022, December 13). *Overview of the Irish education system*. Accessed at www.citizensinformation.ie/en/education/the-irish-education-system/overview-of-the-irish-education-system on November 1, 2023.

Ireland Department of Education and Science. (2023, August 9). *School attendance*. Accessed at www.citizensinformation.ie/en/education/primary-and-post-primary-education/attendance-and-discipline-in-schools/school-attendance on November 1, 2023.

ITS Education Asia. (2020). *Hong Kong education system*. Accessed at www.itseducation.asia/article/hong-kong-education-system on April 20, 2023.

Jackson, A. (2015, May 9). *Here's the one big problem with China's supposedly amazing schools*. Accessed at www.businessinsider.com/china-has-a-major-issue-with-its-educational-system-2015-5 on October 30, 2023.

Jeffreys, B. (2019, December 2). Pisa rankings: Why Estonian pupils shine in global tests. *BBC News*. Accessed at www.bbc.com/news/education-50590581 on April 18, 2023.

Jensen, K. J. (2015). *A meta-analysis of the effects of problem- and project-based learning on academic achievement in grades 6–12 populations* [Doctoral dissertation, Seattle Pacific University]. Digital Commons @ SPU. https://digitalcommons.spu.edu/cgi/viewcontent.cgi?article=1004&context=soe_etd

Johnson, D. W., & Johnson, R. T. (n.d.). *An overview of cooperative learning*. Accessed at www.co-operation.org/what-is-cooperative-learning on April 20, 2023.

Johnson, D. W., & Johnson, R. T. (2005). New developments in social interdependence theory. *Genetic, Social, and General Psychological Monographs, 131*(4), 285–358.

Joseph, N., King, J., & McGlynn, S. (2022, December 11). *Fountas and Pinnell*. Accessed at www.teachingbyscience.com/fountas-and-pinnell-meta-analysis on June 25, 2023.

Just Landed. (n.d.). *Schools in Norway: The Norway education system*. Accessed at www.justlanded.com/english/Norway/Norway-Guide/Education/Schools-in-Norway on April 20, 2023.

Kacmaz, G., & Dubé, A. K. (2022). Examining pedagogical approaches and types of mathematics knowledge in educational games: A meta-analysis and critical review. *Educational Research Review, 35*, Article 100428. https://doi.org/10.1016/j.edurev.2021.100428

Khan, A., Sriyanto, S., Baranovich, D. L., Tahir, L. M., Panatik, S. A., Sasmoko, S., et al. (2023). The relationship between positive mental health, academic stress and suicide ideation among Malaysian adolescents residing in Johor Bahru. *Current Psychology, 42*, 15718–15726. https://doi.org/10.1007/s12144-022-02885-7

Kutsyuruba, B., Christou, T., Heggie, L., Murray, J., & Christophe, D. (2015, October 27). Teacher collaborative inquiry in Ontario elementary schools: An analysis of provincial and school board policies and support documents. *Canadian Journal of Educational Administration and Policy, 172*. Accessed at https://files.eric.ed.gov/fulltext/EJ1083430.pdf on December 19, 2023.

Kyndt, E., Raes, E., Lismont, B., Timmers, F., Cascallar, E., & Dochy, F. (2013). A meta-analysis of the effects of face-to-face cooperative learning: Do recent studies falsify or verify earlier findings? *Educational Research Review, 10*, 133–149. https://doi.org/10.1016/j.edurev.2013.02.002

Lazonder, A. W., & Harmsen, R. (2016). Meta-analysis of inquiry-based learning: Effects of guidance. *Review of Educational Research, 86*(3), 681–718. https://doi.org/10.3102/0034654315627366

Lee, J., & Yoon, S. Y. (2017, March/April). The effects of repeated reading on reading fluency for students with reading disabilities: A meta-analysis. *Journal of Learning Disabilities, 50*(2), 213–224. 10.1177/0022219415605194.

Lee, M. S., Jhone, J. H., Kim, J. B., Kweon, Y. S., & Hong, H. J. (2022). Characteristics of Korean children and adolescents who die by suicide based on teachers' reports. *International Journal of Environmental Research and Public Health, 19*(11), 6812. https://doi.org/10.3390/ijerph19116812

Lee, W., & Hotopf, M. (2012). *Funnel plot.* Accessed at www.sciencedirect.com/topics/medicine-and-dentistry/funnel-plot on March 24, 2023.

Macau Special Administrative Region. (2019, December 3). *Macao-China: High-performing and fast-improving basic education system according to PISA 2018.* Accessed at www.gov.mo/en/news/120558 on April 18, 2023.

MacMaster, K., Donovan, L. A., & MacIntyre, P. D. (2002). The effects of being diagnosed with a learning disability on children's self-esteem. *Child Study Journal, 32*(2), 101–108.

Macnamara, B. N., & Burgoyne, A. P. (2023). Do growth mindset interventions impact students' academic achievement? A systematic review and meta-analysis with recommendations for best practices. *Psychological Bulletin* [Advance online publication], *149*(3–4), 133–173. https://doi.org/10.1037/bul0000352

Mantzicopoulos, P. Y., Neuharth-Pritchett, S., & Morelock, J. B. (1994, April 4–8). *Academic competence, social skills, and behavior among disadvantaged children in developmentally appropriate and inappropriate classrooms* [Conference presentation]. Annual meeting of the American Educational Research Association, New Orleans, LA.

Marcon, R. A. (1992). Differential effects of three preschool models on inner-city 4-year-olds. *Early Childhood Research Quarterly, 7*(4), 517–530.

Marsh, J. H. (2015, March 4). *Eugenics: Pseudo-science based on crude misconceptions of heredity.* Accessed at www.thecanadianencyclopedia.ca/en/article/eugenics-keeping-canada-sane-feature on April 20, 2023.

Marshall, J., Mou, H., & Atkinson, M. (2019, April 18). *Canada's public schools: Are we paying more but getting less?* Accessed at www.schoolofpublicpolicy.sk.ca/research-ideas/publications-and-policy-insight/policy-brief/Canadas%20Public%20Schools%20-%20Are%20we%20paying%20more%20but%20getting%20less.php on April 21, 2023.

Mathes, P. G., & Denton, C. A. (2002). The prevention and identification of reading disability. *Seminars in Pediatric Neurology, 9*(3), 185–191. https://doi.org/10.1053/spen.2002.35498

Mayfield Brain and Spine Clinic. (2018, April). *Anatomy of the brain.* Accessed at https://mayfieldclinic.com/pe-anatbrain.htm on April 20, 2023.

McGill Qualitative Health Research Group. (n.d.). *Qualitative or quantitative research?* Accessed at www.mcgill.ca/mqhrg/resources/what-difference-between-qualitative-and-quantitative-research on April 20, 2023.

McMaster, K. N., & Fuchs, D. (2002). Effects of cooperative learning on the academic achievement of students with learning disabilities: An update of Tateyama-Sniezek's review. *Learning Disabilities Research and Practice, 17*(2), 107–117. https://doi.org/10.1111/1540-5826.00037

Methe, S., Kilgus, S., Neiman, C., & Riley-Tillman, T. C. (2012). Meta-analysis of interventions for basic mathematics computation in single-case research. *Journal of Behavioral Education, 21*(3), 230–253. Accessed at https://link.springer.com/article/10.1007/s10864-012-9161-1 on August 14, 2023.

Ministry of Education of the People's Republic of China. (2018). *China increases education spending in 2017.* Accessed at http://en.moe.gov.cn/News/Top_News/201805/t20180509_335408.html on April 18, 2023.

Morning Future. (2018, March 26). *The Estonia model: The secrets of the best education system in Europe.* Accessed at www.morningfuture.com/en/2018/03/26/estonia-school-coding-social-mobility on April 20, 2023.

Myers, J. A., Brownell, M. T., Griffin, C. C., Hughes, E. M., Witzel, B. S., Gage, N. A., et al. (2021). Mathematics interventions for adolescents with mathematics difficulties: A meta-analysis. *Learning Disabilities Research and Practice, 36*(2), 145–166.

Myers, J. A., Witzel, B. S., Powell, S. R., Li, H., Pigott, T. D., Xin, Y. P., et al. (2022). A meta-analysis of mathematics word-problem solving interventions for elementary students who evidence mathematics difficulties. *Review of Educational Research, 92*(5), 695–742. https://doi.org/10.3102/00346543211070049

Nancekivell, S. (2019, May 30). *Belief in learning styles myth may be detrimental* [Press release]. Accessed at www.apa.org/news/press/releases/2019/05/learning-styles-myth on August 6, 2023.

National Association for the Education of Young Children. (2009). *Developmentally appropriate practice in early childhood programs serving children from birth through age 8* [Position statement]. Accessed at www.naeyc.org/sites/default/files/globally-shared/downloads/PDFs/resources/position-statements/PSDAP.pdf on June 27, 2023.

National Center on Education and the Economy. (2020). *Top-performing countries: Hong Kong.* Accessed at https://ncee.org/country/hong-kong on December 11, 2023.

National Institute for Direct Instruction. (n.d.). *DI vs. di: The term "Direct Instruction."* Accessed at www.nifdi.org/what-is-di/di-vs-di.html on August 7, 2023.

National Institute of Standards and Technology. (2018, August 15). *Dataplot: Hedges G.* Accessed at www.itl.nist.gov/div898/software/dataplot/refman2/auxillar/hedgeg.htm on March 25, 2023.

National Reading Panel. (2000). *Teaching children to read: An evidence-based assessment of the scientific research on reading and its implications for reading instruction.* Washington, DC: National Institute of Child Health and Human Development. Accessed at www.nichd.nih.gov/sites/default/files/publications/pubs/nrp/Documents/report.pdf on April 20, 2023.

Ndlovu, M. (2013). Revisiting the efficacy of constructivism in mathematics education. *Philosophy of Mathematics Education Journal, 27*(April), 1–13. Accessed at https://philarchive.org/rec/NDLRTE on June 27, 2023.

Neitzel, A. J., Lake, C., Pellegrini, M., & Slavin, R. E. (2021). A synthesis of quantitative research on programs for struggling readers in elementary schools. *Reading Research Quarterly, 57*(1), 149–179. https://doi.org/10.1002/rrq.379

New Zealand Ministry of Business, Innovation and Employment. (2022). *The school system.* Accessed at www.newzealandnow.govt.nz/living-in-nz/education/school-system on April 19, 2023.

New Zealand Ministry of Education. (2022). *Education in New Zealand.* Accessed at www.education.govt.nz/our-work/our-role-and-our-people/education-in-nz on April 19, 2023.

Nickerson, C. (2023, May 10). *Labeling theory of deviance in sociology: Definitions and examples.* Accessed at www.simplypsychology.org/labeling-theory.html on June 26, 2023.

Northern Illinois University Center for Innovative Teaching and Learning. (2020). Howard Gardner's theory of multiple intelligences. In *Instructional guide for university faculty and teaching assistants.* Accessed at www.niu.edu/citl/resources/guides/instructional-guide/gardners-theory-of-multiple-intelligences.shtml on June 27, 2023.

Nugent, G., Malik, S., & Hollingsworth, S. (2012). *A practical guide to action research for literacy educators.* Washington, DC: International Reading Association. Accessed at www.literacyworldwide.org/docs/default-source/resource-documents/a-practical-guide-to-action-research-for-literacy-educators.pdf?sfvrsn=4 on April 21, 2023.

Odom, S. L., Brantlinger, E., Gersten, R., Horner, R. H., Thompson, B., & Harris, K. R. (2005). Research in special education: Scientific methods and evidence-based practices. *Exceptional Children, 71*(2), 137–148.

Okkinga, M., van Steensel, R., van Gelderen, A. J. S., van Schooten, E., Sleegers, P. J. C., & Arends, L. R. (2018). Effectiveness of reading-strategy interventions in whole classrooms: A meta-analysis. *Educational Psychology Review, 30*(4), 1215–1239.

Ontario College of Teachers. (2023). *Standards of practice.* Accessed at www.oct.ca/public/professional-standards/standards-of-practice on August 6, 2023.

Ontario Ministry of Education. (2006, June 7). *A guide to effective literacy instruction, grades 4 to 6: Volume 3—Planning and classroom management.* Toronto: Author. Accessed at https://issuu.com/davepotts/docs/guide_lit_456_vol_3_planning on December 11, 2023.

Ontario Ministry of Education. (2008). *Capacity building series.* Toronto: Author. Accessed at www.onted.ca/monographs/capacity-building-series on June 27, 2023.

Ontario Ministry of Education. (2010). *Growing success: Assessment, evaluation, and reporting in Ontario schools—First edition, covering grades 1 to 12.* Toronto: Author. Accessed at www.edu.gov.on.ca/eng/policyfunding/growsuccess.pdf on June 27, 2023.

Ontario Ministry of Education. (2017). *Special education in Ontario, kindergarten to grade 12: Policy and resource guide.* Toronto: Author. Accessed at https://files.ontario.ca/edu-special-education-policy-resource-guide-en-2022-05-30.pdf on June 17, 2023.

Ontario Ministry of Education. (2020, June 12). *High school graduation requirements.* Accessed at www.ontario.ca/page/high-school-graduation-requirements on August 14, 2023.

Ontario Ministry of Education. (2022, April 29). *Learning for all: A guide to effective assessment and instruction for all students, kindergarten to grade 12.* Accessed at www.ontario.ca/page/learning-all-guide-effective-assessment-and-instruction-all-students-kindergarten-grade-12 on August 15, 2023.

Open Science Collaboration. (2015). Estimating the reproducibility of psychological science. *Science, 349*(6251).

Organisation for Economic Co-operation and Development. (n.d.a). *Education spending.* Accessed at https://data.oecd.org/eduresource/education-spending.htm on April 21, 2023.

Organisation for Economic Co-operation and Development. (n.d.b). *What is PISA.* Accessed at www.oecd.org/pisa/#:~:text=OECD%20member%20countries%20and%20Associates, to%20reflect%20post%2DCovid%20difficulties on August 8, 2023.

Organisation for Economic Co-Operation and Development. (2010). *Presentation of the 2010 PISA results.* Accessed at https://web-archive.oecd.org/2012-06-14/61910-presentationofthepisa2010results.htm on December 11, 2023.

Organisation for Economic Co-operation and Development. (2012a). *Education at a glance 2012: Highlights.* Paris: Author. Accessed at www.oecd-ilibrary.org/docserver/eag_highlights-2012-en.pdf?expires=1689278492&id=id&accname=guest&checksum=EFF3B5AFF9C53CB5EF8BD30AE542074F on July 13, 2023.

Organisation for Economic Co-operation and Development. (2012b). *Education at a glance: OECD indicators—Estonia.* Paris: Author. Accessed at https://web-archive.oecd.org/2012-10-17/209977-estonia50.pdf on April 21, 2023.

Organisation for Economic Co-operation and Development. (2018a). *PISA 2018 country-specific overviews.* Accessed at www.oecd.org/pisa/publications/pisa-2018-snapshots.htm on April 21, 2023.

Organisation for Economic Co-operation and Development. (2018b). *PISA 2018 results.* Accessed at www.oecd.org/pisa/publications/pisa-2018-results.htm on June 26, 2023.

Organisation for Economic Co-operation and Development. (2019a). *Education at a glance 2019: Country note—Belgium.* Accessed at www.oecd.org/education/education-at-a-glance/EAG2019_CN_BEL.pdf on April 21, 2023.

Organisation for Economic Co-operation and Development. (2019b). *Education at a glance 2019: Country note—Norway.* Accessed at www.oecd.org/education/education-at-a-glance/EAG2019_CN_NOR.pdf on April 21, 2023.

Pedagogy Non-Grata. (Host). (2019a, December 10). Interview with Dr. Shanahan: The topic of DAP and dyslexia [Audio podcast episode]. In *Pedagogy Non-Grata.* Accessed at https://podcasts.apple.com/us/podcast/interview-with-dr-shanahan-on-the-topic-of-dap-and-dyslexia/id1440404959?i=1000459255502 on April 21, 2023.

Pedagogy Non-Grata. (Host). (2019b, October 29). Interview with Dylan Wiliam: A case for more formative assessment than summative [Audio podcast episode]. In *Pedagogy Non-Grata.* Accessed at https://podcasts.apple.com/us/podcast/interview-with-dylan-wiliam-a-case-for-more/id1440404959?i=1000455437126 on June 27, 2023.

Pedagogy Non-Grata. (Host). (2019c, November 12). Interview with Dylan Wiliam (continued): The limitations of meta-studies [Audio podcast episode]. In *Pedagogy Non-Grata.* Accessed at https://podcasts.apple.com/us/podcast/interview-dylan-wiliam-part-2-limitations-meta-studies/id1440404959?i=1000456643700 on April 21, 2023.

Pedagogy Non-Grata. (Host). (2021, April 17). Interview with Dr. Max Colheart on the different types of dyslexia [Audio podcast episode]. In *Pedagogy Non-Grata.* Accessed at https://podcasts.apple.com/ca/podcast/interview-with-dr-max-colheart-on-the-different/id1448225801?i=1000517538932 on April 18, 2023.

Pedagogy Non-Grata. (Host). (2022, June 2). Interview with Dr. Graham [Audio podcast episode]. In *Pedagogy Non-Grata.* Accessed at https://podcasts.apple.com/ca/podcast/interview-with-dr-graham/id1448225801?i=1000564966230 on June 27, 2023.

Perera, A. (2023, April 20). *The Pygmalion effect: Definition and examples.* Accessed at https://simplysociology.com/pygmalion-effect.html on April 21, 2023.

Piaget, J. (1964). Part I: Cognitive development in children: Piaget development and learning. *Journal Research in Science Teaching, 2*(3), 176–186. https://doi.org/10.1002/tea.3660020306

Plonsky, L., & Oswald, F. L. (2014). How big is "big"? Interpreting effect sizes in L2 research. *Language Learning, 64*(4), 878–912. https://doi.org/10.1111/lang.12079

Powell, S. R., & Fuchs, L. S. (2018). Effective word-problem instruction: Using schemas to facilitate mathematical reasoning. *Teaching Exceptional Children, 51*(1), 31–42.

Powell, S. R., Hughes, E. M., & Peltier, C. (2022, August 11). *Myths that undermine maths teaching* (Analysis Paper 38). Sydney, New South Wales, Australia: The Centre for Independent Studies. Accessed at www.cis.org.au/publication/myths-that-undermine-maths-teaching on June 27, 2023.

Prawat, R. S. (1996). Constructivisms, modern and postmodern. *Educational Psychologist, 31*(3–4), 215–225. https://doi.org/10.1080/00461520.1996.9653268

Puderbaugh, M., & Emmady, P. D. (2022). *Neuroplasticity.* Treasure Island, FL: StatPearls.

Puzio, K., & Colby, G. T. (2013). Cooperative learning and literacy: A meta-analytic review. *Journal of Research on Educational Effectiveness, 6*(4), 339–360. https://doi.org/10.1080/19345747.2013.775683

Puzio, K., Colby, G. T., & Algeo-Nichols, D. (2020). Differentiated literacy instruction: Boondoggle or best practice? *Review of Educational Research, 90*(4), 459–498. https://doi.org/10.3102/0034654320933536

Qin, Z., Johnson, D. W., & Johnson, R. T. (1995). Cooperative versus competitive efforts and problem solving. *Review of Educational Research, 65*(2), 129–143. https://doi.org/10.3102/00346543065002129

Ran, H., Kim, N. J., & Secada, W. G. (2022). A meta-analysis on the effects of technology's functions and roles on students' mathematics achievement in K–12 classrooms. *Journal of Computer Assisted Learning, 38*(1), 258–284.

Rehfeld, D. M., Kirkpatrick, M., O'Guinn, N., & Renbarger, R. (2022). A meta-analysis of phonemic awareness instruction provided to children suspected of having a reading disability. *Language, Speech, and Hearing Services in Schools, 53*(4), 1177–1201. https://doi.org/10.1044/2022_LSHSS-21-00160

Rittle-Johnson, B., & Schneider, M. (2015). Developing conceptual and procedural knowledge of mathematics. In R. C. Kadosh & A. Dowker (Eds.), *The Oxford handbook of numerical cognition* (pp. 1118–1134). New York: Oxford University Press.

Rogers, K. B. (2008, May). *Academic acceleration and giftedness: The research from 1990 to 2008. A best-evidence synthesis* [Conference presentation]. Acceleration Poster Session at the 2008 Wallace Research Symposium on Talent Development, Iowa City, IA. Accessed at www.accelerationinstitute.org/proceedings_2008.pdf on November 6, 2023.

Rosen, P. (n.d.). *What is MTSS?* Accessed at www.understood.org/en/articles/mtss-what-you-need-to-know on June 27, 2023.

Rosenshine, B., & Meister, C. (1994). Reciprocal teaching: A review of the research. *Review of Educational Research, 64*(4), 479–530.

Rosli, R., Capraro, M. M., & Capraro, R. M. (2014). The effects of problem posing on student mathematical learning: A meta-analysis. *International Education Studies, 7*(13), 227–241.

Rousseau, Y. (2022, September 2). *Play and pay: Why Singapore's education system is top of the class.* Accessed at https://worldcrunch.com/culture-society/singapore-education on June 17, 2023.

Rushton, J. P., & Jensen, A. R. (2005). Thirty years of research on race differences in cognitive ability. *Psychology, Public Policy, and Law, 11*(2), 235–294. https://doi.org/10.1037/1076-8971.11.2.235

Ryan, T. (2013, December 5). *The Polish education system is no joke.* Accessed at https://fordhaminstitute.org/national/commentary/polish-education-system-no-joke on April 21, 2023.

Sánchez-Meca, J., & Marín-Martínez, F. (1998). Weighting by inverse variance or by sample size in meta-analysis: A simulation study. *Educational and Psychological Measurement, 58*(2), 211–220.

Saygili, H., & Cetin, H. (2021). The effects of learning management systems (LMS) on mathematics achievement: A meta-analysis study. *Necatibey Faculty of Education Electronic Journal of Science and Mathematics Education, 15*(2), 341–362.

Scammacca, N. K., Roberts, G., Vaughn, S., & Stuebing, K. K. (2015). A meta-analysis of interventions for struggling readers in grades 4–12: 1980–2011. *Journal of Learning Disabilities, 48*(4), 369–390. https://doi.org/10.1177/0022219413504995

Scanlon, D. M., & Anderson, K. L. (2020). Using context as an assist in word solving: The contributions of 25 years of research on the interactive strategies approach. *Reading Research Quarterly, 55*(S1), S19–S34. https://doi.org/10.1002/rrq.335

Scarr, S., & Weinberg, R. A. (1976). IQ test performance of Black children adopted by White families. *American Psychologist, 31*(10), 726–739. https://doi.org/10.1037/0003-066X.31.10.726

Shanahan, T. (2021, June 12). *A question I hate: Should we use pictures (embedded mnemonics) when teaching phonics?* [Blog post]. Accessed at www.shanahanonliteracy.com/blog/a-question-i-hate-should-we-use-pictures-embedded-mnemonics-when-teaching-phonics on July 10, 2023.

Shepherd, J. (2010, December 7). World education rankings: Which country does best at reading, maths and science? *The Guardian.* Accessed at www.theguardian.com/news/datablog/2010/dec/07/world-education-rankings-maths-science-reading on April 21, 2023.

Shepley, C., & Grisham-Brown, J. (2019). Multi-tiered systems of support for preschool-aged children: A review and meta-analysis. *Early Childhood Research Quarterly, 47,* 296–308. Accessed at www.sciencedirect.com/science/article/pii/S0885200619300067 on November 6, 2023.

Sherman, C. W., & Mueller, D. P. (1996, June 20–23). *Developmentally appropriate practice and student achievement in inner-city elementary schools* [Conference presentation]. Third Head Start's National Research Conference, Washington, DC.

Shifrer, D., Muller, C., & Callahan, R. (2011). Disproportionality and learning disabilities: Parsing apart race, socioeconomic status, and language. *Journal of Learning Disabilities, 44*(3), 246–257.

Slavin, R. E. (1987). Mastery learning reconsidered. *Review of Educational Research, 57*(2), 175–213. https://doi.org/10.3102/00346543057002175

Slavin, R. (2018, June 21). *John Hattie is wrong* [Blog post]. Accessed at https://robertslavinsblog.wordpress.com/2018/06/21/john-hattie-is-wrong on April 21, 2023.

Smale-Jacobse, A. E., Meijer, A., Helms-Lorenz, M., & Maulana, R. (2019). Differentiated instruction in secondary education: A systematic review of research evidence. *Frontiers in Psychology, 10,* Article 2366. https://doi.org/10.3389/fpsyg.2019.02366

Small, M. (2008). *Making math meaningful to Canadian students, K–8.* Toronto, Ontario, Canada: Nelson Education.

Snyder, M. (2017, October 26). *Nine facts about education in Taiwan* [Blog post]. Accessed at https://borgenproject.org/education-in-taiwan on April 18, 2023.

Spuler, F. B. (1993). *A meta-analysis of the relative effectiveness of two cooperative learning models in increasing mathematics achievement* [Doctoral dissertation, Old Dominion University]. ODU Digital Commons. Accessed at https://digitalcommons.odu.edu/urbanservices_education_etds/147 on February 5, 2024.

Statista. (2023). *Number of suicides in Finland from 2011 to 2021, by age group.* Accessed at www.statista.com/statistics/524563/finland-total-number-of-suicides-by-age on April 21, 2023.

Steenbergen-Hu, S., Makel, M. C., & Olszewski-Kubilius, P. (2016). What one hundred years of research says about the effects of ability grouping and acceleration on K–12 students' academic achievement: Findings of two second-order meta-analyses. *Review of Educational Research, 86*(4), 849–899. https://doi.org/10.3102/0034654316675417

Stene-Larsen, K., Øien-Ødegaard, C., Straiton, M. L., Reneflot, A., Zahl, P. H., Myklestad, I., et al. (2023, March 31). *Suicide in Norway.* Accessed at www.fhi.no/en/op/hin/mental-health/suicide on April 21, 2023.

Stipek, D., Feiler, R., Daniels, D., & Milburn, S. (1995). Effects of different instructional approaches on young children's achievement and motivation. *Child Development, 66*(1), 209–223.

Stockard, J., Wood, T. W., Coughlin, C., & Khoury, C. R. (2018). The effectiveness of direct instruction curricula: A meta-analysis of a half century of research. *Review of Educational Research, 88*(4), 479–507. https://doi.org/10.3102/0034654317751919

Stough, C. (2015, October 15). *How has intelligence testing changed throughout history?* Accessed at www.weforum.org/agenda/2015/10/how-has-intelligence-testing-changed-throughout-history on April 24, 2023.

Study in the UK. (n.d.). *UK education system guide.* Accessed at www.studying-in-uk.org/uk-education-system-guide on April 21, 2023.

Stuebing, K. K., Barth, A. E., Cirino, P. T., Francis, D. J., & Fletcher, J. M. (2008). A response to recent reanalyses of the National Reading Panel report: Effects of systematic phonics instruction are practically significant. *Journal of Educational Psychology, 100*(1), 123–134. https://doi.org/10.1037/0022-0663.100.1.123

Stuebing, K. K., Barth, A. E., Molfese, P. J., Weiss, B., & Fletcher, J. M. (2009). IQ is *not* strongly related to response to reading instruction: A meta-analytic interpretation. *Exceptional Children, 76*(1), 31–51. https://doi.org/10.1177/001440290907600102

Sullivan, G. M., & Feinn, R. (2012). Using effect size—or why the *p* value is not enough. *Journal of Graduate Medical Education, 4*(3), 279–282. https://doi.org/10.4300/JGME-D-12-00156.1

Suri, H. (2010). *Cooperative learning in secondary mathematics: A meta-analysis.* Saarbrücken, Germany: VDM.

Swanson, E., Vaughn, S., Wanzek, J., Petscher, Y., Heckert, J., Cavanaugh, C., et al. (2011). A synthesis of read-aloud interventions on early reading outcomes among preschool through third graders at risk for reading difficulties. *Journal of Learning Disabilities, 44*(3), 258–275. https://doi.org/10.1177/0022219410378444

Swanson, H. L., & Lussier, C. M. (2001). A selective synthesis of the experimental literature on dynamic assessment. *Review of Educational Research, 71*(2), 321–363. https://doi.org/10.3102/00346543071002321

Tannock, R. (2012). *DSM-5 changes in diagnostic criteria for specific learning disabilities (SLD)1: What are the implications?* Accessed at https://dyslexiaida.org/dsm-5-changes-in-diagnostic-criteria-for-specific-learning-disabilities-sld1-what-are-the-implications on April 20, 2023.

Torgerson, C. J., & Torgerson, D. J. (2001). The need for randomised controlled trials in educational research. *British Journal of Educational Studies, 49*(3), 316–328. https://doi.org/10.1111/1467-8527.t01-1-00178

Torgesen, J. K. (2009, March 3). *Preventing early reading failure and its devastating downward spiral.* Washington, DC: National Center for Learning Disabilities. Accessed at www.bharathiyartamilpalli.org/training/images/downwardspiral.pdf on June 27, 2023.

Trading Economics. (2023). *Netherlands—Public spending on education, total (% of GDP).* Accessed at https://tradingeconomics.com/netherlands/public-spending-on-education-total-percent-of-gdp-wb-data.html on April 21, 2023.

Tran, L., Sanchez, T., Arellano, B., & Swanson, H. L. (2011). A meta-analysis of the RTI literature for children at risk for reading disabilities. *Journal of Learning Disabilities, 44*(3), 283–295. https://doi.org/10.1177/0022219410378447

Tse, H. (2023). *Hong Kong youth suicide on the rise since school began, NGO warns.* Accessed at https://hongkongfp.com/2023/10/27/hong-kong-youth-suicide-on-the-rise-since-school-began-ngo-warns on February 28, 2024.

Turgut, S., & Turgut, I. G. (2018). The effects of cooperative learning on mathematics achievement in Turkey: A meta-analysis study. *International Journal of Instruction, 11*(3), 663–680.

UNICEF. (2019). *Adolescent data portal: Country profile–Ireland.* Accessed at https://data.unicef.org/adp/country/irl on February 28, 2024.

University of Buffalo. (n.d.). *Constructivism.* Accessed at www.buffalo.edu/catt/develop/theory/constructivism.html on April 21, 2023.

University of Connecticut. (2000). *Effect size.* Accessed at https://media.pluto.psy.uconn.edu/stats/es.htm on April 21, 2023.

Van der Kleij, F. M., Feskens, R. C. W., & Eggen, T. J. H. M. (2015). Effects of feedback in a computer-based learning environment on students' learning outcomes: A meta-analysis. *Review of Educational Research, 85*(4), 475–511. https://doi.org/10.3102/0034654314564881

Van Ryzin, M. J., & Roseth, C. J. (2018). Cooperative learning in middle school: A means to improve peer relations and reduce victimization, bullying, and related outcomes. *Journal of Educational Psychology, 110*(8), 1192–1201.

Vernon-Feagans, L., Kainz, K., Amendum, S., Ginsberg, M., Wood, T., & Bock, A. (2012). Targeted reading intervention: A coaching model to help classroom teachers with struggling readers. *Learning Disability Quarterly, 35*(2), 102–114.

Visible Learning. (2018). *Hattie ranking: 252 influences and effect sizes related to student achievement.* Accessed at https://visible-learning.org/hattie-ranking-influences-effect-sizes-learning-achievement on April 19, 2023.

Walker, J. (2019, August 6). *The beautiful simplicity in McGuinness's prototype* [Blog post]. Accessed at https://theliteracyblog.com/2019/08/06/the-beautiful-simplicity-in-mcguinnesss-prototype on October 21, 2023.

Wang, X.-Y., Wang, X., Huang, C.-Q., Guo, Z.-Y., Qian, Y.-F., Yang, Y., et al. (2013). Effects of sleep deprivation on the intelligence structure of school-age children in Changsha, China. *Chinese Journal of Contemporary Pediatrics, 15*(10), 866–869.

Warikoo, N., Sinclair, S., Fei, J., & Jacoby-Senghor, D. (2016). Examining racial bias in education: A new approach. *Educational Researcher, 45*(9), 508–514. https://doi.org/10.3102/0013189X16683408

Wasserman, D., Cheng, Q., & Jiang, G.-X. (2005). Global suicide rates among young people aged 15–19. *World Psychiatry, 4*(2), 114–120.

Watson, K., & Ozanne, W. I. (2010). EDITORIAL: Education, religion and politics: Can they ever be disentangled? *Comparative Education, 46*(3), 267–271. Accessed at www.jstor.org/stable/27856170 on December 19, 2023.

Weale, S. (2017, March 12). *Teachers must ditch "neuromyth" of learning styles, say scientists.* Accessed at www.theguardian.com/education/2017/mar/13/teachers-neuromyth-learning-styles-scientists-neuroscience-education on April 21, 2023.

Wes, M., & Bodewig, C. (2016, January 22). *Poland's education system. Leading in Europe.* Accessed at www.worldbank.org/en/news/opinion/2016/01/22/polands-education-system-leading-in-europe on July 11, 2023.

What Works Clearinghouse. (n.d.). *Baseline equivalence.* Washington, DC: Institute of Education Sciences. Accessed at https://ies.ed.gov/ncee/wwc/Docs/OnlineTraining/wwc_training_m3.pdf on March 25, 2023.

Wiliam, D. (2016, April 28). *Learning styles: What does the research say?* [Blog post]. Accessed at https://deansforimpact.org/learning-styles-what-does-the-research-say on June 27, 2023.

Willingham, D. T. (2018). Ask the cognitive scientist: Does tailoring instruction to "learning styles" help students learn? *American Educator, 42*(2), 28–32, 43. Accessed at www.aft.org/ae/summer2018/willingham on May 5, 2023.

Wise, B. W., Ring, J., & Olson, R. K. (1999). Training phonological awareness with and without explicit attention to articulation. *Journal of Experimental Child Psychology, 72*(4), 271–304. https://doi.org/10.1006/jecp.1999.2490

Wisniewski, B., Zierer, K., & Hattie, J. (2020). The power of feedback revisited: A meta-analysis of educational feedback research. *Frontiers in Psychology, 10*(3087). https://doi.org/10.3389/fpsyg.2019.03087

Wong, T. (2021, May 7). Education officials aim to reduce pupils' homework pressure. *The Macau Post Daily.* Accessed at www.macaupostdaily.com/article10925.html on June 17, 2023.

The World Bank. (n.d.). *GDP growth (annual %)—Macau SAR, China*. Accessed at https://data.worldbank.org/indicator/NY.GDP.MKTP.KD.ZG?locations=MO on April 18, 2023.

Worldometer. (n.d.). *Taiwan population (live).* Accessed at www.worldometers.info/world-population/taiwan-population on April 18, 2023.

Xie, C., Wang, M., & Hu, H. (2018). Effects of constructivist and transmission instructional models on mathematics achievement in mainland China: A meta-analysis. *Frontiers in Psychology, 9,* Article 1923. https://doi.org/10.3389/fpsyg.2018.01923

Yang, P. (2016, December 21). *Why is South Korea education so successful?* Accessed at https://medium.com/@pasuahayang22/why-is-south-korea-education-so-successful-e05abab1a91c on April 21, 2023.

Yi, P. Q. (2022, June 22). *China's education system is notoriously rigid. This school is trying to change that.* Accessed at www.vice.com/en/article/bvm8aq/china-education-rigid-gaokao-alternative-learning-beijing-school on October 30, 2023.

Zong, S. (2014). A study on adolescent suicide ideation in South Korea. *Procedia—Social Behavioral and Sciences, 174,* 1949–1956. https://doi.org/10.1016/j.sbspro.2015.01.860

INDEX

A

B

C

D

E

G

H

I

J

N

O

Q

R

S

T

U

V

W

X

Z